# BOWHUNTER'S DIGEST

## 2nd Edition

## By Chuck Adams

DBI BOOKS, INC.

**ON THE COVER:** A successful bowhunter uses the latest in equipment to improve his odds of success. Expert archer Ron Hawkins displays proper modern hunting gear here: a factory-camouflaged two-wheel compound bow, four-pin bowsight, bow-shooting stabilizer, eight-arrow bow quiver, dull two-tone aluminum arrow shafts, sharp four-blade factory-sharpened broadheads, bowhunting rangefinder on belt, and head-to-toe hunting camouflage.

**Publisher**
SHELDON FACTOR

**Editorial Director**
JACK LEWIS

**Art Director**
SONYA KAISER

**Production Coordinator**
BETTY BURRIS

**Copy Editor**
DORINE IMBACH

**Contributing Editor**
MARK THIFFAULT

**Produced by**

*Charger Productions*

ISBN 0-910676-29-1                    Library of Congress Catalog Card # 73-91589

# CONTENTS

*To My Own Personal*

*R.D.A.C.W.*

# ACKNOWLEDGEMENTS

One seldom gets far in life or career without the help of friends. Good friends within the archery industry have helped me tremendously over the past few years, and these same friends came through with photographs, technical information, and abundant encouragement during the writing of this book. They deserve special credit here.

Jim Easton, Joe Johnston, Dave Feil, and Kathy O'Brien at Easton Aluminum have been of tremendous help in providing accurate data on the precision manufacture of arrows, shooting stabilizers, and other quality aluminum archery products. Duke Savora at Savora Archery has provided abundant technical data on the design and manufacture of hunting broadheads and broadhead steels. Mike Murray of Ranging, Incorporated, generously contributed the arrow-trajectory data and technical rangefinder information included in this book. Jim Baker of Baker Manufacturing provided the excellent line drawings and many of the specific facts concerning commercial tree stands and tree-stand accessories. Don Garbow of Buck Stop Lure Company contributed photos and facts about commercial odor-masking scents.

Also of great help to me in compiling this book were Bill McIntosh of Bear Archery, Tom Jennings of Jennings Compound Bow, Jim Dougherty of Jim Dougherty Archery, Ken Brown of Ken Brown Publications, and Ken Elliott of *Petersen's Hunting* Magazine.

*Chuck Adams*

# GENERAL INTRODUCTION

A COOL early morning fog swirled in unexpectedly and closed its clammy fist about the ridgetop, blotting out the canyon in front of me and the hillside beyond. I leaned back to wait, knowing the relentless summer sun would burn away the mist in less than an hour. The wait was not a particularly patient one, for less than three hundred yards away a nice four-point muley buck was alternately feeding and loafing on a juniper-studded hillside. Now all I could do was fidget and hope the animal stayed put until the sun cut through the low-scudding clouds.

Half an hour later, the visibility began to improve, bright patches of clear blue sky flashing momentarily overhead as the sun cut through the haze. After a few moments, the canyon in front of me popped into sight, a gray, out-of-focus hole in the gloom. Meanwhile the distant hillside beyond was drifting in and out of view as the mist performed a few dying swirls and finally, begrudgingly gave up the ghost.

I began glassing across the canyon intently, growing more and more perplexed as I swept the terrain repeatedly. The buck had vanished, either long gone from the hillside or motionless behind bushes or trees.

The sun finally stabbed through the clouds for good, chasing away the last drooping fingers of mist and quickly warming the landscape. Still I continued to probe the distant slope, intent on finding the buck or another like him. With luck, the sunlight might trigger a brief morning feeding flurry as the deer grabbed a few extra calories and soaked up a few bone-warming rays.

Suddenly the animal stood out like a diamond against a gray velvet cloth. One instant he was nowhere to be seen and the next he was filling the objective lenses of my binoculars. It was the same deer I'd seen before the fog — a fat, mature four-by-four with long, heavy tines. I settled back to watch the animal, a nervous but enjoyable time as I tried to figure out what he was going to do next.

My decision came surprisingly easy. After less than a minute he wheeled directly away, walked three steps, then lay down behind a log. All I could see were his antlers and his fanny. I was up, plunging into the canyon at a trot, planning my approach route up the far side.

The breeze was blowing strongly in my face as I waded the creek in the canyon and began easing up the slope the deer was on. I knew the downdraft would hold for a while, but past experience told me it would begin rambling aimlessly before long. I had the toughest chore facing me a bowhunter can tackle: go fast, but go quietly.

The damp, fog-drenched soil helped, as did the heavily used deer trail I blundered onto halfway up the hill. The trail was miraculously angling directly toward the bedded buck and I gratefully took this animal highway with a sigh of relief. The footing on the path was quiet and it kept me away from the noisy bushes and trees that littered the slope.

Soon a familiar downed spruce I had seen from across the canyon loomed fifty yards ahead, indicating that the

*Chuck Adams has taken plenty of trophies using the bow, such as this heavy mule deer.*
*Most of his success is attributed to hard work, time spent in the field, and knowledge of*
*equipment. By reading his instructive comments, it's hoped that you, too, will taste success!*

buck should be just over a little rise in front of me. The way things looked, he might actually be bedded in the very trail I was on. The breeze still strongly in my face. I down-shifted to a slow, cautious crawl. Take a step, look around, then take another. The deer should be within long distance bow range now.

The seconds and minutes oozed by like molasses, as I slipped upward toward the buck. He still was bedded out of sight beyond a wrinkle in the ridge; at least I hoped he was. I double-checked my arrow on the string, gripping the bow with clammy hands. My pulse was starting to surge as the long, tense minutes rolled by.

Suddenly, the tips of a massive deer rack loomed in front of me, silhouetted against the azure summer sky. They were barely thirty yards away. My heart rocketed to my throat, and I half wondered why the buck didn't hear my pounding pump and flee. I stopped a minute to calm down, all the while eyeballing the tips of the rack. They were rocking methodically as the deer breathed and chewed his cud and I noted with satisfaction that the animal was still facing the other way. So far, so good.

The next five yards came slowly and painfully, each step taken gingerly, tentatively as I started upward toward the buck. The back of the animal's butt rolled into view above the ridgetop, and I realized the deer was indeed lying in the trail I was on.

I gently eased my bowhunting rangefinder from its padded belt pouch, raised it slowly, and whirled the distance dial. When the antlertip images in the viewfinder popped together, the distance scale said exactly twenty-five yards. My only problem now was getting a shot at the animal's vitals.

I slipped the rangefinder away, pondering my problem. As if on cue, I felt the fickle morning breeze swirl, subside, then gently fan the back of my neck. My muscles tensed for the events I knew would follow.

The buck was on his feet in a flash, staring down the hillside past me. The sunlight glistened off his wet, sensitive nostrils as he sniffed the wind currents intently. I was in the open, but my camouflage outfit and cotton headnet were apparently enough to fool his eyes.

The damnable wind reversed direction again, this time with a strong, steady flow. The deer wasted no time at all, his large, beautiful rack rolling methodically as he wheeled and fled around the hill. I drew, anchored and released in one fluid motion, a mindless reflex learned from hours of shooting at running rabbits and squirrels. The orange aluminum shaft followed the buck over a little rise out of sight. The dull, watermelon plunk that followed told me I had either scored a hit or smacked a particularly soft bank of dirt. I scrambled around the hillside in time to see the deer cross a little ravine, lunge up the far side...then collapse. The red fletching on my arrow flashed like a beacon as the animal rolled tail over tea-kettle down the hillside. I let out an Indian war whoop and did a little jig.

The razor-sharp broadhead had entered dead-center between the hams, slicing forward to nearly cut the heart in two. The buck later field dressed 175 pounds, a mature, above-average trophy with a rack spreading 27½ inches between the widest points.

This was my latest adventure in an ongoing love affair with bowhunting in particular and the out-of-doors in general. This experience was as exciting as my first bowhunt many years ago; perhaps more so, because I knew what I was doing and felt at least partially in control of the situation. That eventful mule deer stalk reinforced the conviction that I'll never become tired or bored with this exciting, fascinating, and challenging archery sport. As with any true love affair, the enjoyment and the appreciation only deepen as time goes along.

Bowhunting is different things to different people: an escape from hectic modern life for some, a chance to scout gun-hunting areas for others, and a simple excuse to commune with nature for still others. However, I firmly believe the majority of serious hunting archers are mainly concerned with bagging the game they're after, for meat, for trophy, for challenge, or for all three combined. The abundant fringe benefits associated with bowhunting are extremely worthwhile, too — the chance to relax, to enjoy nature, to scout likely areas for gun hunting later on. However, this is not a book about nature, about mental therapy, or how to prepare for shooting deer with a rifle. It is a book about how to become a successful, versatile bowhunter with well-practiced shooting skills and the solid ability to find game, approach game, and set up decent shots at success. It is also a book about the modern equipment needed to accomplish these goals — equipment that is more sophisticated and more troublefree than ever before in the long history of hunting with bent stick and pointed shaft.

This book also is meant to stress the high level of proficiency that can be reached by a serious, thoughtful and hard-working bowhunter. All too often we are told by lackadaisical or misinformed archers that it is impossible to shoot ultra-tight target groups with a hunting bow, that it is foolhardy to shoot at animals past fifty yards, or that it constitutes a major miracle whenever a bowhunter on his two hind legs manages to move within solid bow range of an alert animal like a deer. The fact is, a bowhunter who has taken the time to get good at his sport can regularly shoot three-inch target groups at twenty yards with hunting broadheads, can consistently kill deer-sized critters out to seventy yards, and can purposefully steal within twenty yards of any animal alive if the wind and other uncontrollable factors do not sour the process. Such a fellow has developed a firm grip on his sport, leaving very little to chance and scoring on game with consistency that would rival that of anyone toting a modern high-powered rifle. Bowhunting is a serious, exacting sport — a sport a dedicated woodsman can become incredibly good at with quality equipment, proper technique, and lots of experience in the field.

This book has been written to provide a solid, complete basis for becoming a skillful and consistently successful bowhunter. It is just a starting point, however, because the most important lessons are always learned on the target range and in the woods. I can only hope that after reading this *Bowhunter's Digest* and spending some pleasant time with a bow in your mitts, you too will join the ranks of serious and dedicated bowhunters. For enjoyment, for challenge, for self-satisfaction, there's simply no finer way to go!

*Chuck Adams*

# Introduction
# CHOOSING AND USING SHOOTING GEAR

**P**INPOINT ACCURACY with a hunting bow does not happen by accident. The archer who consistently hits targets and animals leaves little to chance, carefully choosing his shooting gear, tuning this gear to perfection, and practicing throughout the year to maintain and steadily improve his fine-honed shooting ability. Being able to hit what you aim at is half the battle in successful bowhunting and any would-be expert at this sport should strive to become the very best shot he can possibly be.

There are two major keys to becoming a fine shot with a bow. One is using well-designed bow-and-arrow equipment and adjusting this equipment properly to achieve maximum performance. The other is mastering the art of shooting a bow, a process that requires sound basic shooting form and plenty of diligent practice on the range and in the field. These two ingredients — accurate shooting equipment and well-developed shooting ability — will definitely stack the odds in any bowhunter's favor no matter what the situation or the species being hunted. Never underestimate the importance of your shooting equipment or the necessity of using it well.

I'll never forget the first time I shot at a deer with a bow. It was a humbling and maddening experience, but it taught me early how important shooting skill is, no matter how good at hunting you happen to be.

It was one of those colorful late-summer dawns, a crimson stain slowly oozing across the eastern sky as pitch black night turned to the fuzzy, exciting gray of legal hunting time. I was perched atop a rockpile overlooking a freshly burned manzanita hillside, the tender green shoots of deer feed carpeting the ground between dead, fire-blackened stumps. It was a prime spot for blacktail deer, a spot I had carefully scouted prior to bow season.

Daylight had hardly begun seeping into the canyon when my 8X30 glasses picked up a telltale red-brown spot two hundred yards away. An instant later the spot moved and materialized into a fat deer, its light summer coat glowing softly in the weak, indirect light. I strained my eyes to see antlers, and when the deer dropped its head in front of a pepperwood tree its velvet rack leaped out like a neon sign. Just a forked horn, but big enough to be legal in my home state of California.

I quickly assessed the situation, checked the wind, then began a circular stalk along a thin strip of pine trees that petered out about thirty yards below the buck. I knew the pre-sunrise wind would be perfect for the sneak, but once the sun cleared the mountains the breezes would become unstable and eventually shift 180 degrees. I had to hurry, but be quiet and unobtrusive in the process — a tall order to fill.

Things worked out perfectly. The trees followed a seam of weathered lava rock, footing that made travel swift and silent. The pines and the roll of the mountain hid me from

*A handsome trophy at close range will certainly make your muscles rubbery and set your heart pounding; if you can't control these reactions to place a shot accurately, your story may resemble that of author Adams on his first bowhunting venture. You need more than just hunting skill.*

*The craggy profile of master bowhunter, Fred Bear, designing a bow in his workshop. This archer, who has taken game all over the world, has repeatedly stressed the necessity for practice under field conditions, and the need for accuracy. The products that bear his name are capable of downing game, if the hunter does his share.*

the deer entirely, and I had the good fortune not to bump into other deer along the way. Before I knew it, I found myself within fifty yards of the buck's position. I slowed to a snail's pace, nocked an arrow, and crept forward like a bobcat after a mouse.

I had barely left the trees when four fat, hairy antler tips suddenly popped above a bush not twenty yards away. My heart did a double handspring as the little buck strode around the bush into full view, apparently heading for the trees to bed. I froze like a stump, completely numb with surprise. The animal angled past me, then suddenly stopped and looked the other way. His sleek red sides glittered like the mouth of hell as I weakly drew the bow, and his little forked-horn rack seemed immense at the point-blank range. I somehow anchored despite my rubbery muscles and shattered nerves, pointed the bow in the buck's direction, and let fly unceremoniously.

As if in slow motion, the aluminum arrow floated out of the bow, covered the fifteen-odd yards separating the animal and me...and passed harmlessly between his antlers! The next instant the deer was gone on frantically flying hooves, leaving behind a giant cloud of dust and bitter disappointment. As it turned out, the deer had been less than twelve steps away.

Because of careful scouting, good camouflage clothing, some knowledge about deer gleaned from past gun-hunting trips and more than a little good luck, I had managed to set up the ideal shot at a buck first crack out of the box.

However, a careful inspection of my bow/arrow combo the next day plus some serious target shooting during midday hours over the next two weeks of deer season clearly showed me the error of my ways.

My old recurve bow was coupled with arrow shafts of the wrong size — which meant it shot fairly well with target points but sent broadheads absolutely nuts even at close range. After buying proper arrows, I could hit bull's-eye targets fairly well, but couldn't seem to hit the vitals on a commercial animal target because there was no aiming spot with which to line up. I practiced hard during the rest of the deer season and finally bagged the smallest forked horn I saw on the entire trip only two days before season was over. I counted myself fortunate, especially since my buck was an honest forty-five yards away when the arrow laced his heart. I vowed then and there to be a competent field shot before another archery season rolled around.

There is no substitute for accurate, well-chosen shooting equipment and plenty of sensible shooting practice in a variety of situations. The following ten chapters will serve as a guide in choosing bowhunting equipment, tuning and maintaining it properly for best results, and learning to use it like an expert on the target range and in the field. As I found out so many years ago, well-developed hunting skill alone is not enough to fill the freezer with meat. A hunter must hit what he's shooting at...something that seldom happens by mistake!

# CHAPTER 1

# BASIC SHOOTING EQUIPMENT

I N THE good ol' days, bowhunting was a relatively simple sport. Prior to the 1950s, the choice of bows at archery stores was somewhat limited, and the differences between various hunting-bow models was not all that tough to grasp — even for the rank beginner. Good-quality aluminum hunting arrows were already on the scene at this point, but the selection of sizes was severely limited. Most bowhunters aimed without bowsights, most carried their arrows in simple shoulder quivers, and most did not have the slightest idea what a shooting stabilizer could

possibly be. Things have changed one heckuva lot in the past twenty-five or thirty years.

Actually, the good ol' days were not so good, all things considered. Bowhunting was simple then, true, but equipment was not as accurate, efficient, or convenient to use as it is today. Bows had to be strung immediately before a hunt and unstrung again at nightfall, hunting broadheads had to be meticulously sharpened by hand and quickly became dull again in crude arrow quivers, feather fletching on arrows had to be burned to proper shape with the foul odor of

*Your local archery shop is the best place to purchase the bowhunting equipment you need. Such a store has a broad selection of gear, as well as qualified personnel to help you make the right choices for the type of game you want.*

*The compound bow is favored by most hunters today because it is powerful yet easy to shoot. The author bagged this big bull elk with the help of a fast-shooting compound design and proper arrows matched to this type of hunting.*

# There Is Good Tackle, There Is Poor Tackle; Recognizing The Difference Means Bowhunting Success!

sizzling hair, and bows were incredibly difficult to draw despite the fact that they shot arrows slowly and inefficiently. Simple is not always best, and the old days proved this dramatically.

Modern archery stores are jam-packed with an incredible array of bows, arrows, and bow-shooting accessories — a selection guaranteed to confuse any would-be bowhunter. However, with some proper guidance a beginner can choose basic shooting equipment which will serve him well on both targets and game. Because there are so many bow models, arrow sizes, and accessory designs available today, a beginning bowhunter is best advised to purchase his shooting equipment at an archery pro shop which has qualified personnel on duty to help with proper selection. The best of such shops have indoor or outdoor shooting facilities so customers can try out bows and arrows before actually making a purchase. There are several thousand such shops in the United States and Canada, so chances are there's one not far from where you live.

The following guidelines are meant to help any

bowhunter choose basic, good-quality shooting equipment. The equipment recommended here is all anyone needs to begin shooting at targets and slowly perfecting his accuracy. Later on, with some additional gear, this same basic shooting setup can be used successfully in all sorts of bowhunting situations.

### HUNTING BOWS AND BOW EQUIPMENT

Immediately prior to the late 1960s, the recurve hunting bow was the overwhelming choice of serious bowhunters. A few die-hard nimrods still used the even older style longbow, but the recurve bow's S-shaped limbs shot arrows faster and smoother than the longbow's straight or mildly curving limbs. Nonetheless, choosing a proper hunting bow was not a difficult task.

Around 1968, several archery manufacturers dropped a bomb on the bowhunting public by introducing a bizarre-looking, revolutionary bow design. This design used short, stubby limbs, steel cables, and pulley wheels to give the archer mechanical advantage in drawing and achieving

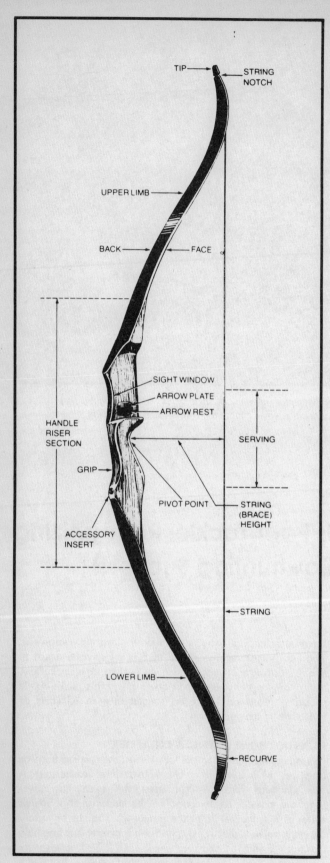

TIP — STRING NOTCH

UPPER LIMB

BACK — FACE

SIGHT WINDOW
ARROW PLATE
ARROW REST

HANDLE RISER SECTION

SERVING

GRIP

PIVOT POINT

STRING (BRACE) HEIGHT

ACCESSORY INSERT

STRING

LOWER LIMB

RECURVE

*This artist's drawing indicates the parts of a recurve bow of the type that has been popular for several decades.*

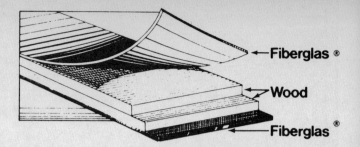

Fiberglas®

Wood

Fiberglas®

*The best recurve bows have laminated limbs consisting of one or more layers of wood sandwiched between layers of fiberglass to produce fast, consistent flight of arrows.*

faster arrow velocities. By the early 1970s, older-style recurve "stick bows" were rapidly falling off in popularity among dedicated bowhunters, and today some eighty-five to ninety percent of all bowhunters head for the deer woods with compound bows in their mitts. However, simpler recurve bows still have their fans, and still take plenty of game in experienced hands. In addition, a few nostalgia buffs continue to hunt with longbows for fun and extra challenge. As a matter of fact, longbow hunting has recently enjoyed a strong spurt of popularity in some parts of the country. Here are some facts about all three bow designs which should help you make a sensible choice.

A longbow or recurve bow is a simple, aesthetically appealing design consisting of a central grip section called a handle riser and a flexible limb on either end. Such a bow is braced or strung by slipping a bowstring into string notches near the tips of both limbs. This flexes the limbs to a certain degree, bringing the bowstring taut and bending the bow into a bowed, arching shape. The terms "archery" and "bow" were originally derived from the curving shape of a longbow when strung and drawn to shoot.

Although there are certain differences between longbows and recurve bows, both designs can be considered together when outlining their strong and weak points. A longbow has a considerably greater overall length than a recurve bow because its limbs are relatively straight and because they have to be longer to produce decent cast (arrow velocity). Modern longbows sold by specialty companies usually measure something over sixty-eight inches tip to tip. By contrast, the average hunting recurve bow measures fifty-eight to sixty-two inches long from tip-to-tip — an advantage when packing it about the woods — and casts an arrow faster and with much flatter trajectory than a longbow because of its mathematically superior S-shaped limbs. Other differences between these two basic stick-bow designs are also noticeable to the experienced archer, including grip shape, sight window depth, and handle vibration level when shot. However, such differences are not of major consequence to the average bowhunter. Longbows are generally shot today by experts who have backpeddled from recurve bows to increase their shooting and hunting challenge by using a slower-shooting tool. Most practical-minded modern bowhunters use either the recurve bow or the compound bow instead.

The recurve bow is a fine hunting tool, provided it is a well-made product of proven design. Available recurve bows run the gamut from cheap, poor-shooting models with

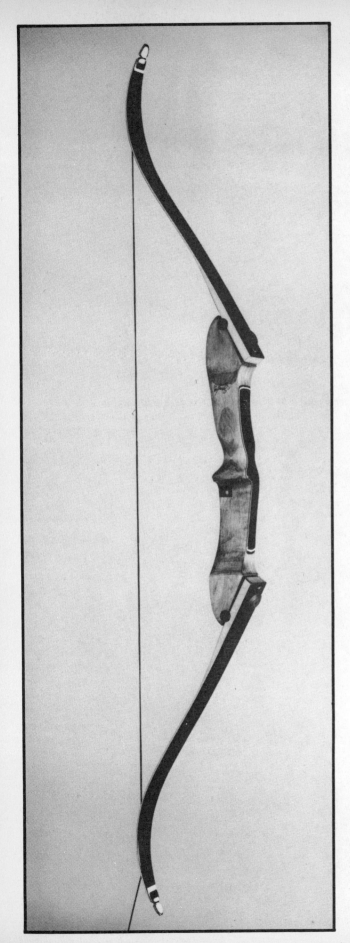

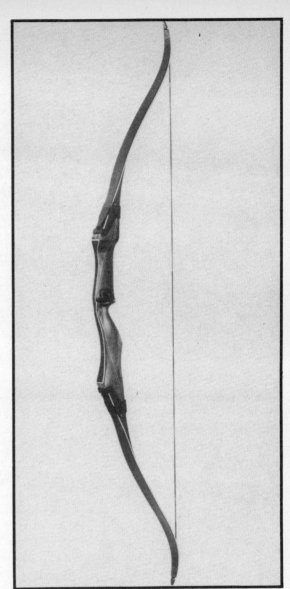

*Recurve bows are simple but elegant shooting tools. Both models shown take down into three pieces for transport.*

plastic grips and fiberglass limbs to fine works of art with exotic hardwood handles and pleasantly curving wood-and-fiberglass laminated limbs which easily detach to facilitate transport and storage.

Because a laminated recurve limb snaps forward more smartly than a heavier, more sluggish solid fiberglass limb, a prospective recurve buyer should only consider hunting recurves incorporating laminated limbs with outer fiberglass layers glued to an inner core of hardwood like maple. Laminated-limb recurves shoot faster, smoother, and more accurately than cheaper bows with all-fiberglass limbs, increasing the hunter's chances of success.

The handle risers on recurve bows vary considerably in length and shape. Most are made of quality hardwood, but some are composed of lightweight aluminum or magnesium. Since a hunting bow should be spray-painted in dull colors

*Hunting bows with threaded quiver holes allow fast, easy, and solid attachment of quality bow quivers.*

*Fred Bear has taken hundreds of game animals with his recurve bows, including many fine trophies such as this record-class Alaskan caribou which was downed in 1959. Author feels that one never should underrate recurves.*

to camouflage its shiny surfaces, the eye appeal of a beautiful recurve handle riser should not be a factor in choosing a practical hunting bow model.

Although recurve bows of extremely short overall length are all the rage among some groups of bowhunters, such bows are grossly inferior in performance and practicality to recurves of longer length. Manufacturers of recurves normally push ultra-short designs with the sales pitch that such bows are easier to carry, easier to stow in a car, and easier to shoot in tight quarters like from a tree stand. However, a recurve bow which is only fifty inches long shoots arrows slower than a longer bow, severely pinches a hunter's fingers with its short bowstring when he draws to shoot, and is light enough in physical weight to hinder steady, accurate shooting. A hunting recurve bow should ideally be between fifty-eight and sixty-six inches long for best accuracy, flattest trajectory, and most comfortable shooting. All else being equal, one recurve bow of a particular length (say sixty-two inches) will shoot smoother and faster than another bow of the same length if the first bow has longer limbs and a shorter handle riser. Longer working limbs generally cast arrows faster and more pleasantly than shorter limbs around a longer handle section.

Aside from laminated limbs, an overall length of at least fifty-eight inches, and a relatively short handle riser between relatively long limbs, a bowhunter shopping for a recurve bow should pay attention to several other features he'll probably need for best shooting and hunting results. One is a threaded stabilizer hole positioned below the bow grip in the front of the handle riser. Such a hole allows easy attachment of a shooting stabilizer — a weighted rod that usually improves arrow accuracy and makes a bow quieter to shoot. In addition, a stabilizer hole is the ideal place to attach a bowfishing reel for shooting at rough fish like carp, and also accepts various forms of bow lights for shooting varmints at night. If at all possible, buy a recurve bow with a stabilizer hole in front.

The vast majority of bowhunters carry their arrows in quivers that attach directly to bows. These so-called "bow quivers" are most easily and most solidly attached with screws or bolts, and many modern recurve bows come complete with steel or brass bushings tapped into their handles to accept suitable bow quivers. Quivers are available that tape or lock in place with spring-steel arms, but threaded quiver holes are a convenience well worth asking your archery dealer about. Some archery stores will install recurve quiver bushings if these have not been installed at the factory.

Although not important to most bowhunters, a takedown recurve bow can be a godsend for the archer who plans to backpack into remote country or regularly transport his bow by air. Takedown recurve bows are usually more expensive than one-piece models, but when dismantled into two or three pieces they can be stuffed in a compact transport case, duffle bag, or pack sack with

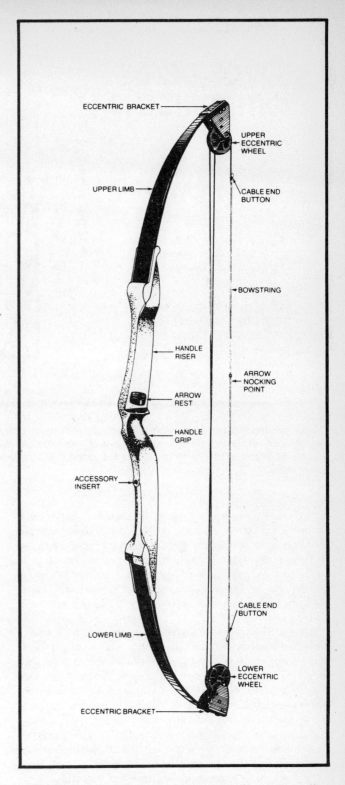

incredible ease. Several companies offer top-quality takedown recurve bows, and such bows are especially handy for any regularly traveling bowhunter.

A suitable hunting recurve bow with the desirable characteristics just described will regularly take game in practiced hands. It is a graceful, eye-appealing design, and has the important plus of being simple and extremely trouble-free. A well-made recurve bow is also very quiet to shoot — an important factor in hunting most kinds of game.

Why then, you might ask, is the recurve bow presently

# FORCE-DRAW COMPARISON

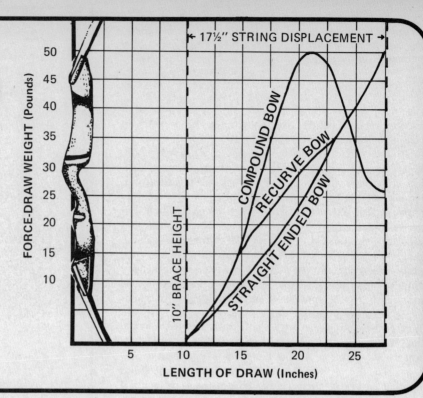

**COMPOUND BOW: 50 lb.**
ARROW: 402.5 grains
VELOCITY: 204 fps

**RECURVE BOW: 50 lb.**
ARROW: 402.5 grains
VELOCITY: 184 fps

**STRAIGHT ENDED BOW: 50 lb.**
ARROW: 402.5 grains
VELOCITY: 159 fps

*This simple force-draw chart graphically compares drawing characteristics of a straight-ended bow (longbow). recurve bow, and compound model. As draw length increases back to 27½ inches, the "stick bows" increase in draw weight, while the compound increases at first, then lets off. Note the significant differences in arrow velocities.*

used by such a small percentage of bowhunters? The answer is simple enough — the recurve is considerably harder on shooting muscles than the more modern compound bow. A recurve is every bit as accurate as a compound when a shooter is in condition to use it, but as the following section on compound bows clearly proves, the more complex compound bow is a superior performer for most hunting archers.

When compound bows first hit the market, manufacturers made some incredible claims about how much superior these were to conventional recurve bows and longbows. The most common claims centered on the lightning speed with which a compound would shoot an arrow. As is often the case, manufacturers' boasts were sometimes way out of line with reality. An average compound bow is a slightly faster shooter than a recurve bow of the same draw weight, but the compound's major advantage has to do with shooting ease — not huge improvements in arrow speed or flatness of trajectory.

Comparing recurve bows and compounds is every bit as impractical as trying to compare lemons and cucumbers. Both kinds of bows are hand-held when shot, and both are aimed and shot in the same basic way. However, the designs are extremely different when it comes to how they cast an arrow and how they affect a hunter's muscles as he draws and aims to shoot.

A recurve's draw weight (often called draw force) is defined as the amount of pressure it takes to pull the bowstring back twenty-eight inches. For example, a typical

deer-hunting recurve bow requires between fifty and sixty pounds of pull on the bowstring to draw back a twenty-eight-inch hunting arrow. The exact twenty-eight-inch draw weight of an individual recurve bow is normally determined at the factory and marked somewhere on the bow's handle riser. This draw weight (draw force) increases steadily as the bowstring is pulled farther and farther back — approximately three pounds per inch of draw in a hunting-weight recurve. For instance, a fifty-pound recurve at twenty-eight inches requires about fifty-three pounds to draw it back to twenty-nine inches, fifty-six pounds to draw it back to thirty inches, et cetera. All this draw weight must be held with a hunter's fingers, arm muscles, and shoulder muscles as he aims prior to releasing an arrow.

By contrast, a compound bow's so-called draw weight or draw force is a different thing entirely. Because of its system of wheels and cables, a compound bow reaches a peak draw weight at about half draw and relaxes in draw weight from twenty-five to fifty percent as the archer pulls the bowstring on back to full draw. For example, a fifty-pound compound bow with a fifty-percent draw-weight relaxation (often called draw-weight let-off) requires fifty pounds of finger pull on the bowstring to draw it halfway, but then this pressure drops quickly to only twenty-five pounds (fifty percent of fifty pounds) at full draw. A bowhunter with a recurve bow of fifty pounds holds a full fifty pounds with his fingers as he aims to shoot. By comparison, a bowhunter with a compound bow

*Independent arrow velocity testing with accurate chronographs has proved that average compound bows shoot only 5 to 10 percent faster than average recurve bows of the same draw weight.*

A compound bow is far easier to hold back than a recurve; this is to the hunter's advantage when aiming or waiting for an animal to walk out.

of fifty pounds and a fifty-percent let-off will only hold twenty-five pounds of bowstring pressure as he aims to shoot.

A visual comparison of the draw-weight or draw-force characteristics of longbows (straight-ended bows), recurve bows, and compound bows is made possible with a simple force-draw chart. The chart on page 12 for fifty-pound bows clearly shows that the draw weight of "stick bows" steadily increases as they are drawn back while the compound's draw weight increases at first and then subsides.

Early compound-bow manufacturers were fond of saying that a compound bow with a fifty-pound draw-weight shot arrows considerably faster than an average recurve bow with the same draw weight. Independent testing during the past few years has proven that the average good-quality compound bow shoots arrows only five to ten percent faster than an average recurve bow with the same draw weight, and that some especially well-designed recurve bows shoot every bit as fast as top-notch compound bows. However, the compound bow *is* superior because it is so easy to hold back and aim with when compared to the recurve bow.

Strained, tired, and wobbly arm and shoulder muscles are the major cause of poor bow-shooting, and it stands to reason that the fellow shooting a fifty-pound recurve bow is

but it is far easier to shoot a compound well because muscle strain while aiming is cut by twenty-five to fifty percent.

The bowstring let-off of a compound bow provides obvious shooting advantages for any serious bowhunter. For one thing, a hunter with a compound bow can remain at full draw for a longer period of time if he has to wait for an animal to move into the open prior to taking a shot. For another, he can generally buy a bow with a heavier draw weight than he can handle in a recurve bow while still reducing the weight he holds on his bowstring fingers at full draw.

As an example, I prefer to shoot a recurve bow of fifty-two or fifty-three pounds, because at fifty-five pounds, my fingers begin to bruise and my muscles begin to wobble during extended target-practice sessions. By contrast, my favorite hunting compound bow has a draw weight of seventy-four pounds, yet I only hold forty-two pounds when this bow is at full draw. The effort required to draw my bow through the seventy-four-pound peak weight is over in the blink of an eye — not enough to tire me out — and aiming with this bow is far easier than aiming with a fifty-two-pound recurve bow because I'm holding ten pounds less on my fingers at full draw. The seventy-four-pound compound shoots arrows with considerably more energy and speed than any

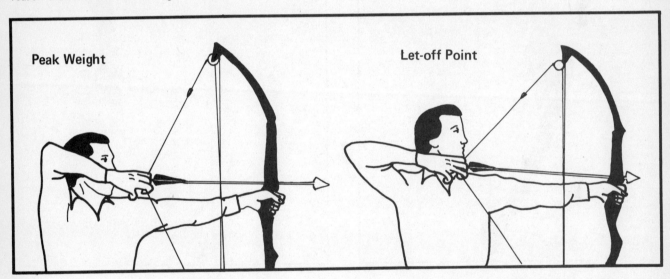

*A compound bow reaches a peak weight at about half of the full draw, then subsides from 25 to 50 percent at what is called the full-draw let-off point. This is the primary advantage of using a compound bow over a recurve model.*

under considerably more strain as he aims than the fellow with a fifty-pound compound — twice as much strain, to be exact, when the compound is a model which lets off a full fifty percent. It takes a split second to draw a bow, but a full three to five seconds to aim it once the arrow is drawn all the way back. A fifty-pound compound bow definitely exerts the muscles during the instant the hunter pulls through half draw, but this strain is minor compared to the constant strain of holding a full fifty pounds of recurve-bow pressure as you aim. A bowhunter who practices long and hard can shoot a recurve bow quite well,

fifty-two-pound recurve, too, which produces flatter arrow trajectory for easier aiming on animals and results in substantially better arrow penetration and stopping power on larger game like deer and elk.

As you can see, comparing recurve bows and compound bows by so-called "draw weight" makes no sense at all because the draw weight of a recurve is held at full draw while the draw weight of a compound occurs for a split-instant at half draw. Because of this drastic difference in the two bow designs, the average hunting compound bow is far easier to aim with because of reduced holding weight

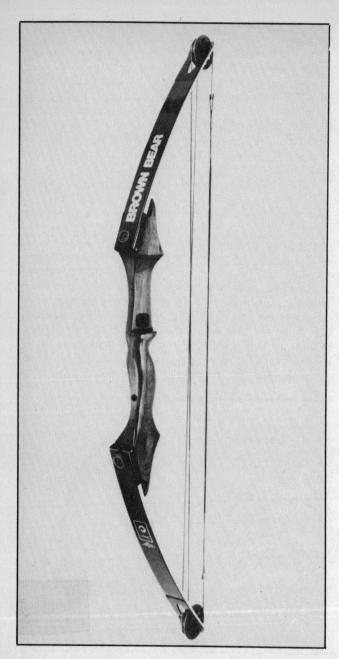

*Compound bows take many forms, including this relatively inexpensive two-wheel version, which is simple in design.*

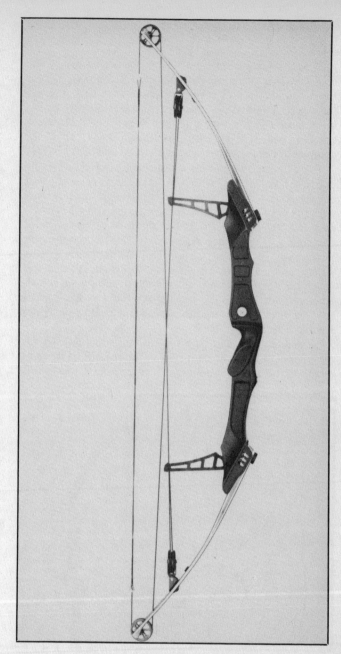

*The bow shown above is somewhat more complicated because it utilizes four wheels in its compound configuration.*

at full draw, and also casts an arrow much faster, because a hunter can easily shoot a compound bow with a draw weight ten or fifteen pounds heavier than is comfortable in a recurve bow.

Although the compound bow does provide some shooting advantages over the older-style recurve bow, the compound *is not* a wonder machine that ensures accurate shooting or game in the bag. A shooter with a compound must still learn to shoot properly, and must still practice solid, time-tested hunting techniques. As a matter of fact, national bowhunter-success percentages on deer have not risen significantly since the compound has become popular. There are many variables in bowhunting, and the aiming advantages provided by a compound bow are not enough to

heavily stack the odds in the compound-user's favor.

A wide variety of compound-bow designs are available these days, and only the Lord knows what mechanical monstrosities are likely to pop up as time goes by. However, the best compounds have relatively short, stubby limbs attached to wooden or metal handle risers. This handle/limb setup is laced together under low tension with steel cables and a bowstring — a network that incorporates somewhere between two and six pulley wheels that provide mechanical advantage when drawing the bow.

Although originally plagued with breakage problems and excessive noise when shooting, modern compound bows produced by reputable companies are now perfected and nearly as trouble-free as old-style recurve bows. They are

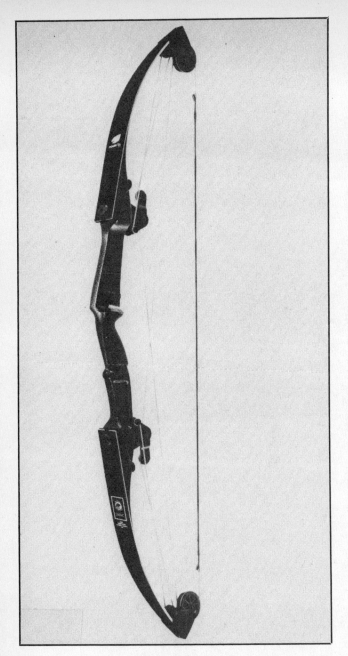

*This intricate design has about as many pulleys as one can pack on one bow, with a total of six for more efficiency.*

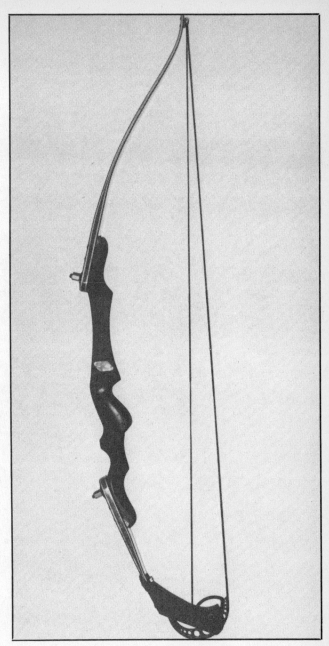

*The designer of this bow seemingly was attempting to use the best of two designs, one wheel and one recurve limb.*

considerably heavier in physical weight than recurves, are not as pleasing to the eye, and often make slightly more noise when shot than simple "stick bows" — a factor that can spook distant animals before the arrow arrives. However, their superior aiming qualities and higher arrow speeds more than make up for these minus traits in the minds of most dedicated bowhunters.

When purchasing a compound hunting bow, you should look for the same stabilizer hole and quiver-attachment bushings desirable in a recurve. You should also buy a bow with handy threaded sight-mounting holes in the handle riser — a feature seldom seen on recurves. In addition, many compound bows feature adjustable draw weights over a ten or fifteen-pound range — a real plus if you aren't sure what

draw weight you want to shoot or if you plan to lower the poundage for target shooting and raise it during big-game hunting season.

Most compound bows measure less than fifty inches in overall length, but length isn't the important consideration it is with recurves because the compound does not rely on limb length for arrow speed and does not increase bowstring pinch on the shooting fingers as bow length decreases.

Because compound bow designs are constantly changing, it is best to rely on your local archery dealer's suggestions when choosing an adequate hunting bow. Some excellent compounds with all-fiberglass limbs are now available, so laminated limbs are not necessarily the way to go. The most

*Left: Reduced holding weight of a compound bow helped the author nail this nice record-size California black bear.*

common choice of good bowhunters today is the so-called two-wheel compound, a simple, accurate design that usually lets off a full forty-five or fifty percent in draw weight, features a ten or fifteen-pound draw-weight adjustment range, and operates with the aid of one eccentric wheel on each limb tip that attaches to a simple network of cables and a bowstring. Ask your archery dealer for details on the latest compound offerings and their design peculiarities.

Aside from the basic choice of a recurve or compound design, several other things must be determined before purchasing a sensible hunting bow. The first and foremost is whether you need a left-hand or a right-hand bow. This choice is not always as easy as one might think. Every person has a dominant eye called a master eye which is stronger and most natural to aim with. Most right-handed people have right master eyes, and most left-handed people have left master eyes. However, a few have master eyes opposite to their favorite hands — a circumstance which can lead to a severe aiming problem called crossfiring.

To determine your master eye, simply point your index finger at a distant object with both eyes open. Shut your left eye, open it, then shut your right eye. The eye that is lined up with the object you are pointing at is your master eye (see photo).

If your master eye is your right eye, buy a right-hand bow. If your master eye is your left eye, buy a left-hand bow. It is always a bit awkward for a right-handed person with a left master eye or a left-handed person with a right master eye to learn to shoot the proper bow, but a right-hander or left-hander with a master eye on the opposite side can never aim well if he buys a bow that matches his favorite hand instead of his master eye. As is explained in Chapter 3, a shooter must have his master eye directly in line with the bowstring for decent accuracy.

After you determine your master eye, the next step is deciding what draw weight your hunting bow should be.

*Determining which is your master eye is a simple procedure described in the text, but a must for hunting accuracy.*

## Recommended Recurve Hunting Bow Draw Weights

| | Young Teenagers | Adult Women | Adult Men |
|---|---|---|---|
| **To Begin With** | 25-35 | 30-40 | 35-50 |
| **After Lots Of Regular Practice** | 30-40 | 35-45 | 45-60 |

Proficiency Level

## Recommended Compound Hunting Bow Draw Weights

| | Young Teenagers | Adult Women | Adult Men |
|---|---|---|---|
| **To Begin With** | 30-40 | 35-45 | 45-60 |
| **After Lots Of Regular Practice** | 35-45 | 45-60 | 50-75 |

Proficiency Level

## Recommended Bow Weights For Various Animals

| Draw Weights | Rabbits, Woodchucks | Bobcats, Coyotes | Deer, Black Bear | Elk, Moose |
|---|---|---|---|---|
| 30-40 | X | | | |
| 40-50 | X | X | X | |
| 50-60 | X | X | X | |
| 60-70 | | X | X | X |
| 70-80 | | | | X |

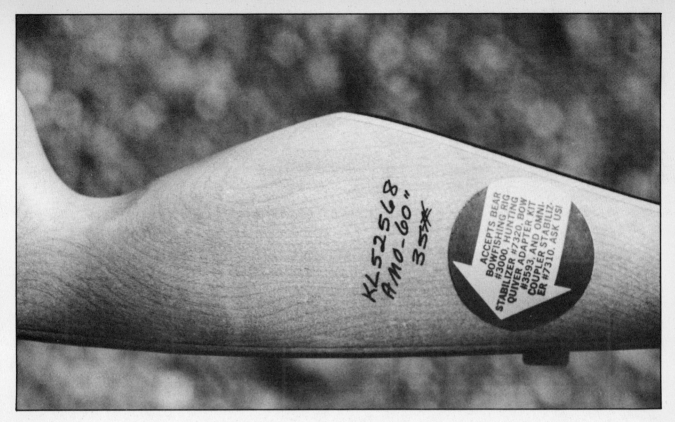

Most recurve bows are marked with the poundage or draw force required for a 28-inch draw. If draw length is longer or shorter, one must compute his personal draw weight by adding or subtracting three pounds per inch.

The accompanying charts for recurve and compound bows should serve as an accurate guide. The most important thing when deciding upon a hunting-bow draw weight is making sure not to "overbow" yourself and degrade accuracy because of excess muscle strain when shooting. Also important is matching your draw weight to the size of animals being hunted to ensure adequate arrow penetration and quick, humane kills. If forced to make a choice between accuracy and penetrating power, always choose the more accurate bow with the lighter draw weight. Proper shot placement on game is far more important than raw penetrating power.

Before buying a specific hunting bow, you must know your exact hunting draw length. This is determined by your physical size and the length of your arms. Compound bows are factory-set for specific draw lengths, so buying a bow set for the wrong draw length will make that bow difficult or impossible for you to shoot with comfort and accuracy. Since draw length directly determines the draw weight of a recurve bow, knowing your draw length is absolutely necessary when buying a recurve bow to ensure that you end up holding a correct, comfortable poundage at full draw. As a rough rule of thumb, a hunting recurve bow marked for a specific draw weight at a twenty-eight-inch draw pulls three pounds heavier per inch of draw over twenty-eight inches and three pounds lighter per inch of draw under twenty-eight inches. For example, a fifty-pound recurve at twenty-eight inches is a forty-seven-pound recurve when drawn twenty-seven inches and a fifty-three-pound recurve when drawn twenty-nine inches.

There are two accurate methods a beginner can use to determine his personal draw length. One is by holding one end of a yardstick lightly against the bottom of his throat with the fingertips of both hands extended along the sides of the yardstick and the yardstick parallel with the ground. The distance from the shooter's throat to the tips of the fingers will be his correct draw length. A similar method requires a person to stand at right angles to a wall with the clenched fist of his left hand (for a shooter with a right master eye) touching the wall. The distance from the wall to the right corner of the mouth is also the shooter's correct draw length (again, see photo). The commonly used method of determining draw length by actually having a person draw a bow is not very accurate for beginners because a novice's muscles are not strong enough or his bow-shooting form sound enough to tell how long an arrow he is likely to shoot once he becomes proficient with a bow.

Once you (1) decide on a specific bow design, (2) check your master eye, (3) settle on a practical hunting-bow draw weight, and (4) determine your draw length, you have the necessary information to buy the proper hunting bow. An archery dealer will normally help you make these decisions. Never, but never buy any hunting bow without considering these four basic bow-buying steps. They are the major keys to comfortable shooting and consistent success once you begin shooting at targets and game.

Aside from a well-designed hunting bow, a beginning archer needs to purchase four important bow accessories prior to learning how to shoot and hunt. These are a bowsight, an accurate arrow rest, a bowstringing tool, and a nocking point for the bowstring.

Although bowhunters of yesteryear with longbows and recurve bows often aimed without the aid of bowsights, the overwhelming majority of modern hunters prefer the accuracy and aiming ease afforded by a simple, durable sight attached to a bow. A small percentage of archers shoot better *without* bowsights, either by using the point of the arrow as a crude form of sight (called gap-shooting) or by shooting by pure instinct without consciously seeing anything but the target as they shoot. The ability to shoot by pure instinct is a rare gift akin to being able to throw a baseball exactly where you want to every single time. Gap-shooting by placing the arrow point different distances below the target at different ranges is at best a rough-hewn way to aim — a much less accurate way for most bowhunters than using a regular bowsight. Some long-time bowhunters are so used to shooting without sights that trying sights ruins their accuracy. However, virtually any beginner will shoot a bow best with a sight — especially a compound bow, which is usually shot slowly and deliberately after a careful aim at the target. As a

*The yardstick-against-the-throat method of determining draw length is fast, easy and accurate. (Right) Method known as knuckles-on-the-wall for determining draw length requires a helper, but provides a pinpoint measurement.*

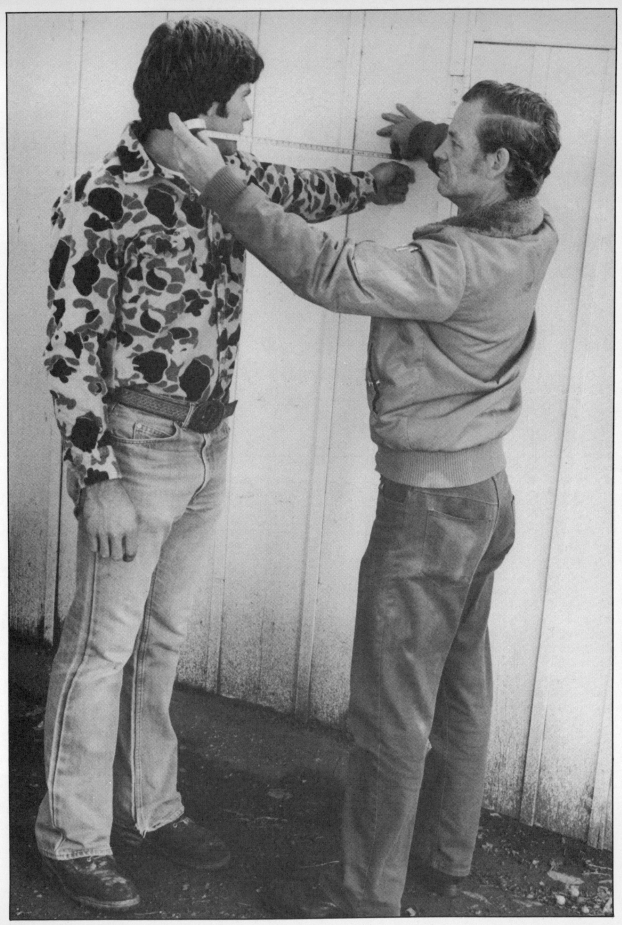

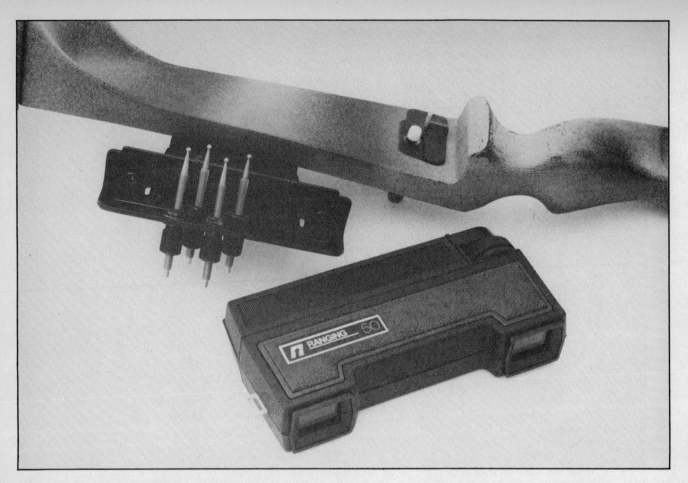

*Ranging Model 20-20 bowsight combines sturdy all-metal construction, four fully adjustable sight pins, and simple, rugged design. This particular sight is color-coded to be used with the color-coded Model 50 bowhunting rangefinder.*

result, every beginner should buy a bowsight prior to learning how to shoot.

A hunting bowsight should be a simple, rugged affair consisting of a metal sight bracket and four or five metal sight pins which can be set for several different shooting distances. Quite a few bowsights available at archery stores are completely ill-suited for bowhunting, either because they are fragile one-pin target sights or because they are simply low-cost, ill-designed contraptions made of plastic or another easily broken material. The best hunting bowsights mount solidly to a bow with bolts or screws, feature fully adjustable sight pins made of stainless steel or brass, and display a rugged simplicity any practical person can spot. A

hunting bow receives considerable rough-and-tumble abuse in the woods — abuse a sight must be able to resist.

Although so-called "rangefinder bowsights" with intricate rangefinding grids, sliding sight pins, or wire-ring aiming devices might appeal to the uninitiated, these gimmicks are not as effective as one might desire in practical hunting situations. As is discussed in Chapter 8, a bowhunter is best advised to use a separate rangefinding tool instead of relying on sight-attached rangefinding gizmos.

A bow's arrow rest consists of two parts — a shelf, which the bottom of the arrow rests upon, and a plate, which the

*Semi-rigid, adhesive-backed arrow rests sometimes produce decent arrow flight, but don't afford the plate adjustability or the flexibility of better designs.*

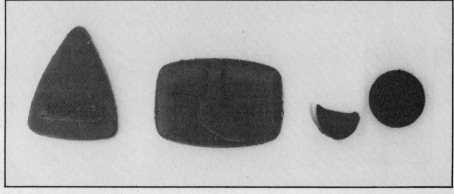

side of the arrow rides against. Unfortunately, most bow manufacturers attach relatively poor rests to their bows — a way of cutting costs that normally penalizes beginning, uneducated bowhunters. A well-designed arrow rest ensures good shooting accuracy; a poor one prevents decent shooting no matter how hard an archer tries.

The typical factory arrow rest provided with a new, good-quality bow is a one-piece rubber design with a semi-rigid shelf arm and a raised ridge or bump which serves as a plate. Such a rest is attached to the bow with adhesive — a fortunate circumstance because the rest can be easily peeled off and tossed in the nearest trash can. Such a rest does not offer the plate adjustability needed to make arrows fly well and tends to wear away or break from regular shooting. The relatively unyielding shelf on such a rest also collides with modern plastic arrow fletching during a shot and makes an arrow wobble haphazardly toward the target.

Buy a decent arrow rest for your bow before you ever shoot it. You'll be glad you did. No matter what specific kind of rest you decide to use, it should have the following general characteristics: First, the shelf section should be sturdy enough to hold up the arrow but horizontally flexible to prevent collision with arrow fletching as the arrow leaves the bow. Second, the rest's plate should be horizontally adjustable by screwing it in and out of the bow, by shimming it with adhesive spacers, or by cutting it down with a knife or file. Third, the rest should be waterproof and quiet to draw an arrow across. Fourth, the rest should be made of durable, long-wearing material like nylon, Teflon, leather, steel, and/or brass. In addition to the one-piece rubber or plastic rests often supplied by bow manufacturers, other wretched, poor-shooting, inflexible rests to avoid include so-called "rug rests" often installed on recurve bows and any other rest design that is rigid, fragile, noisy, or prone to rust or soak up water.

If your bow's handle riser is drilled and tapped to accept a screw-adjustable rest, buy such a rest at the archery store. The two very best rests of this sort are the cushion plunger/flipper rest, made by several different companies, and the springy rest. The plunger/flipper is a two-piece setup with a spring-loaded, collapsing shelf section that sticks to the bow with adhesive and a fully screw-adjustable spring-loaded plunger plate section that screws into the bow. The springy rest is a simpler one-piece affair with a flexible spring-wire shelf and a fully adjustable spring-coil plate. Springy rests of different wire diameters and different resulting flexibilities are sold to match hunting

*The two-piece plunger/flipper arrow rest (right) consists of a white, spring-loaded Teflon plate and a collapsing Teflon-covered shelf; springy rest (left) is more simple one-piece unit with spring-coil plate and a flexible spring-wire shelf arm. Most bowhunters cover the springy rest's shelf arm and first coil with commercial Teflon arrow-rest sleeves to prevent game-spooking noise when arrow is drawn. Both types are excellent for bowhunting.*

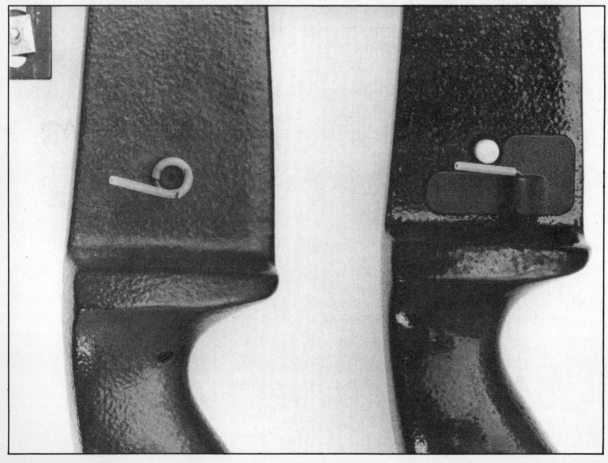

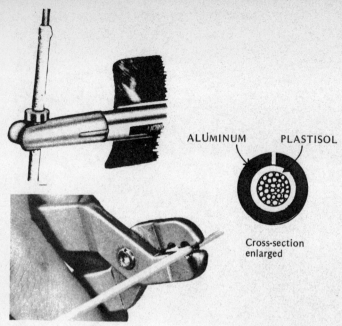

ALUMINUM    PLASTISOL

Cross-section
enlarged

*Author contends the best commercial nocking point consists
of an aluminum ring with a layer of plastisol beneath.
This nocking point is clamped in place with special pliers
and can be loosened easily and moved for best flight of
the arrow. Nock arrow directly under such a nocking point.*

bows of different draw weights. For bows without threaded
rest holes in the handles, use a flexible, well-designed
adhesive-mounting rest like the all-nylon Hoyt Super Pro,
the Bear bristle rest (with leather plate), or the Flipper II
rest with a plate of stacking felt pads. Most but not all
compound bows are drilled to accept a springy or cushion
plunger rest; most recurve bows are not drilled and must be
installed with a flexible adhesive-backed rest.

Every bowhunter needs a bowstringing tool
(bowstringer) which matches the kind of bow he hunts
with. A bowstringer is especially important for the recurve
or longbow user because a stick bow should be strung at the
start of each hunting day and unstrung again each night.
This procedure prevents unnecessary strain on the bow
limbs which can eventually weaken them.

Although some bowhunters string and unstring their
longbows or recurve bows by hand using tricky,
muscle-straining techniques like the push-pull method or

*Left: Changing bowstrings on a two-wheel compound is safe
and easy with a steel-cable bowstringer requiring the use
of one foot, both hands. Be certain to buy a bowstringer,
however, that will match the design of your hunting bow.*

the step-through method, incorrectly hand-stringing a bow
can easily twist and permanently damage its fragile limbs,
and can also put out a person's eye with the upper limb tip
if the bow slips or breaks during the stringing process. If
you plan to use a recurve bow or longbow, buy a
bowstringer to avoid problems.

A wide variety of bowstringing tools is available to
match the current wide variety of compound bows on the
market. Ask your archery dealer to set you up with a
proper bowstringing tool for the compound you intend to
use. A compound bowstring normally lasts at least a year of
regular shooting unless accidentally cut with a sharp
hunting broadhead, which means the beginning archer with
a compound bow won't need to use his bowstringer until
after he perfects his basic shooting form. Then, as discussed
in Chapter 7, he'll want to buy a couple of extra bowstrings
for the field and set them up properly with the aid of his
bowstringing tool.

The final necessary piece of bow equipment you need to
begin shooting is some sort of nocking point (sometimes
called a nock locator) that attaches to the bowstring to
ensure consistent arrow placement on the string. Consistent
arrow nocking is a must for good accuracy. The best
commercial nocking point is a compact design consisting of
an aluminum ring with a layer of rubber underneath. Such a
nocking point is clamped in place with inexpensive
nocking-point pliers and is easily loosened and moved about
to achieve the best arrow accuracy. Purchase one or two
such nocking points with your bow, and either buy a pair
of nocking-point pliers or have your archery dealer clamp
the nocking point in place to begin with. It's probably best
to go ahead and purchase the nocking-point pliers because
you'll need them later on to fine-tune your bow/arrow
combination once you have a solid handle on bow-shooting
basics. In Chapter 3, we'll discuss where and how to install
this nocking point for best shooting accuracy.

## HUNTING ARROWS

Choosing the proper arrow to match your hunting bow

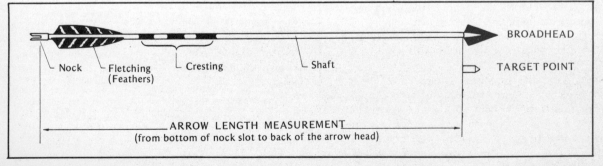

ARROW LENGTH MEASUREMENT
(from bottom of nock slot to back of the arrow head)

*Quality arrows are assembled by several reputable firms. One of the oldest and largest suppliers is Bear Archery, whose arrow division annually produces many thousands of well fletched aluminum hunting arrows in various lengths.*

is the single most important step you'll have to make on the way to a well-matched bow-shooting setup. A wide variety of hunting bows can be used successfully to take game, but only one or two arrow shaft sizes will fly accurately from a particular hunting bow. Determining which shaft size is best and selecting well-made arrows of this shaft size is not all that difficult with the following tips, but this selection is vital to decent accuracy on targets and game.

An arrow consists of a central shaft with a nock and fletching on one end and some sort of arrowhead on the other end. Let's discuss these arrow components one at a time to determine which kind of arrow is best for bowhunting sport.

The shaft of an arrow is the most important ingredient in consistent arrow accuracy and flat arrow trajectory. Arrow shafts have traditionally been made of three materials — wood (usually cedar), fiberglass, and aluminum. All these shaft materials have been used successfully on game in the past, but all are not of equal quality — not by a long shot.

Cedar shafts were the traditional choice of longbow users in years gone by, and many recurve shooters also used these with fair results. Such shafts are light in weight for flat arrow trajectory, but tend to vary considerably in stiffness (spine), straightness, and weight — the three major ingredients which must be consistent to achieve

bow-shooting accuracy. In addition, cedar is prone to warp in damp conditions, requiring regular inspection by a hunter. Cedar tends to break on impact with bone or other hard objects, too, another major drawback. So-called compressed cedar shafts are more consistent in stiffness and weight than regular wooden shafts, but are considerably heavier and still not as uniform or weatherproof as other shaft materials. Cedar arrow shafts are the least expensive of those available — a plus — but are not used much these days. They are especially ill-suited for use with compound bows because compounds tend to shoot best with stiff, quickly flexing shafts of thin-wall aluminum. Wood is

**NOTES TO CHART ON PAGE 33**

*Available in XX75 only. **Available in GameGetter only.
☐Indicates Jim Doughtery "Naturals"
† NOTE: The shaft sizes 8185 through 2419 are contractions of actual physical dimensions of the tubes — example: **2016** has a **20/64"** outside diameter and a **.016"** wall thickness.
‡ NOTE: The arrow weight in grains (437.5 grains per ounce) includes a 125 grain broadhead, 30 grain insert and 35 grains (average between plastic vanes and feathers) for nock and fletching.
8.4M, 8.5M and 8.7M are Bear Metric Magnum & Metric Hunter shaft sizes. The indicated spines are recommended by Bear Archery.

The chart indicates that more than one shaft size may shoot well from your bow. The shaft size in the unshaded or white area of the box is the most widely used, but you may decide to shoot a lighter shaft for flatter trajectory, or a heavier shaft for greater durability. Also, large variations in bow efficiency, bow design, shooting style, and release may require special bow tuning or a shaft size change to accommodate these variations.

# EASTON ALUMINUM HUNTING SHAFT SELECTION CHART

(Most popular size selection is shown in the unshaded area of each box)

**CORRECT HUNTING ARROW LENGTH** (Your Draw Length Plus ½ to ¾ Inch Clearance)

| ACTUAL BOW WEIGHT (At Your Draw Length) | 26½-27½ / 27" Shaft Size | Arrow Weight | 27½-28½ / 28" Shaft Size | Arrow Weight | 28½-29½ / 29" Shaft Size | Arrow Weight | 29½-30½ / 30" Shaft Size | Arrow Weight | 30½-31½ / 31" Shaft Size | Arrow Weight | 31½-32½ / 32" Shaft Size | Arrow Weight | 32½-33½ / 33" Shaft Size | Arrow Weight | 33½-34½ / 34" Shaft Size | Arrow Weight | COMPOUND BOW PEAK WEIGHT 30% Let-off | 50% Let-off |
|---|---|---|---|---|---|---|---|---|---|---|---|---|---|---|---|---|---|---|
| 35-39 | 1913*<br>1815□<br>1816 | 415<br>424<br>440 | 1913*<br>1915□<br>1916<br>1818 | 426<br>447<br>471<br>490 | 2013*<br>1916<br>1917□ | 451<br>481<br>501 | 2114<br>2016<br>8.4M<br>1917□<br>1918 | 486<br>507<br>508<br>511<br>537 | 2114<br>2016<br>2115□<br>1918<br>8.5M | 496<br>517<br>524<br>549<br>565 | 2213*<br>2115□<br>2018<br>8.6M | 505<br>535<br>583<br>619 | 2213*<br>2117 | 514<br>587 | | | 41-46 | 47-52 |
| 40-44 | 1913*<br>1915□<br>1916<br>1818 | 415<br>438<br>461<br>478 | 2013*<br>1916<br>1917□<br>1820** | 442<br>471<br>490<br>530 | 2114<br>2016<br>8.4M<br>1917□<br>1918 | 476<br>496<br>497<br>501<br>526 | 2114<br>2016<br>2115□<br>1918<br>8.5M | 486<br>507<br>513<br>537<br>553 | 2213*<br>2115□<br>2018<br>8.6M | 495<br>524<br>571<br>612 | 2213*<br>2117<br>2018<br>8.7M | 505<br>575<br>583<br>675 | 2117<br>2216 | 587<br>587 | | | 47-52 | 53-59 |
| 45-49 | 2013*<br>1916<br>1917□<br>1820** | 433<br>461<br>479<br>517 | 2114<br>2016<br>8.4M<br>1917□<br>1918 | 466<br>486<br>487<br>490<br>514 | 2114<br>2016<br>2115□<br>8.5M<br>1920** | 476<br>496<br>502<br>541<br>559 | 2213*<br>2115□<br>2018<br>8.6M | 485<br>513<br>558<br>598 | 2213*<br>2117<br>2018<br>2020<br>8.7M | 495<br>563<br>571<br>609<br>660 | 2117<br>2216<br>2020<br>8.7M | 575<br>575<br>622<br>675 | 2216<br>2217□ | 587<br>609 | 2219 | 658 | 53-58 | 60-66 |
| 50-54 | 2114<br>2016<br>1917□<br>1918 | 456<br>475<br>470<br>503 | 2114<br>2016<br>8.4M<br>2115□<br>1920** | 466<br>486<br>487<br>492<br>546 | 2213*<br>2115□<br>8.5M<br>2018<br>1920** | 475<br>502<br>541<br>546<br>559 | 2213*<br>2117<br>2018<br>2020<br>8.6M | 485<br>551<br>558<br>595<br>598 | 2117<br>2216<br>2020<br>8.7M | 563<br>563<br>609<br>660 | 2216<br>2217□<br>8.7M | 575<br>596<br>675 | 2216<br>2217□<br>2219 | 587<br>609<br>644 | 2219 | 658 | 59-64 | 67-72 |
| 55-59 | 2114<br>2016<br>8.4M<br>2115□<br>1920** | 456<br>475<br>477<br>481<br>534 | 2213*<br>2115□<br>8.5M<br>2018<br>1920** | 465<br>492<br>529<br>534<br>546 | 2213*<br>2117<br>2018<br>2020<br>8.6M | 475<br>539<br>534<br>582<br>585 | 2117<br>2216<br>2020<br>8.7M | 551<br>551<br>595<br>645 | 2216<br>2217□<br>8.7M | 563<br>584<br>660 | 2216<br>2217□<br>2219 | 575<br>596<br>631 | 2217□<br>2219 | 609<br>644 | 2317<br>2219 | 648<br>658 | 65-70 | 73-79 |
| 60-64 | 2213*<br>8.4M<br>2115□<br>2018<br>1920** | 455<br>477<br>481<br>522<br>534 | 2213*<br>2117<br>8.5M<br>2018<br>2020 | 465<br>527<br>529<br>534<br>568 | 2117<br>2216<br>2020<br>8.6M | 539<br>539<br>582<br>585 | 2216<br>2217□<br>8.7M | 551<br>571<br>645 | 2216<br>2217□<br>2219<br>8.7M | 563<br>584<br>617<br>660 | 2217□<br>2219 | 596<br>631 | 2317<br>2219 | 634<br>644 | 2317 | 648 | 71-76 | 80-86 |
| 65-69 | 2213*<br>2117<br>2018<br>2020 | 455<br>515<br>522<br>555 | 2117<br>2216<br>2020<br>8.6M | 527<br>527<br>568<br>571 | 2216<br>2217□<br>8.7M | 539<br>558<br>629 | 2216<br>2217□<br>2219<br>8.7M | 551<br>571<br>603<br>645 | 2217□<br>2219 | 584<br>617 | 2317<br>2219 | 621<br>631 | 2317 | 634 | 2317 | 648 | 77-82 | 87-93 |
| 70-74 | 2117<br>2216<br>2020 | 515<br>515<br>555 | 2216<br>2217□ | 527<br>546 | 2216<br>2217□<br>2219 | 539<br>558<br>589 | 2217□<br>2219 | 571<br>603 | 2317<br>2219 | 607<br>617 | 2317 | 621 | 2317 | 634 | 2419 | 685 | 83-88 | 94-100 |
| 75-79 | 2216<br>2217□ | 515<br>533 | 2216<br>2217□<br>2219 | 527<br>546<br>575 | 2217□<br>2219 | 558<br>589 | 2317<br>2219 | 594<br>603 | 2317 | 607 | 2317 | 621 | 2419 | 670 | 2419 | 685 | 89-94 | 101-107 |
| 80-84 | 2216<br>2217□<br>2219 | 515<br>533<br>562 | 2217□<br>2219 | 546<br>575 | 2317<br>2219 | 580<br>589 | 2317 | 594 | 2317 | 607 | 2419 | 656 | 2419 | 670 | 2419 | 685 | 95-100 | 108-114 |
| 85-89 | 2217□<br>2219 | 533<br>562 | 2317<br>2219 | 567<br>575 | 2317 | 580 | 2317 | 594 | 2419 | 641 | 2419 | 656 | 2419 | 670 | | | 101-106 | 115-121 |
| 90-94 | 2317<br>2219 | 553<br>562 | 2317 | 567 | 2317 | 580 | 2419 | 627 | 2419 | 641 | 2419 | 656 | | | | | 107-112 | 122-128 |
| 95-99 | 2317 | 553 | 2317 | 567 | 2419 | 612 | 2419 | 627 | 2419 | 641 | | | | | | | 113-118 | 129-135 |
| 100-109 | 2317 | 553 | 2419 | 597 | 2419 | 612 | 2419 | 627 | | | | | | | | | 119-129 | 136-149 |
| 110-119 | 2419 | 583 | 2419 | 597 | 2419 | 612 | | | | | | | | | | | 130-142 | 150-163 |

anything but stiff in normal shaft sizes, and bends sluggishly instead of recovering to straightness quickly after the bowstring slams it in the rear and bends it during a shot.

Fiberglass shafts are an improvement over wood, but tend to be extremely heavy in weight and are seldom rigidly uniform in weight, straightness, or stiffness. These shafts are waterproof, and do resist breakage better than cedar shafts. However, like wooden shafts, they tend to recover to straightness sluggishly after leaving a bow, a phenomenon which impedes the accuracy of a compound bow. Fiberglass shafts are not nearly as popular as aluminum, the third major kind of shaft material. Aside from weight and accuracy considerations, aluminum shafts are more popular than fiberglass because they can be restraightened if they collide with a rock or another solid obstacle. In contrast, solid impact breaks and forever ruins a shaft made of fiberglass.

According to official archery-shop surveys, some eighty percent of all bowhunting arrows currently purchased have shafts made of aluminum. Aluminum has a number of things going for it. For one, it is the most rigidly consistent shaft in straightness, stiffness, and weight, which leads to superior accuracy. For another, aluminum shafts are available in more sizes than any other shaft material, easing the bowhunter's quest for an especially accurate hunting arrow. In addition, modern aluminum arrow shafts are incredibly durable, and when they *are* bent they can be easily restraightened and used again. In addition, modern aluminum shafts are anodized in a variety of dull hunting colors, providing the ultimate in camouflage as well as protection for the shafts. Like the compound bow, the aluminum shaft is a current standard in the bowhunting field by which all other products are judged.

Matching the proper arrow size to your hunting bow is very easy, thanks to arrow-shaft selection charts published by arrow manufacturers. Shaft stiffness is the most important factor in achieving accurate arrow flight from a particular bow, with shaft weight being a secondary but also important factor in hunting situations.

To determine which arrow shaft size you need to shoot, you must know the exact draw weight of your hunting bow, the approximate percentage let-off at full draw (if it is a compound bow), and your exact draw length (discussed earlier in this chapter). The Easton Hunting Shaft Selection Chart is an industry standard which includes all presently offered sizes of aluminum hunting arrows sold in North America. It can be used directly to determine which size or sizes of arrow shafts will best match your bow.

Like a rifle, a bow will normally shoot several sizes of "ammunition" with excellent accuracy. Determining which of the three or four acceptable arrow sizes listed on the Easton Chart will work the best for you should be based on how much these shafts weigh. This chart includes the weight (in grains) of each arrow size at your draw length, and as a general rule the medium-weight to heaviest shafts recommended represent the most practical choices for hunting. A heavier arrow is normally superior to a lighter one because it retains energy better for deeper penetration on game, flies more accurately with big-game broadheads, shoots more quietly from a bow than a lighter-weight shaft, and causes less strain and vibration on the limbs and other parts of a hunting bow. Vibration and strain can eventually cause bow failure if excessively light arrows are used.

The lighter shaft sizes recommended on the accompanying shaft-selection chart are primarily used by competitive archers who demand ultra-fast arrow speeds to minimize wind drift and to flatten out arrow trajectory for easier aiming. These lighter shaft sizes can be extremely accurate when used with field points or other target-shooting arrowheads, but are not the best choices

*Every aluminum arrow shaft is marked clearly with the alloy of which it is made (such as XX75, an extremely durable hunting alloy) and the size (such as 2219 or 2117). The arrow manufacturer's name often appears on the shaft, too.*

*Relatively heavy aluminum arrow shafts are needed when bowhunting large, tough-to-penetrate animals. The author used 2219 shafts in a 70-pound compound bow to bag this record-size 60-inch Alaska moose. The heavy shaft/bow combo dropped the animal with one shot in the lungs. The mass of a shaft yields the energy for penetration.*

when hunting because of the reasons already stated.

There currently exists what I call a "speed cult" among modern bowhunters. The fellows in this cult are completely possessed with the desire to shoot the fastest arrows they can find — which means the arrows of the lightest physical weight. The philosophy behind this cult is that flat arrow trajectory is by far the most important thing in hunting animals. It *is* true that a faster, flatter-flying arrow is easier to hit with at unknown ranges (see Chapter 8 for arrow-trajectory facts). However, light, fast-flying arrows create a whole set of problems that more than cancel out the appeal of their slightly flatter flight. They shed energy like ping-pong balls at longer ranges, cutting down

drastically on animal penetration. They fly erratically with all but the smallest-diameter hunting broadheads...and the smaller the broadhead, the less deadly it tends to be. This is not to mention the shooting noise and strain on equipment which light arrows cause.

A specialized big-game bowhunter who concentrates on pronghorn antelope, mule deer, and other small to medium-sized big game in wide-open country might be best off with an ultra-speedy, lightweight arrow, but a heavier arrow is far more practical in the vast majority of cases. When using shaft-selection charts for arrows other than aluminum, these same basic selection principles should apply.

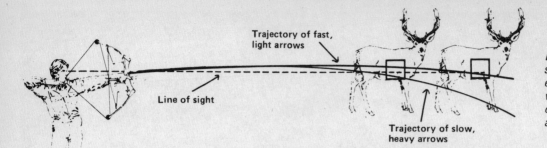

Trajectory of fast, light arrows

Line of sight

Trajectory of slow, heavy arrows

*Lightweight aluminum shaft will produce an extra-flat trajectory which can ease the job of hitting open-area animals like mule deer.*

*With hunting bows drawing over 50 pounds, arrow fletching should be a full five inches long to ensure good arrow stability. Fletching should be spiraled around shaft to further enhance accuracy.*

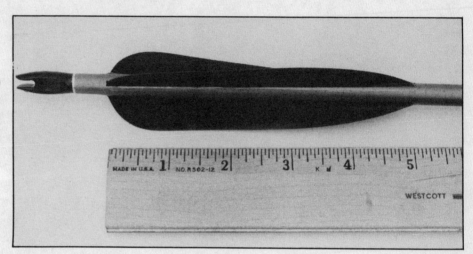

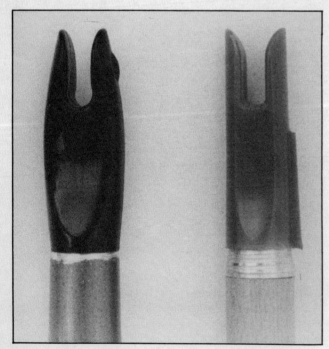

*Bjorn-type snap-on nock (left) is standard equipment on modern quality hunting arrows. The older index type (right) does not hug the bowstring as firmly and often retards arrow accuracy, especially if it is installed crookedly.*

A good-quality, well-assembled hunting arrow has certain traits a bowhunter should insist upon. One is full-sized, strongly spiraled fletching on the rear end. This fletching should be at least four inches long on arrow sizes for hunting bows under fifty pounds, and should be a full five inches long on arrows for bows over fifty pounds. Quite a few second-rate arrows sold over the counter today carry fletching that is not spiraled on the shaft at all, and such arrows should be avoided like the plague. The fletching on an arrow is supposed to stabilize it in flight, and in order to do this it must be fairly large in surface area (hence the need for fletching four or five inches long) and must also spiral around the shaft to rotate it in flight.

Most modern hunting arrows carry plastic fletching, normally called "vanes." Such fletching usually flies well from a properly tuned compound bow, but older-style feather fletching generally shoots better from a recurve bow or longbow because it flattens out as it passes the bow's handle during a shot. Handles on most compound bows are recessed (centershot) to allow adequate handle clearance of plastic vanes. Plastic vanes are most practical to hunt with if they'll fly well from your bow because they are impervious to moisture and outwear feathers during extended periods of regular shooting. By contrast, feathers become ratty with age and wilt in the rain unless soaked with silicone or another effective waterproofing agent.

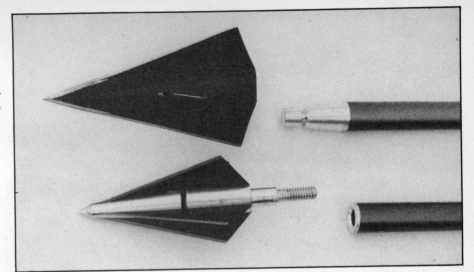

Old-style glue-on point adapter (top) is less convenient to use than a modern screw-in adapter.

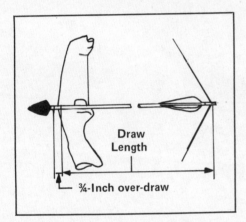

Hunting arrows should be cut 3/4-inch longer than your draw length. This prevents broadhead from bumping the front of your bow during your shot.

The same speed cult that favors ultra-light arrow shafts also tends to favor small, lightly spiraled fletching on arrows because this sort of setup creates less tail-end drag and results in slightly faster arrow flight. The trouble is, it also results in wretched accuracy and requires dinky, poorly performing hunting broadheads for even mediocre target groups.

Most modern hunting arrows are fletched with three plastic vanes or feathers. A few bowhunters prefer four-fletched arrows, but these do not normally shoot one whit better than standard arrows unless compound-bow cables collide with the higher-profile three-fletch configuration.

Extensive testing by Easton Aluminum, the largest arrow-shaft manufacturer in the world, indicates that a crooked or poorly designed arrow nock can completely destroy the accuracy of an otherwise perfect hunting arrow. A bowhunter should make sure his arrows are installed with snap-on, Bjorn-type nocks — nocks that hug a bowstring for safety and convenience and that glue uniformly, concentrically to an arrow shaft. Such nocks are standard equipment on modern aluminum hunting arrows.

Another standard fixture on a modern aluminum

hunting arrow is a screw-in point adapter which glues into the front end of the tubular shaft. Such an adapter allows instant screw-interchangeability of various kinds of arrowheads. Older-style or off-brand arrows often require points to be glued to tapered point adapters — a tedious, time-consuming, and completely unnecessary process today.

Once you have selected a good-quality set of arrows to match your bow, these arrows must be cut off to the proper length. This length is your draw length (which you determined earlier) plus an extra three-quarters-inch to make sure hunting broadheads or other wide arrowheads do not bump the front of your bow when you draw. Arrow length is measured from the bottom of the nock slot on the arrow to the cut-off point on the front of the shaft. It is standard practice for archery dealers to cut their customers' arrows to length and install screw-in point adapters with hot-melt arrow-point cement.

To begin shooting your bow/arrow combination, the only arrowheads you need are standard 125-grain field

Standard 125-grain field points are the only arrowheads a beginner needs to learn the basics of bow-shooting.

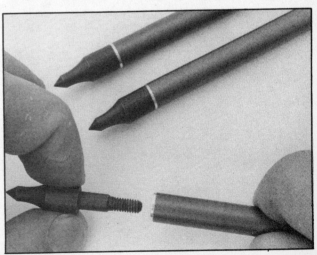

*A simple tube-type hip quiver can be handy for carrying arrows during your sessions at casual target practice.*

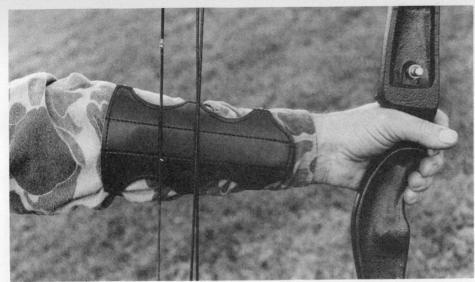

Armguard flattens a baggy sleeve, protects the forearm from painful bowstring slap when you're shooting.

Shooting tab protects an archer's bowstring fingers, while providing a smooth, accurate arrow release.

points that instantly screw into the ends of your arrows. Later on, after some shooting practice, you can purchase other arrowhead designs that suit various forms of bowhunting. See Chapter 6 for details on specific bowhunting arrowheads and their uses.

## OTHER NECESSARY BOW-SHOOTING GEAR

Before you can set up your bow/arrow combination and begin to shoot, you'll need three other important items. The first is an inexpensive, tube-type hip quiver to carry your arrows while practicing on targets. Such a quiver is available at any archery store, and eliminates the need to lay arrows on the ground or stuff them unceremoniously and precariously in a hip pocket as some beginners end up doing.

The second thing you'll need is a simple, inexpensive armguard for the forearm of the arm you use to hold your bow. Such an armguard performs two basic functions — it

flattens out the baggy sleeve of a shirt or jacket to prevent the bowstring from catching it and throwing a shot wild, and it protects the forearm from painful bowstring slap that can severely bruise any shooter's arm. Although larger armguards are available, most experienced shooters prefer an armguard about six inches long and four inches wide.

The third and last piece of basic shooting gear every bowhunter needs is either a shooting glove or a tab to protect his bowstring fingers as he shoots. A glove is initially easier for most beginning shooters to use, but a tab provides a slicker, smoother bowstring release and significantly better accuracy. Try out both forms of finger protection at the archery store, then choose the one that feels most comfortable and allows the easiest shooting. If you're starting out, you'll probably choose the glove. However, after you master bow-shooting basics you should give the tab a serious workout because it improves most hunters' shooting performance on both targets and game.

# CHAPTER 2

# EQUIPMENT: READY OR NOT?

## There Are Things To Know If Your Tackle Is To Shoot Properly!

ONCE A would-be bowhunter has carefully selected a bow, arrows, and other necessary items outlined in Chapter 1, the next step is preparing this equipment for shooting on the target range.

Since hunting bows vary greatly in design today — especially compound bows — it is impossible to outline one specific setup procedure that works well for all bows. A hunter is best advised to carefully read whatever manufacturer's literature has been included with his bow, and then to enlist as much equipment setup help as he can from the dealer who has sold him his basic shooting gear.

Nonetheless, there are six basic steps every archer should follow when setting up his bow prior to actual shooting. These ensure adequate accuracy from the outset and

*Before shooting the compound bow, friction points such as the axles of the compound wheels all should be lubricated carefully using a top-grade lubricant.*

provide a solid base for tuning the bow/arrow combination to shooting perfection as time goes by.

First, an archer should oil or grease all friction points on his bow as recommended by the manufacturer. This procedure applies primarily to compound bows, but some takedown recurve bows have locking knuckle joints or assembly bolts and lock pins which need lubrication to prevent rust and wear. On a compound bow, the primary lubrication points are the threads on draw-weight adjustment bolts and the axles of eccentric wheels. A light automotive grease works well on bolts, and a penetrating lubricant like WD-40 is fine where axles and wheels come together.

In addition, an archer should lubricate his bowstring before starting to shoot. This is accomplished by rubbing the string strands thoroughly with beeswax or another commercial bowstring wax available at any archery store. *Do not* wax the wrapped central "serving" section of the string where you grip the string to shoot. Waxing a bowstring prevents wear-causing friction between individual string strands and also protects the surface of the string from minor scrapes and bumps. Coating a bowstring with wax every month or two will at least triple the life of the string.

Once a bow is lubricated, the next step is setting it up according to manufacturer's instructions. Actually, any archery dealer worth his salt should personally supervise this particular detail. For example, most two-wheel and four-wheel compound bows with adjustable draw weights must be "tillered" prior to shooting — a process which balances the upper bow-limb against the lower bow-limb to ensure good accuracy. This is a relatively simple process accomplished by tightening the lower draw-weight adjustment bolt approximately one turn tighter than the upper bolt to put the lower limb under slightly greater pressure than the upper limb. Such a tiller adjustment compensates for the fact that a bowhunter grips the bow and the bowstring slightly off the vertical center of the bow, equalizing the amount of bend and thrust in each bow limb when the bow is drawn and released. Recommended setups of this sort for compound bows are usually simple and fully spelled out in manufacturer's literature.

Next, the bow should be set at a desired draw weight if it is an adjustable-weight bow. Some bows are factory-set at your desired weight and others have pre-marked settings that make reaching a particular draw weight a snap.

40

BOWHUNTER'S DIGESTBOWHUNTER'S DIGEST

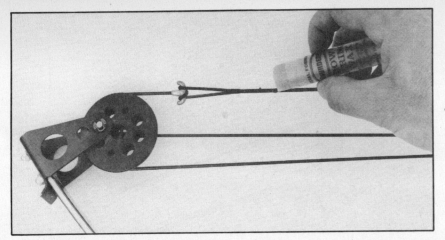

*A bowstring which is waxed regularly resists surface scrapes and normally outlasts an unwaxed bowstring on an average of two or three to one.*

*Most compound bows being manufactured today are set for the proper draw weight at the factory by means of a set of sophisticated scales. But the bowhunter still should check his bow to be certain that the draw weight has been set properly prior to shooting. Even sophisticated factory equipment has been known to go astray in measuring.*

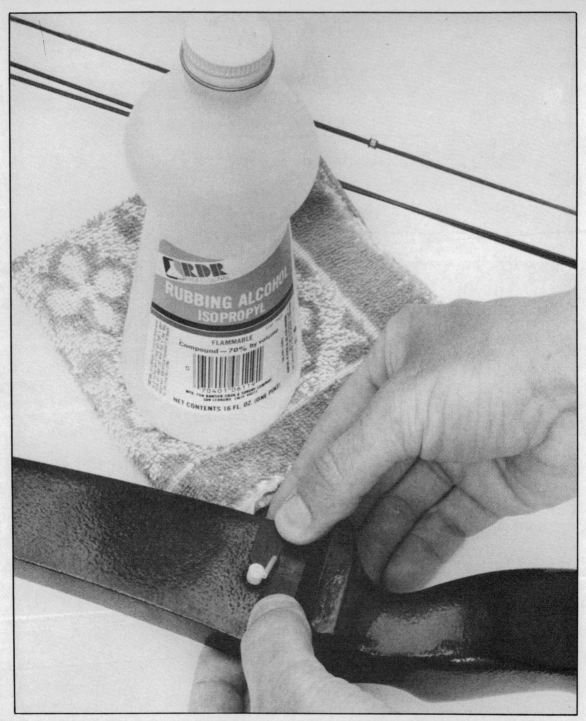

*An adhesive-backed arrow rest such as the Flipper II can be installed easily once the installation area on the bow has been cleaned thoroughly with rubbing alcohol. This is a necessary step to ensure the positive bond that is needed.*

However, the draw weights of most compound bows must be checked and rechecked on an archery-shop bow scale until the desired draw weights are exactly achieved by rotating draw-weight adjustment bolts.

After a bow is set at a particular draw weight, it is time to install a practical arrow rest on the handle riser. Note: a one-piece, adhesive-backed rest like the Flipper II or Hoyt Super Pro should be installed in the same spot on the handle where the factory rest originally was. This precaution ensures good accuracy. Prior to installation, a

little rubbing alcohol should be scrubbed on the surface where the rest will be placed with cotton or a clean paper towel. This will degrease and clean the handle's rest area, ensuring solid rest adhesion.

A cushion plunger/flipper rest combo or a springy rest is even easier to install. The springy is simply screwed into place with the wire shelf at approximate right angles to the bowstring and the plate portion about one-quarter-inch out from the bow. Likewise, the cushion plunger is screwed into place with the button slightly protruding from the

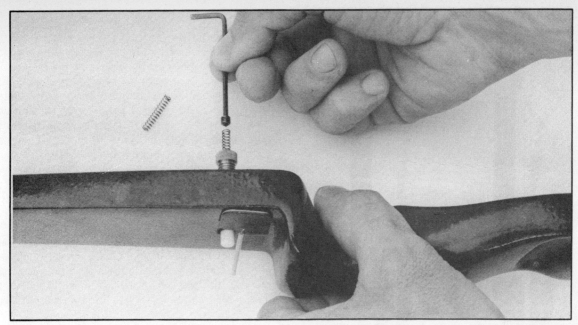

*Most cushion plungers come complete with several plunger springs to ensure easy bow-tuning. The spring of the proper stiffness should be inserted in the plunger prior to shooting the bow, author's findings indicate.*

bow, and the flipper is affixed directly beneath it after an alcohol scrub of the handle riser. When properly installed, the flipper arm of the plunger/flipper rest should be about one-thirty-second-inch below the plunger button so the side of the arrow centers the button as it rides across the flipper. This button-centered setup yields the smoothest plunger operation and the best accuracy.

If a cushion plunger comes complete with three springs of varying stiffness — as plungers often do — then you should install the lightest spring for a hunting bow between

forty and fifty pounds, the medium spring for a bow between fifty and sixty pounds, and the heavy spring for a bow sixty pounds or above. No matter which spring you install or if only one is supplied to begin with, it should be set for a medium tension by tightening down the plunger's tension set-screw all the way and then backing this screw out about half the possible distance. Such a setting will normally yield decent arrow flight until you are ready to get nitpicky and fine-tune your shooting combo. (See Chapter 4 for details.)

*A nocking point — or nock locator — should be installed on the bowstring about half an inch above 90 degrees to the arrow rest. Such nocking height normally will produce proper arrow flight.*

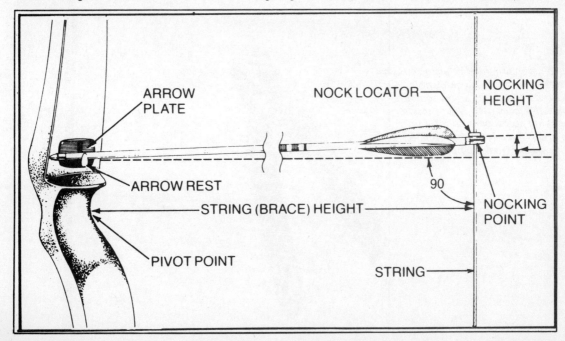

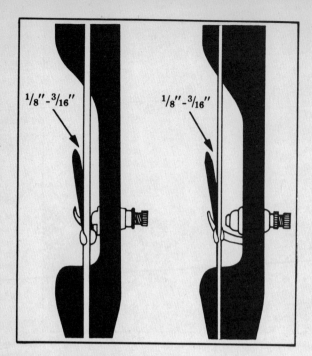

1/8″ - 3/16″          1/8″ - 3/16″

Once the arrow rest is in place, a nocking point should be affixed to the bowstring so the bottom of this point is one-half-inch above ninety degrees to the arrow shelf. This nocking-point placement is roughly correct on both recurve and compound bows, although some minor adjustments might have to be made as a shooter perfects his accuracy. (See Chapter 4.) Your archery dealer can install the nocking point properly for you, or you can do it yourself with nocking-point pliers and a common carpenter's square or a regular commercial bow square that snaps onto the bowstring. A bow square is far more convenient to use, and most serious bowhunters own such a square to set up and check nocking point placement.

From here, one other adjustment might have to be made prior to shooting the bow. This adjustment is called the centershot adjustment, and is made by screwing the cushion plunger, springy rest, or another screw-adjustable rest in or out to the position which is most likely to produce non-wobbly arrow flight. This initial centershot adjustment

*Centershot adjustment of arrow plate is made by visually lining up the bowstring with the back of the upper limb, then moving arrow plate in or out until the point of the arrow is clearly visible on outside of the string. For recurves (left), string should be lined up with exact center of the upper limb. For compound bows (right), string should be lined up a third of the way from left side of the limb if bow is a right-hand model.*

*An ordinary carpenter's square can be used to install the nocking point in the proper place, but a bow square makes the job easier. Once proper nocking point location is found, clamp-on nock locater is installed with special nocking-point pliers.*

is not normally necessary on recurve bows or compound bows without screw-adjustable arrow plates, although such bows sometimes require minor rest adjustments after a hunter perfects his shooting ability and starts using a variety of hunting arrowheads. (See Chapter 6.)

How far out springy, cushion plunger, or similar arrow plates should be set from the sight window of the bow is sometimes included in manufacturer's instructions, but if it

designed to be installed immediately forward of the handle riser, and the forward placement is also best for sights that can be installed either ahead or behind the riser because a sight in front of the bow places sight pins farther from a shooter's eye and thus makes them less fuzzy (more defined) and easier to aim with. The superior sight definition of a front-mounted bowsight can slightly improve both target scores and kill percentages on game.

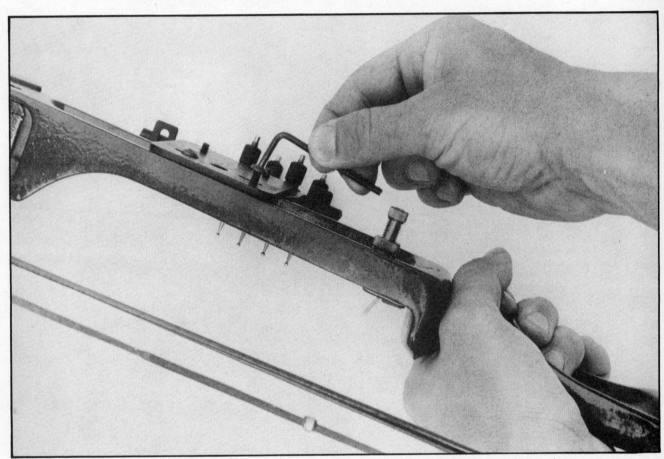

A hunting bowsight normally is installed forward of the handle riser of the bow. This helps ensure sharp sight definition and optimum accuracy. Most sights of this type are easily installed and are not overly expensive today.

is not, the accompanying diagrams show where the arrow plate should be set initially on both recurve and compound bows. This setting can be fine-tuned later on, as outlined in Chapter 4.

The only other thing which needs to be done to the bow at this point is to install the bowsight. Most sights are

Once the bow is set up in the foregoing fashion, it is time to learn basic bow-shooting form. Make sure your arrows are tipped with 125-grain field points, strap on your armguard, slip on your shooting glove or tab, stuff the arrows in your belt quiver...and head for the target range for some slow, thoughtful shooting practice.

# CHAPTER 3

# The How Of Shooting

## This Step-By-Step Procedure Will Help In The Game Fields

LEARNING TO SHOOT a hunting bow well is not all that difficult, provided a shooter carefully follows the basic, time-tested steps of correct shooting.

Shooting practice should begin slowly and deliberately, with the archer thinking about every step of his shooting form to make sure he develops sound shooting habits. It is also important for a shooter not to overtax his arm and shoulder muscles when he first starts out, shooting until muscles get slightly tired and then quitting a couple of days before trying again.

Shooting too much at the outset can strain a beginner's body to the point where he begins to flinch when releasing the bowstring or quits paying close attention to proper shooting form — both of which lead to poor accuracy and potential bad habits that can be a solid chore to break.

The obvious first step in learning to shoot your bow is finding a place to shoot safely and conveniently. Many archery stores maintain indoor or outdoor target-range facilities for their customers, and such ranges are ideal places to learn because they are handy and because an archery dealer can help a shooter start out on the right foot. Similarly, many towns have recreational facilities complete with archery ranges. Either of these will provide the necessary setting to begin practicing with your hunting bow.

An excellent alternative to a public shooting facility is a simple backyard range. All that is needed for such a range is fifteen or twenty yards of open space to shoot across and some sort of target butt to shoot arrows into. The cheapest and most durable butt for beginning practice is

made of three tightly bound straw or hay bales stacked on top of each other like building blocks. To keep ground moisture out of these bales, they should be set on a wooden pallet or two old automobile tires.

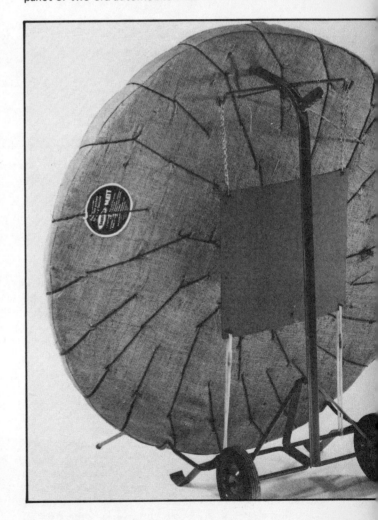

*Joanne Kinsey proves good accuracy with a hunting bow is not difficult to achieve with proper shooting form and sensible shooting practice. (Right) An excellent target butt for the beginner is the round Indian rope-grass matt with a commercial easel. Just as effective is the simple straw-bale butt which is pictured in this chapter.*

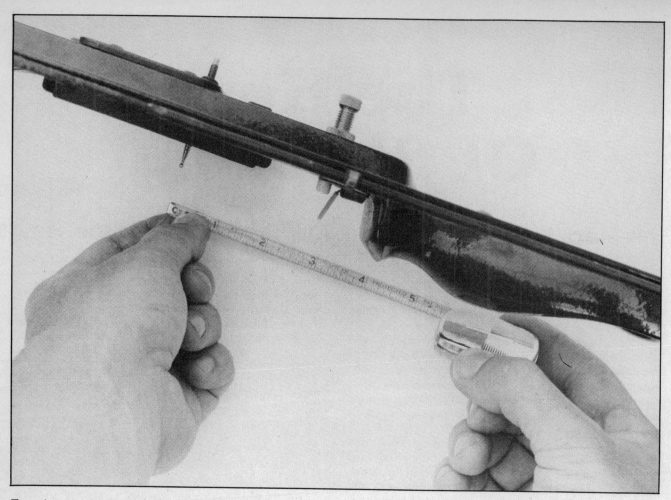

To make sure you hit the target butt with your first shot from ten yards, place your sight pin about three inches above the arrow shelf and about one-half inch inside the sight window of bow. This is a point at which to start.

A decent, although somewhat more expensive alternate target butt is a round, commercial Indian rope-grass matt about three feet in diameter. Such a matt must be set on some sort of easel — an added expense — and cannot be shot with hunting broadheads later on. It is also less durable than straw or hay, although a rope-grass matt is probably the most durable of target butts sold by archery companies. A matt is far more portable and more easily stored if you prefer not to have your backyard archery target in view at all times or don't want to put up with the hassle of covering your target butt with plastic every time it rains.

After you become proficient with your bow, you might want to investigate the use of other target butts like a sand-trap butt, styrofoam broadhead butt, or cotton-filled butt. However, straw, hay, or a rope-grass matt will serve you well to begin with. As a matter of fact, many expert bowhunters prefer a straw-bale butt over all others for all their backyard target-shooting needs.

No matter where you decide to practice basic shooting form, the procedure should be the same. You should begin shooting at a very close range — ten yards is about right —

and you should shoot at a fairly large bull's-eye target available at any archery store. As your shooting improves, you can graduate to smaller targets and longer shooting distances.

Before you begin step-by-step shooting practice, you must roughly set the top pin on your bowsight for ten yards to prevent you from completely missing the target butt. Exact sight setting varies considerably from shooter to shooter, but an average setting is to vertically place the pin bead three inches above the shelf of the arrow rest and horizontally place it about one-half-inch inside the sight window of the bow (one-half-inch to the left of the sight window on a right-hand bow). See diagram for clarification. This sight placement is likely to be somewhat off from where it is supposed to be for dead-center hits, but it will be close enough to prevent totally missing the target butt.

Once your bowsight is roughly set, it is time to begin shooting. My special thanks to model Joanne Kinsey for the following ten-step photo sequence on how to shoot a bow. Joanne is an excellent archer in addition to being a very nice and a very pretty lady!

## Step 1 — Stance

Stand facing at ninety degrees to the target with your feet spread comfortably between twelve and eighteen inches apart. Your body weight should be distributed evenly on both feet.

Grip the bow firmly but not tightly in your left hand (for a right-hand shooter), letting it hang comfortably along your left side. Turn your head to face the target, and pull an arrow from your quiver.

## Step 2 — Nocking The Arrow

Snap an arrow on the bowstring with the nock directly beneath the nocking point on the string. Make sure the off-color vane on the arrow — called the cock vane — is pointing away from the bow (pointing to the left in a right-hand bow). This allows the other two vanes (called hen vanes) to pass the bow during a shot without colliding with the bow handle or the arrow rest.

Once the arrow is properly nocked, place it on the arrow rest with the index finger of your bow hand.

*Model Joanne Kinsey illustrates the proper stance when facing the target. With sufficient practice, using the proper stance will become second nature even in hunting.*

*An arrow should be nocked directly below the nock locator on the bowstring to ensure consistent accuracy from shot to shot. The cock vane should point away from the bow.*

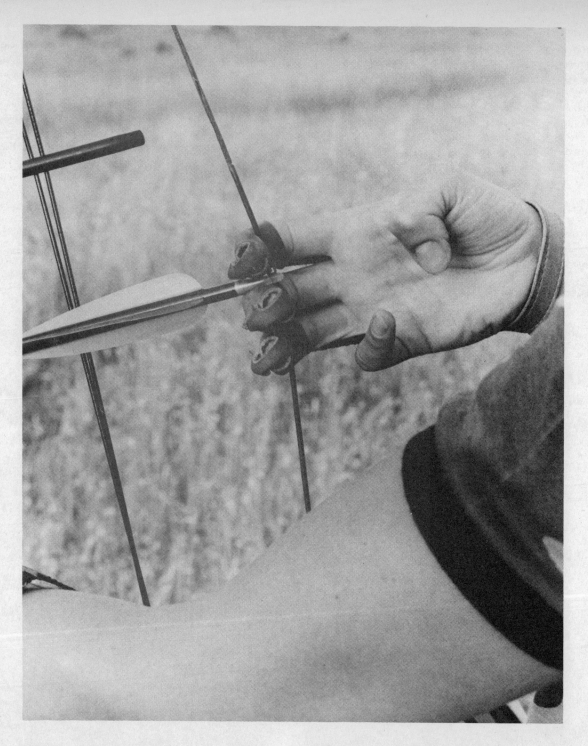

*Proper way to grip bowstring is by placing index finger above arrow and next two fingers below it. String should be cradled snugly in first two joints.*

## Step 3 — Gripping The Bowstring

After the arrow is on the arrow rest, you should grip the bowstring in the first joints of your first three fingers with the index finger above the arrow and the other two fingers below it. This is by far the most common method of gripping the bowstring, although a few bowhunters who shoot without bowsights prefer to grip the string with all three fingers below the arrow so they can sight down the arrow like a gunbarrel. This three-fingers-under grip is called the Apache draw.

When the bowstring is properly gripped, your bowstring hand should form a modified Boy Scout salute as is shown in the photograph.

### Step 4 — Beginning The Draw

Fully extend your bow arm directly at the target, canting the bow slightly and rolling the bowstring in your fingers to make sure the arrow stays on the arrow rest. The most common problem of beginners is keeping the arrow from falling off the arrow rest. A little practice perfects this technique as an archer learns to roll the string to slightly pressure the arrow against the plate portion of the arrow rest.

### Step 5 — Drawing The Bow

Draw the bowstring smoothly back to the side of your face (the right side for right-hand shooters). During the draw, the wrist, forearm, and elbow of your bowstring arm should be lined up exactly with the arrow to give maximum drawing leverage. Keep your bow arm straight and pointed at the target as you draw, and straighten the bow up vertically as you near full draw. The arrow often persists in falling off the arrow rest during this step for a beginning shooter, especially when he rotates the bow to a completely vertical position. Again, a little practice at rolling the bowstring in the string fingers quickly cures this problem.

*Joanne Kinsey starts the draw by extending her bow arm toward the target, slightly canting her bow to one side, then rolling her fingers to keep the arrow on the rest.*

*In coming to full draw, Joanne keeps her wrist, forearm, and elbow in close alignment with the arrow to maximize drawing leverage. The draw should be swift and smooth.*

This comely miss finds her anchor point for consistent accuracy. Each archer tends to experiment until he has found the anchor that affords him the best accuracy, then continues to use that same point as an accuracy reference.

### Step 6 — The Anchor

Anchor your bowstring hand solidly against the side of your face so your master eye (aiming eye) is in the same place in relation to the arrow from shot to shot. The most common hunting anchor point is placing the index finger of the bowstring hand in the right corner of the mouth (for a right-hand shooter). When this anchor is properly assumed, the point of the jawbone is normally nestled in the pocket between the index finger and the thumb. Such an anchor transfers some of the bow's draw weight from the arm and shoulder muscles to the neck muscles, which results in steadier shooting. The anchor point on an archer's face corresponds to the back sight on a rifle, and must be consistent for decent accuracy. When the bowstring hand is properly anchored, a bowhunter should be looking directly around the left or right edge of the bowstring with his master eye.

The correct method of gripping the bow is firmly but not too tight. An overly tight grip tenses the hand and arm muscles, which results in an accuracy-destroying flinch.

### Step 7 — Gripping The Bow For The Shot

After you have reached full draw and have established the anchor, the bow should be gripped firmly but not tightly. Most of the hand pressure on the grip should be in the web of the hand between the thumb and the forefinger. If you grip the bow too loosely during a shot it may fly out of your hand when you release the arrow; if you grip the bow too tightly you'll probably "throw" your bow arm to the side when you shoot because of overly tense arm and wrist muscles — an event which always results in an inaccurate shot.

*When aiming at the target, Joanne's eye is closely aligned with the bowstring to ensure accuracy with every shot.*

### Step 8 — Aiming At The Target

Aim at the target by smoothly swinging your ten-yard sight pin to the center of the bull's-eye. Keep both eyes open when aiming. A bowhunter's master eye should line up closely with the bowstring as he aims with a bowsight — the string should be visible as a fuzzy line in the corner of his eye as he aims at the target.

Most bowhunters move their sights smoothly on target from directly above or directly below, but a few draw slightly off to one side and swing on target from the right or left. Where your sights are when you finish drawing and begin swinging the proper sight toward the target makes no difference as long as your technique is consistent from shot to shot. I personally prefer a "low draw" which requires me to raise the sights on target because this lets me clearly see a target or animal above my sight pins prior to shooting, and also lets me count through my sight pins on longer shots to make sure I use the proper pin for the distance I am shooting.

## Step 10 — The Follow-Through

An important key to consistent bow-shooting accuracy is a proper follow-through. To follow through correctly, you should try to keep the sight pin on the target and your bowstring hand against your face until the arrow hits the mark. The bow will naturally recoil to the side during a shot, but not until after the arrow is out of the bow and well on its way. When a bowhunter is properly following through his shots, the arrow rises above his line of sight after it leaves the bow, completely disappearing from view on longer shots as it arches upward and then drops back

Model Joanne accomplishes a smooth, accurate bowstring release by simply relaxing her fingers and letting the string slide free. Her hand stays snug along her face.

Follow-through is essential to bow-shooting accuracy. If you try to hold your sight pin on the target until the arrow hits, pinpoint shooting will be the result.

## Step 9 — The Bowstring Release

When you think you're on target, relax your bowstring fingers to let the bowstring slide free. A smooth, relaxed string release is a major ingredient in accurate shooting. Concentrate on keeping the bowsight on target as you release and keeping your bowstring hand solidly against your face as the string slips out of your fingers. Your hand will naturally slide backward along your face after you release because of backward-thrusting arm and shoulder tension; however, you should not let your hand jump sideways away from your face during the release. This causes a sloppy, high-friction string release called a "pluck" — a release that results in an inaccurate and often noisy shot.

54

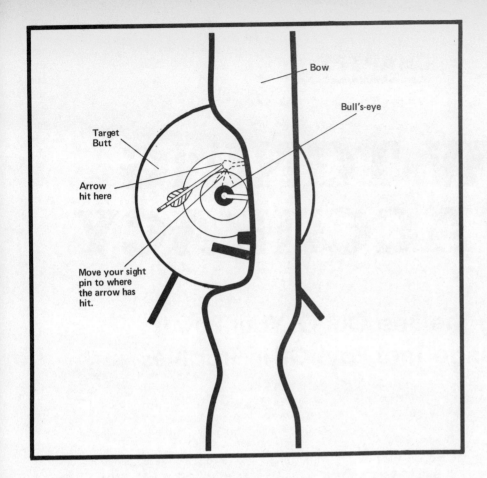

Target
Butt

Bow

Bull's-eye

Arrow
hit here

Move your sight
pin to where
the arrow has
hit.

*To sight in a bowsight for a given yardage, simply shoot a few arrows, then move the sight in the direction. the arrows are hitting. In this case, the arrow has hit high and to right; thus, the sight must go up, to right.*

into the target. A shooter should never try to watch his arrows fly after a shot — to do so ruins his concentration on the target and usually results in poor shooting.

## Sighting In A Bowsight

After you shoot a few times to determine the general area your arrows are hitting on the target, you should adjust your bowsight so the arrows group in the center of the target. To sight in your bow, simply move the sight pin in the direction the arrows are hitting. For example, if they are hitting above and to the right of the bull's-eye, move your ten-yard sight pin up and to the right. Readjust your sight until the arrows are hitting more or less in the center of the target. A properly adjusted bowsight pin builds up a shooter's confidence and helps him concentrate on shooting well because he knows a smooth, well-aimed shot will hit the bull's-eye instead of striking some other part of the target.

After a shooter becomes proficient at hitting a ten-yard bull's-eye, he should gradually increase his shooting distance to fifteen yards, twenty yards, thirty yards, and beyond. Although ten yards is an ideal distance to begin shooting, most experienced bowhunters sight in their pins for twenty yards, thirty yards, forty yards, and so on. The uppermost pin on any sight corresponds to the closest sighting distance, the bottom pin to the farthest distance. For shots closer than twenty yards, a bowhunter simply holds a few inches below the target with his twenty-yard sight pin.

After mastering basic bow-shooting form, many hunters experiment with variations in this form which may or may not improve their accuracy. For example, some archers find that they perform best if they shoot from a so-called open stance with toes angling slightly toward the target. Similarly, the corner-of-the-mouth anchor point is the most common bow-shooting anchor among hunters but is by no means the only one.

Many shooters anchor somewhere below the mouth or place their middle instead of their index finger in the corner of the mouth. Any anchor style works well if it is consistent and closely aligns your master eye with the bowstring.

As mentioned before, some bowhunters also deviate from the standard bowstring grip, using a three-fingers-below-the-arrow grip to more closely align the arrow with the eye when shooting without bowsights. In addition, the exact way good bowhunters grip their bows varies considerably, from extremely loose grips to fairly firm grips and from so-called "high wrist" grips with the hand pointed downward to "low wrist" grips with the palm of the bow hand pressed low on the bow grip. These and similar shooting variations often suit an individual bowhunter better than standard, textbook shooting form, but every archer should learn the basics before deviating from the norm.

A serious bowhunter first masters standard bow-shooting basics, then settles into an individual style that works best for him. One of the main pleasures of shooting a bow is experimenting with style variations in an ongoing attempt to improve accuracy on both targets and game.

# CHAPTER 4

# BOW-TUNING FOR ACCURACY

## Getting The Best Out Of Your Bow Is A Challenge That Pays Off In Trophies

AFTER A month or two of dedicated shooting practice, the average beginning archer with normal eyesight and coordination should be able to shoot most of his arrows into six-inch groups at twenty yards. Once he achieves this level of shooting expertise, it is time to fine-tune his bow/arrow combination to improve accuracy even more and further bolster his confidence. At this point his shooting form will be reasonably consistent and his bowstring release reasonably smooth, allowing him to adjust his bow to match his new-found shooting style so arrows fly cleanly without visible wobble between the bow and the target.

If a shooter's equipment is initially set up as outlined in Chapter 2, his arrows should be flying fairly well from his bow when he begins to fine-tune his gear. However, it would be a minor miracle if his arrows were leaving the bow with perfect smoothness, mainly because every shooter's form requires a slightly different equipment setup for good arrow flight and because hitting upon this exact setup seldom happens by chance.

The objective of fine-tuning a bow-and-arrow combo is to make sure arrows do not wobble at all after they leave the bow. The importance of clean, non-wobbly arrow flight cannot be over-stressed. Even badly wobbling arrows can be grouped into six inches at twenty yards, but tightening twenty-yard groups to four inches or less requires careful tuning to eliminate visible arrow wobble. A wobbly arrow is simply more erratic in the way it leaves the bow and flies toward the target, preventing the best accuracy no matter how good a shot an archer happens to be. Wobbling arrows group poorly enough when tipped with streamlined field points, but go absolutely nuts when installed with large, multi-bladed big-game broadheads.

Eliminating visible arrow wobble by carefully adjusting your bow is an extremely important step in achieving consistent accuracy on targets and game. It also increases arrow speed and arrow energy, flattening out trajectory for easier hits at unknown distances and dramatically increasing arrow penetration and killing efficiency on game.

There are two basic kinds of arrow wobble an archer has to contend with. *Porpoising* occurs when an arrow wobbles up and down in flight. *Fishtailing* occurs when an arrow wobbles from side to side. These two forms of arrow wobble often occur together, causing the tail of an arrow to wag in a circle as it flies. Every intermediate or advanced bowhunter must determine whether or not his arrows wobble, then correct any wobbling problems he discovers. If he does not do so, he'll never be a top-notch shot with his bow.

The first step in correcting wobbly arrow flight is discovering it in the first place. There are several common methods used to determine whether or not arrows are wobbling — methods described in various books and manufacturer's brochures. However, most are not worth a hill of beans to the average bowhunter. Take for example the famous "bare-shaft test" touted by several prominent archery manufacturers.

To test arrow flight in this manner, an archer first strips the vanes from an arrow, then shoots the naked shaft into a "non-directional target butt" at the distance of six feet. If the rear of the shaft is pointing slightly upward, the bow's nocking point should be lowered to correct potential porpoising. If the end of the shaft is pointed downward, the nocking point should be raised. If the end of the shaft is pointing to the right, the bow's arrow-rest plate should be moved to the right. If the end of the shaft is cocked to the

Pinpoint shooting enhanced by proper bow-tuning helped the author arrow this 22-pound wild turkey. A properly tuned bow is essential when hunting smart, elusive targets of this type with relatively small vital areas.

left, the bow's arrow-rest plate should be moved to the left. This method sounds nifty indeed, for when the bare shaft finally enters the butt straight the regular fletched shafts should fly as straight as a string.

There are only two things wrong with the bare-shaft method of taking the wobble out of arrow flight. First, it requires a hunter to wreck a perfectly good fletched arrow to tune his bow. Second, the method doesn't work worth a hoot. There is no such thing as a perfectly non-directional target butt available to the general shooting public, so it is never possible to tell whether an arrow has really entered a bale or matt tail-high or whether the grain of the straw, rope-grass, or similar butt material has flipped the tail of the arrow up after the arrow has entered the butt. The bare-shaft test can be used to improve grossly wobbling arrow flight, but is not exact enough to adequately fine-tune any bow.

By far the best way I've found to determine whether arrows are wobbling is simply watching them fly in good lighting conditions. An experienced bowhunter can see a badly fishtailing arrow after he shoots it because the arrow wags its tail visibly as it rises through his line of sight on the way to the target. However, he can seldom spot a porpoising arrow because it wobbles up and down almost invisibly when viewed directly from the rear.

A shooter should not try to watch his own arrows fly anyway, because this can ruin his shooting form by destroying his follow-through on the target. The only practical way to determine whether or not your arrows are porpoising and/or fishtailing is to have a sharp-eyed friend watch them fly. This friend need not know anything about archery, as long as he has good eyes, the lighting is favorable, and you tell him where to stand and what to look for.

The ideal lighting condition for watching arrows fly is when the sun is low and directly behind or slightly to one side of the target. Shooting toward the sun is not the easiest situation for the shooter, but such a back-lit situation lets an observer see the slightest wiggle on an arrow as it flies. The best place to stand to watch for fishtailing (sideways wobble) is directly behind the shooter so you can peer along the back (right) side of his bow (see photo). Porpoising (up-and-down wobble) is nearly impossible to detect from this position, so to watch for it an observer must move two or three feet to the side of the shooter where he can clearly see whether or not the tails of arrows bob up and down in flight as they leave the bow.

A person with normal vision can watch a few shots from each position and not only determine whether or not the arrows are fishtailing and/or porpoising — he can sometimes also tell whether arrows are leaving the bow tail high, tail low, tail right, or tail left. Once a visible sideways or up-and-down wobble is detected, correcting this wobble is usually very easy.

Arrow porpoise (up-and-down wobble) is normally corrected by relocating the nocking point on the bowstring. If arrows are leaving the bow tail high, the nocking point must be moved down. If arrows are leaving the bow tail low, the nocking point must be moved up. This same basic procedure works well for all bow designs, including longbows, recurve bows, and various kinds of compound bows. If you know that arrows are porpoising but aren't

*Above: Up-and-down arrow wobble is termed porpoising, while side-to-side arrow wobble (below) is known as fishtailing by archers. There are steps in tuning that can be used to cure both.*

58

*To detect a fishtailing arrow, stand directly behind an archer so you can see along the back of his bow as the arrow speeds away toward the target.*

To detect a porpoising arrow, one must stand two or three feet to the side of the archer, eyes focused halfway between the shooter and the target.

sure whether they're leaving the bow tail high or tail low, simply begin experimenting with nocking-point locations. If a move in one direction makes arrow flight worse, you know you've gone the wrong way. Some thoughtful, systematic experimentation with nocking-point location on the bowstring will quickly eliminate any visible arrow porpoise. To systematically zero in on a perfect nocking point location, it is best to move the nocking point on the bowstring no more than one-eighth-inch at a time.

To correct arrows that fishtail (wobble side to side), you must either move the arrow-plate portion of your arrow rest in or out, or change the spring tension of your cushion plunger (if you use one). If an arrow is leaving the bow tail-right, then you must either move the arrow plate to the

right or weaken the spring tension on your cushion plunger (increase spring tension on a left-hand bow). If an arrow is leaving the bow tail-left, the arrow plate must be moved to the left or the spring tension increased on your cushion plunger. As with porpoising, if you aren't sure which way the tail of the arrow is leaving the bow you must experiment by moving the arrow plate or cushion-plunger adjustment in both directions to see which direction minimizes and eventually eliminates visible fishtailing.

Correcting side-to-side wobble in arrows is a breeze with a fully adjustable arrow rest like a springy rest or a plunger/flipper combination. If you detect fishtailing and have an adhesive-backed, one-piece arrow rest to deal with, the plate portion of this rest must be shimmed away from the bow, cut down to cure the problem, or otherwise altered by good ol' American ingenuity. If all else fails, replace your old rest with one that is easier to adjust.

Arrow porpoise can always be eliminated by moving the nocking point. However, if arrows persist in fishtailing despite some serious tinkering with the arrow rest, chances are good that your arrow shafts are not the correct size to be shot from your bow at your particular draw length. In such a case, double-check manufacturers' arrow-shaft selection charts and if necessary consult your archery dealer to isolate and solve the problem.

It is necessary to note here that any major change in a shooter's equipment or shooting style is likely to unbalance arrow flight and necessitate another bow-tuning session. For example, the addition of a bow quiver or shooting stabilizer to a bow will often cause arrows to fishtail that flew perfectly from the unadorned bow. Similarly, if a shooter switches from a shooting glove to a shooting tab or alters the way he grips the bow, arrows are apt to begin porpoising and/or fishtailing again because they are not leaving the bow exactly as they were before these changes were made. One of the most surefire ways of destroying a compound bow's tune is changing the draw weight. Even a slight draw-weight alteration will normally cause arrows to fishtail and fly erratically.

A cleanly flying arrow from a well-tuned hunting bow is beautiful to watch, turning perfectly on its axis as it sizzles toward the target. The results on targets and game are also beautiful because a wobble-free arrow is incredibly accurate when shot by a decent archer. The serious bowhunter who has never fine-tuned his bow-and-arrow generally figures that six-inch arrow groups at twenty yards are the best he can possibly shoot. He'd be absolutely amazed at the dramatic improvement in accuracy that comes from an hour or less of simple nocking-point and arrow-rest adjustment with the help of a sharp-eyed friend standing behind his shoulder.

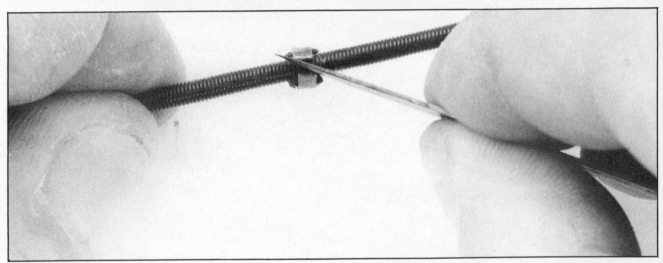

*Above: Moving the nocking point up and down on the bowstring with aid of nocking-point pliers will eliminate arrow porpoise. Quality clamp-on nocking point is easily loosened with back of knife blade. (Right) Moving the arrow plate in or out experimentally normally will correct a fishtailing arrow.*

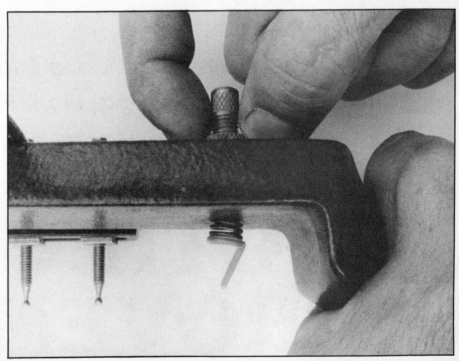

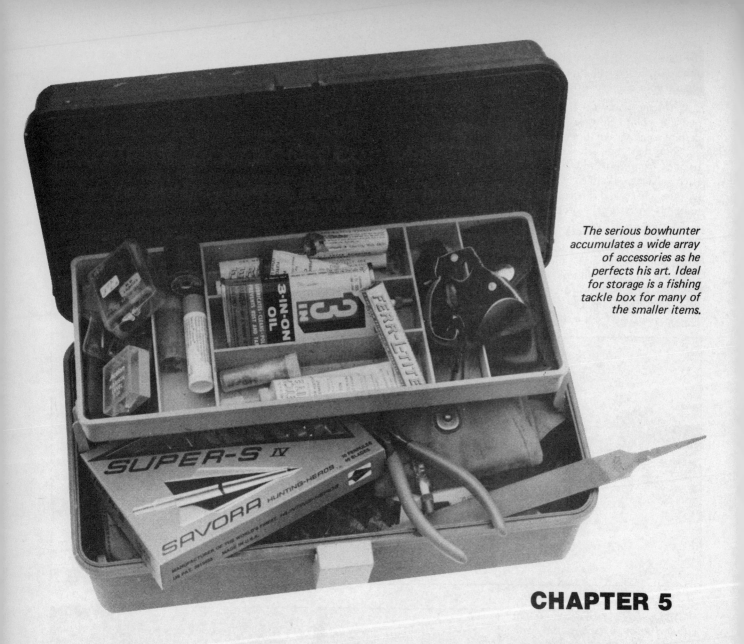

The serious bowhunter accumulates a wide array of accessories as he perfects his art. Ideal for storage is a fishing tackle box for many of the smaller items.

## CHAPTER 5

### These Accessories Can Make Shooting For Accuracy More Satisfying, More Pleasant

# AIDS TO SHOOTING IMPROVEMENT

**B**EGINNING bowhunters need just a few pieces of equipment to learn shooting fundamentals. However, once these fundamentals are mastered, a person should turn his attention to other shooting items which may or may not help his score on targets and game. Some of these items are time-tested, almost standard gear with archers in the know — others are specialized gizmos which may or may not help the individual shooter. A bowhunter must pick and choose to suit himself, experimenting until a solid, practical set of shooting gear is decided upon. The following are a few of the more common shooting accessories found at well-stocked archery stores.

### Arrow Quivers

Every bowhunter needs some sort of quiver to hold arrows as he stalks about the woods or sits patiently on stand. Several quiver designs are commonly available these days, and each has certain advantages and disadvantages every archer should carefully consider.

The shoulder quiver is a simple elongated container slung high scross the shooter's back. This quiver was the kind supposedly used by Robin Hood and his fictional merry men, and was in fact popular for several hundred years with English longbowmen and other archers of yesteryear. The shoulder quiver was used successfully as recently as the 1940s, when it was the standard arrow holder for such bowhunting pioneers as Art Young, Alexander Pope, Howard Hill, and Fred Bear. However, the shoulder quiver is seldom used today because it embodies some major disadvantages.

The shoulder quiver's primary advantage is fast, easy arrow access. Old-style longbowmen using this quiver could put as many as five arrows into the air before the first one

*A shoulder quiver can provide fast, easy access to arrows, but requires arm movement that spooks game. Also, arrows tend to rattle and snag the brush.*

A hip quiver is quiet, handy, inexpensive. For these reasons, it has found popularity with the bowhunting clan.

Bow quivers have become standard equipment for most of today's bowhunters. Using such quivers, Jim Dougherty (left) and the author downed a pair of Rocky Mountain goats during a hunt in British Columbia.

hit the ground, reaching smoothly over the shoulder to pluck another arrow free between shots. However, the shoulder quiver and the arrows inside are prone to snag noisily and obnoxiously on brush as a hunter moves along, and the long arm movement needed to pull arrows from this quiver tends to spook the daylights out of game. In addition, the shoulder quiver does not hold hunting arrows snugly in place, which creates noisy arrow rattle and quickly dulls sharp hunting broadheads. Because of these problems, most modern bowhunters use a hip quiver or a bow quiver instead.

A hip quiver attaches to a hunter's belt and ideally holds six or eight arrows close at hand. Such a quiver normally has an arrowhead cup at the bottom to snugly and safely house hunting broadheads, and also has metal or rubber arrow clips that hold arrows firmly apart so shafts do not

rattle and fletching does not vibrate together. A hip quiver does not protect broadheads from rainwater, dust, and debris because the arrowhead cup is open on the top side, and such a quiver can also snag on undergrowth as a hunter walks along. However, the hip quiver is a favorite of some serious bowhunters.

By far the most popular bowhunting quiver is the bow quiver, which attaches directly to the side of a hunting bow with bolts, screws, spring-steel arms, or tape. Such a quiver holds arrows close at hand and lets a hunter maneuver these arrows silently through the heaviest cover because they are attached to the bow itself. A bow quiver is by far the best choice for most serious hunters, provided it is a sturdy, safe, and easy-to-use design.

When shopping for a bow quiver, look for these important features. First, the quiver should attach solidly

A quiver attached to a bow makes
handling the bow-and-arrow setup
less awkward, especially when an
archer finds himself on a horse!

*Approaching game is made easier with the use of a bow quiver, and so is access to a second arrow. Such a quiver also comes in handy when a trophy is being packed out.*

to a bow to prevent noise caused by vibration. Second, it should have a roomy arrowhead cap on top that fully encloses sharp hunting broadheads. This feature protects the hunter from accidental cuts, and also protects broadheads from edge-dulling moisture and grime. Never use a bow quiver that does not fully enclose broadheads — such a quiver is extremely dangerous and invariably dulls sharp hunting broadheads.

A third feature every bow quiver should have is a six to eight-arrow capacity and snug, silent rubber clips that hold these arrows firmly apart to prevent game-spooking rattle. If a bow quiver has these features, it should serve a hunter well.

Several special-purpose arrow quivers should be mentioned here, although they are not generally used by hunters. One is the ground quiver, a simple metal ring at the

end of a stake that arrows are dropped into on a target range. A ground quiver can be handy to have on the twenty-yard mark of a backyard range, but most bowhunters prefer a tube-type hip quiver instead. Another target-shooting quiver is a pocket quiver, a simple leather sheath that slips inside a hip pocket and accepts five or six arrows with streamlined field points attached. Such a quiver is desirable primarily because it is cheap.

One other arrow quiver is occasionally used today. This is the back quiver, a backpack-type quiver that straps in the middle of a bowhunter's back with the aid of a shoulder harness. A back quiver is designed to hold a large quantity of hunting arrows under a weather-protective hood, and is ideal for the bow-bending duck hunter, wilderness backpacker, or any other nimrod who expects to shoot and perhaps lose more than six or eight arrows per outing.

## Bow Stabilizers

A bow stabilizer is a relatively heavy rod that screws into the front of a bow's handle just below the grip area. Such a stabilizer does two things: It minimizes handle torque when a bow is shot, which improves accuracy; and it dampens bow vibration during a shot, which reduces game-spooking noise. Stabilizers for tournament shooting are sometimes up to four feet long, but a hunting stabilizer must be short and stubby to facilitate moving about in the woods. A stabilizer makes a bow somewhat less compact and some bowhunters feel it hinders their movement in heavy woods. However, a stabilizer will slightly improve any hunter's shooting, and most serious archers regard this aid as standard equipment.

## Mechanical Bowstring Releases

Releasing the bowstring smoothly and consistently with the fingers is one of the most critical factors in achieving good accuracy with a bow. In recent years various mechanical "trigger releases" that grip the bowstring have become increasingly popular with archers because these mechanical bowstring releases let go of the string crisply and consistently each time a shooter trips the release trigger. Bowstring releases are most definitely more accurate in practiced hands than shooting with the fingers on the bowstring, but tend to be slower to use and noisier to shoot. As a result, they have a limited following among bowhunters in spite of their popularity with target archers.

*A bow stabilizer such as the Gamegetter II improves shots by preventing bow torque and dampens vibration noises.*

*A simple wrist sling ties a hunter's hand to his bow so he can shoot open handed, avoid throwing shots astray. (Below) String peep should be slipped between strands of bowstring in line with the hunter's eye. Peep ensures consistent anchoring, eye alignment with the bowstring.*

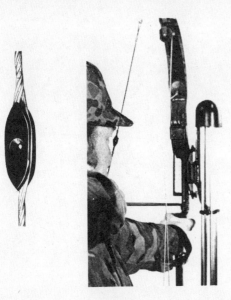

Hunters who have severe problems releasing the string cleanly with their fingers might try a bowstring release to improve accuracy, especially if they plan to hunt primarily on stand where there is usually plenty of time to use a release and where shots are close enough so the extra bowstring "twang" caused by a release will not cause an animal to duck an arrow.

### Wrist Slings And Finger Straps

One accuracy problem some bowhunters have is involuntarily grabbing or squeezing the bow as they release the bowstring. This torques the bow as the arrow leaves it, and severely degrades accuracy. To solve this problem, some archers strap their wrists or fingers to the bow so they can shoot with an open, non-torquing hand without having the bow fly out of their hand during a shot. Having your hand literally tied to a bow can be somewhat cumbersome and inconvenient in the field, but might be worth the trouble if it puts shots on the mark. A wrist sling

or finger strap is only practical if you tend to grab or squeeze your bow during a shot at the expense of accurate shooting.

### String Peeps

A string peep is a metal or plastic oval with a hole in the middle that is sandwiched between the strands of a bowstring and lashed in place with thread. Such a peep allows a shooter to exactly line up his eye with the bowstring on every shot, and also helps ensure the same anchor on the face because the shooter must look through the small peep hole on the string before he can shoot. A bowstring peep cuts down light transmission to a shooter's eye, which can make shooting in poor light difficult or impossible. However, a peep used temporarily or all the time can cure the bad, inaccurate shooting habit of anchoring in slightly different places from shot to shot. A special nocking point is normally used with a string peep to ensure that the peep is rotated squarely with the eye on each and every shot. This allows the shooter to see clearly through the hole in the peep.

### Bow Lights

A powerful light attached to a bow with the beam in line with the sights is the ultimate aid when hunting for predators, rough fish, and similar critters that are legal to take at night. Alternatives like a miner's headlamp or a light held by a friend do not provide the instant, perfectly aimed light necessary to consistently hit targets at night. The

*A compact shooting light attached to a bow is ideal for predator calling and other forms of legal night hunting. This Burnham Brothers model clamps to a bow stabilizer to cast a bright beam out to seventy-five yards or more.*

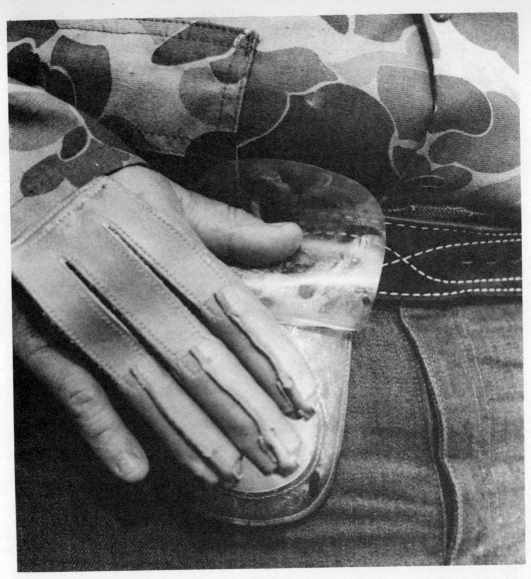

*A powder pouch allows instant lubrication of a shooting glove, also reveals exact wind direction as talcum powder floats away. (Left) A simple bow rack can be important addition on the target range to protect your tackle.*

all-around bowhunter owns at least one such light to hunt coyotes, foxes, barn pigeons, dump rats, alligator gar, carp, and other species most easily bowhunted under the veil of darkness.

### Light-Up Sight Pins

The bowhunter with eye problems or the hunter after late-moving animals like black bear or whitetail deer can benefit by simple bowsight pins illuminated with small batteries. Such light-up pins allow clear aiming visibility in low-light situations such as those encountered around a bear bait or a deer trail just prior to darkness.

### Target-Range Bow Racks

Some sort of bow rack on a backyard target range eliminates the need to carry a bow to the target after every round of shooting. Commercial racks are available for hanging compound and recurve bows, and similar racks are also easy for the do-it-yourselfer to make. A bow rack is not a shooting necessity by any means, but is certainly a nicety every archer should consider.

### Powder Pouches

A powder pouch is a simple commercial belt pouch designed to hold talcum powder and filter out a little of this dry lubricant every time the pouch is slapped by a shooting glove or tab. Talcum powder from such a pouch provides an extra-slick bowstring release for many archers, a release that results in superior accuracy. In addition, a little cloud of talc patted from a powder pouch instantly drifts with the slightest breeze, indicating wind direction and helping the bowhunter avoid the razor-keen noses of deer and similar game. A powder pouch is an inexpensive item and just might help your shooting and hunting.

*A lightweight target butt such as the Lightarget from Bear is ideal for use in a remote hunting camp. Such a target holds up well when it is shot with field points; don't use broadheads.*

### Alternative Target Butts

Although rope-grass matts and straw-bale butts are most popular with bowhunters, a variety of other commercial and homegrown butts are commonly used by archers. Some of these are worthwhile to consider because of compact size, light weight, or another unique advantage. For example, a commercial target butt made of styrofoam may not last as long as a straw bale, but might be handy to haul into a relatively remote hunting camp. A careful look at commercial target-butt alternatives might turn up something of value to you.

### Targets

A wide variety of commercial targets are available at archery stores, from simple black-and-white bull's-eye targets and colorful bull's-eye targets to life-like animal and bird targets. A dedicated bowhunter learns to shoot well on a wide variety of targets, mastering basic shooting skills on bull's-eye targets and perfecting field-shooting ability on game targets without specific round aiming spots. The versatile hunter takes full advantage of all kinds of targets at his local archery shop or sporting goods outlet, knowing full well that practice on such targets will improve his performance on game as well as increasing his enjoyment during practice sessions.

## Rangefinders

As will be discussed in Chapter 8, a quality bowhunting rangefinder is essential to pinpoint shooting on targets and game. Only recently has optical technology reached the point where small bowhunting rangefinders have become dependable and sufficiently accurate to yield consistently good results. Such rangefinders are already considered necessary equipment by many modern bowhunters, and are likely to become as standard as bowsights as more and more archers discover their merits.

## Other Shooting Equipment

A myriad of other gizmos meant to improve bow shooting are constantly appearing on the archery market. Among these are spine testers to ensure consistent shaft stiffness in wood and fiberglass shafts, arrow holders that keep an arrow on a bow's arrow rest until the bow is drawn, and dozens of other interesting inventions. Some of these are universally worthwhile, some are beneficial to specific bowhunters in specific situations, and others are solid wastes of time and money. A thoughtful study of bowhunting catalogs and the shelves of your local archery store will provide hours of enjoyment and is likely to turn up at least a few shooting aids of importance to you.

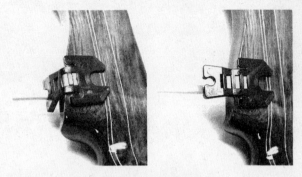

*An arrow holder is an adhesive-attachable, flexible unit that holds a shaft firmly on the arrow rest prior to a shot. When hunter starts to draw, holder flips out of the way.*

*A simple spine tester accurately measures the stiffness of all sorts of arrow shafts. Such a tool is handy in matching wood and fiberglass arrows for serious shooting in the outdoors.*

*Arrowheads are a constant subject of conversation among dedicated bowhunters. Preferences vary somewhat from one individual to another, but certain arrowhead designs are clear favorites among those with broad experience, skill.*

## CHAPTER 6

# HEAD 'EM UP!

### Choosing The Right Arrowhead For The Game You Intend To Hunt Makes A Decisive Difference

**T**HE ARROWHEAD is the single most important part of any hunting arrow. How this head is designed is primarily responsible for what happens when the arrow hits the mark, and in many instances also plays a critical role in whether or not the arrow hits home in the first place.

The average hunting arrow leaves a bow with less than 50 foot-pounds of energy (fpe), a mere drop in the bucket when compared to the power of even the tiniest rimfire rifle cartridge. For example, the dinky .22 Short rimfire round measures a scant three-quarters-inch long and less than one-quarter-inch in diameter, yet shoots a 29-grain bullet with over 100 fpe. This cartridge is generally considered to be inferior for hunting even small animals like ground squirrels, yet a 550-grain hunting arrow with only 45 fpe will regularly poleax everything from ground squirrels to moose. The key to success with any hunting arrow is tipping that arrow with the kind of head that best utilizes the meager energy in a speeding shaft.

Aside from raw effectiveness on a particular kind of game, an arrowhead should be chosen with a few other features in mind as well. For one thing, a head must be inherently accurate enough to hit the intended target. For another, it should be convenient to attach to a shaft. On top of these characteristics, it should be reasonably durable to withstand regular shooting without falling apart, becoming misshapen, or dulling down to the point where it no longer takes game efficiently. Here's a brief look at the common kinds of arrowheads on the market and their primary applications in the field.

### Field Points

Field points are simple, pointed arrowheads made of durable steel. They are available in both screw-in and glue-on configurations, and are also available in several weights besides the standard 125 grains to match broadheads of heavier weights.

Field points are the standard points used for regular

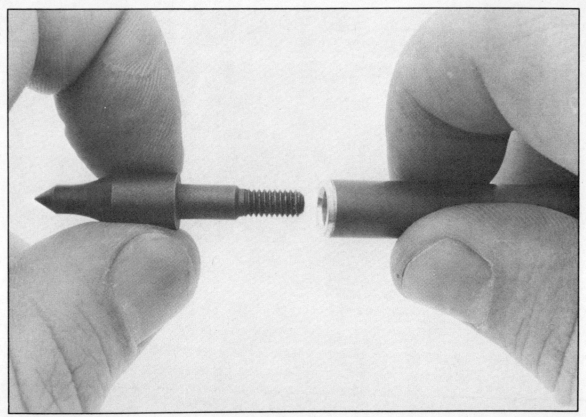

*Interchangeable heads are in common use today. A simple, durable screw-in field point is ideal for field target shooting as well as for hunting small animals and birds. It can be replaced with a broadhead for trophy hunting.*

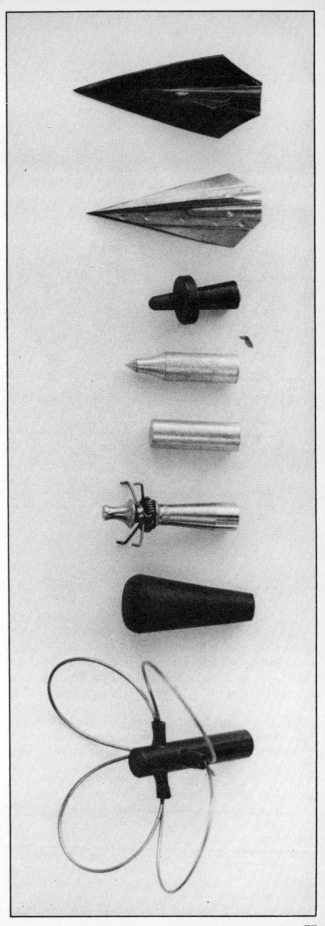

target practice and competitive shooting with hunting bows. These points are shaped to penetrate a target butt deeply enough to hold arrows, but not so deeply as to bury arrows out of sight. Field points are the most aerodynamically sound of all hunting arrowheads, providing decent accuracy even when a hunting bow is not perfectly tuned.

In addition to target shooting, a field point can be neatly used to take small game like rats, ground squirrels, magpies, and other critters under two pounds. This head does not impart enough shock to stun larger game, and does not cut a large enough hole to drop sizable animals and birds. It is strictly a head for the smallest huntable game.

### Blunt Arrowheads

Blunt arrowheads take many forms, from standard flat-nosed steel blunts to cone-shaped rubber blunts to more elaborately shaped blunts made of steel and/or plastic. A blunt head has two basic uses in the field.

First, it is ideal for practice shooting at stumps, dirt banks, grass clumps, and similar objects because it does not glance wildly into space, burrow deeply under grass or leaves, or bury tightly in wood. These particular problems are associated with the field point. A steel blunt with parallel sides is especially suited to shooting at stumps and other wooden targets because it penetrates enough to hold an arrow in place but is easily removed because it is not wedged in place.

The second major use of a blunt arrowhead is in hunting animals from jackrabbit size on down, provided its frontal surface is fairly small in diameter and provided the hunting bow used has a draw weight of sixty to seventy pounds. Such a blunt converts every bit of an arrow's energy into shocking power in game, and literally knocks the starch out of animals with solid hits.

### Bird-Hunting Heads

Most birds are best taken with big-game broadheads which cut a large, killing hole even when targets are flying quickly away. However, several other special-purpose arrowheads are also popular for shooting at airborne birds. One is the Snaro head, a steel blunt with large piano-wire loops attached to greatly increase the frontal impact zone

*If one is to be a success at bowfishing, he should make certain that his fish points are streamlined, rugged and heavily barbed. Note the barbs on these styles which Adams prefers for his own serious bowfishing efforts.*

of the head. This makes hitting a flying bird easier because the arrow can miss the mark by a couple of inches and still rake the bird with lethal effect. Another popular bird-hunting head is the Judo point, a spaceship-looking design with spring-steel arms that extend away from the central section of the head. The Judo's enlarged frontal zone makes hits slightly easier on birds, and also prevents an arrow from skipping out of sight in heavy weeds, grass, or leaves. The Judo is called an "unlosable point" by its manufacturer, and this trait makes it popular with small-game hunters as well as bird hunters.

More about bird hunting in Chapter 17.

## Fish Points

Bowfishing is becoming increasingly popular in modern times. This interesting sport will be discussed in detail in Chapter 17. The arrowheads used on fish are unique because they have a unique job to do — to penetrate a fish completely, which requires a streamlined design; to resist regular pounding on the rocky bottoms of lakes and streams, which requires rugged construction; and to hold fish securely with stout barbs or blades until these fish are played and landed. A wide variety of bowfishing heads are sold at archery stores, and each design has its strong and weak points. More on this subject later on.

## Hunting Broadheads

Hunting broadheads comprise the most widely diversified and most highly controversial group of

*Well-known bowhunter Bob Brandau took this giant wild boar in California's wilds with four-blade broadhead he had hand-sharpened. The carefully chosen head penetrated the massive hog completely, rewarding this bowhunter with one of the best boars ever taken with archery hunting gear.*

bowhunting arrowheads. Literally dozens of broadhead designs are sold at archery stores, and each has its gallery of fans. There are very good broadheads, mediocre broadheads, and very bad broadheads, but all have certain basic things in common.

A broadhead consists of a central section called a ferrule surrounded by two to six cutting blades. Such a head is designed to cut a large wound channel in an animal — a channel sufficient to result in quick, humane death. A broadhead is absolutely necessary to take any kind of big game, and is also necessary for all game over five or six pounds. This includes wild turkey, woodchucks, coyotes, foxes, raccoons, and similar mid-sized critters. As

mentioned earlier, a hunting arrow simply does not have the raw energy to drop game like a bullet does — a fact that requires a carefully designed broadhead to cause major damage in animals or birds larger than squirrels and rabbits.

A broadhead must have certain traits to be an effective hunting choice. It is safe to say that every broadhead on the market has at least a few fans, even the most horribly designed abortion ever seen on an archery pro shop shelf. The reason is simple enough. Most half-hearted bowhunters seldom if ever hit anything with their broadheads, and are therefore flying blind when they speculate about how their favorite broadhead might perform on game. A large percentage of manufacturers' literature about broadheads

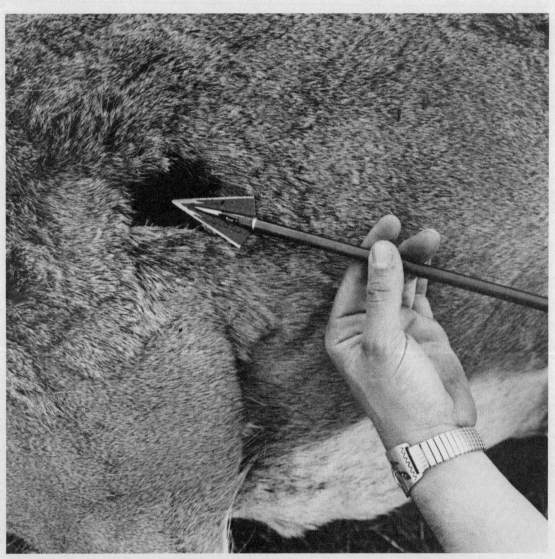

*A big-cutting four-blade head such as the Zwickey Black Diamond Delta creates a devastatingly large hole in game, as it passes through the animal. The only problem is that this type of head must be sharpened properly by hand.*

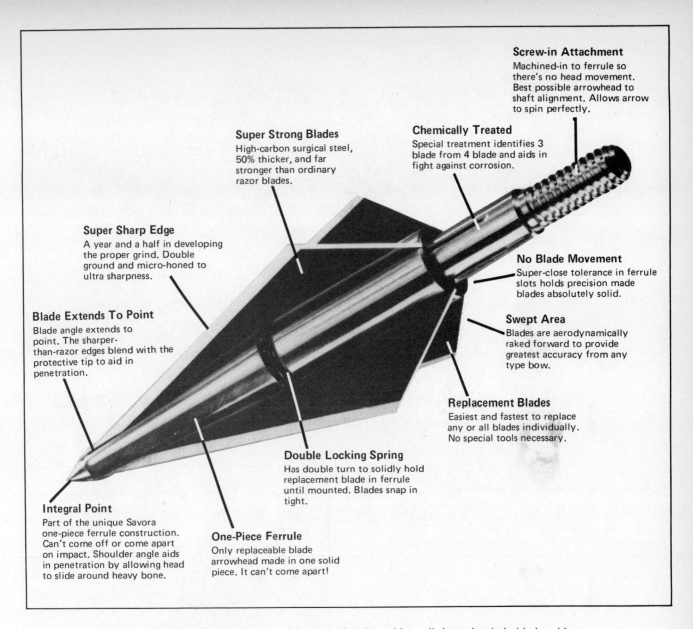

**Screw-in Attachment**
Machined-in to ferrule so there's no head movement. Best possible arrowhead to shaft alignment. Allows arrow to spin perfectly.

**Super Strong Blades**
High-carbon surgical steel, 50% thicker, and far stronger than ordinary razor blades.

**Chemically Treated**
Special treatment identifies 3 blade from 4 blade and aids in fight against corrosion.

**Super Sharp Edge**
A year and a half in developing the proper grind. Double ground and micro-honed to ultra sharpness.

**No Blade Movement**
Super-close tolerance in ferrule slots holds precision made blades absolutely solid.

**Blade Extends To Point**
Blade angle extends to point. The sharper-than-razor edges blend with the protective tip to aid in penetration.

**Swept Area**
Blades are aerodynamically raked forward to provide greatest accuracy from any type bow.

**Replacement Blades**
Easiest and fastest to replace any or all blades individually. No special tools necessary.

**Integral Point**
Part of the unique Savora one-piece ferrule construction. Can't come off or come apart on impact. Shoulder angle aids in penetration by allowing head to slide around heavy bone.

**Double Locking Spring**
Has double turn to solidly hold replacement blade in ferrule until mounted. Blades snap in tight.

**One-Piece Ferrule**
Only replaceable blade arrowhead made in one solid piece. It can't come apart!

*The popular Savora Super-S factory-sharpened hunting broadhead combines all the traits desirable in a big-game broadhead. This combination leads to both accuracy and deadly performance on big game with proper shooting.*

has been dreamed up in some high-rise marketing office by sales people who know next to nothing about the woods and the animals that live there. Enough inexperienced bowhunters are likely to fall for such bunk to make a particular broadhead a fair seller even if a regular old steel blunt would do just as good a job on deer.

The following recommendations about broadhead design are based on several hundred big-game kills I have personally witnessed and several thousand I have heard about through reliable sources. Any broadhead will kill game with perfect hits, but some designs are clearly superior to others.

First, the broadhead must have three or more blades to promote an acceptable level of tissue damage. Quite a few bowhunters swear by various two-blade designs, but three or more blades will perform better than two. As I said before, there is no accounting for broadhead taste because many archers have nothing but their imaginations to guide them.

Second, a broadhead should cut a hole *at least* one inch in diameter to ensure quick, humane kills. Quite a few smaller designs are available and legal to hunt with, but these are marginal at best. Smallish broadheads *do* tend to fly most accurately when a bow is not tuned up or when a bowhunter is obsessed with shooting light arrows at maximum speed. However, a larger, soundly designed head can be made to fly well and always produces superior results on game.

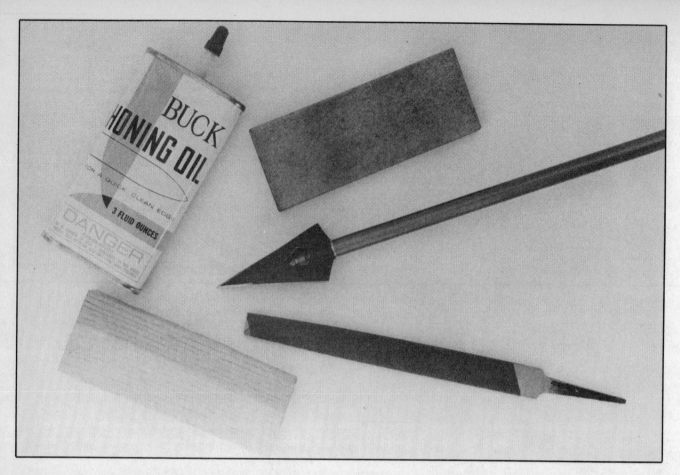

*Tools necessary to sharpen a broadhead are inexpensive and simple. Needed are good-quality honing oil; medium-grain whetstone, the broadhead attached to its shaft; a coarse-toothed mill file; plus a small block of wood. The last item is utilized to strop the blades of head.*

Third, hunting broadheads must be uniformly constructed so they can be installed concentrically on shafts and so they all weigh about the same. As discussed in Chapter 7, a broadhead must be installed with the point in exact line with the centerline of the shaft to prevent erratic arrow flight and dismal accuracy. Similarly, broadheads that do not weigh within a few grains of each other will not all shoot accurately from even the best-tuned hunting bow. A brief common-sense look at various broadhead designs in an archery store will weed out the most poorly constructed heads with crooked blades, off-center ferrules, etc. From there, it is best to stick with a widely used, brand-name broadhead recommended by your dealer and/or several serious bowhunting friends.

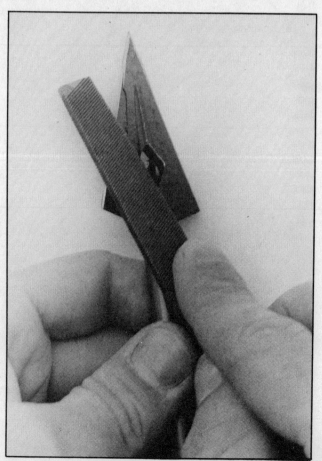

*First step in sharpening is to file the main broadhead blades to a 20 or 22-degree angle by using the back of the broadhead ferrule as a file guide. This angle will provide the sharpest, most durable edge, author says.*

As a general rule, any aerodynamic, good-flying broadhead will also penetrate well on game. However, there are some notable exceptions to this rule. A broadhead must have smooth, sharp blades and a streamlined, relatively sharp point to ensure deep penetration. I have seen a few blunt-nosed, replaceable-blade hunting broadheads actually bounce off deer and wild pigs when shot from bows in the fifty- to sixty-pound range — bows that will normally drive a streamlined, sharp-pointed arrow clear through a deer's body in the twinkle of an eye. When choosing a hunting broadhead, be sure it is sharp all the way around the end, as is the case with the Bear Razorhead and the Zwickey Black Diamond, or has a fairly sharp point with blades that come close to this point, as is the case with the Savora Swept-Wing broadhead.

Normally, the more streamlined arrowheads are also the

*Once the main blades of the broadhead have been filed to proper angle, one should lightly spade the point. This will ensure that the tip of the broadhead will not curl over if the broadhead should impact on animal's heavier bones.*

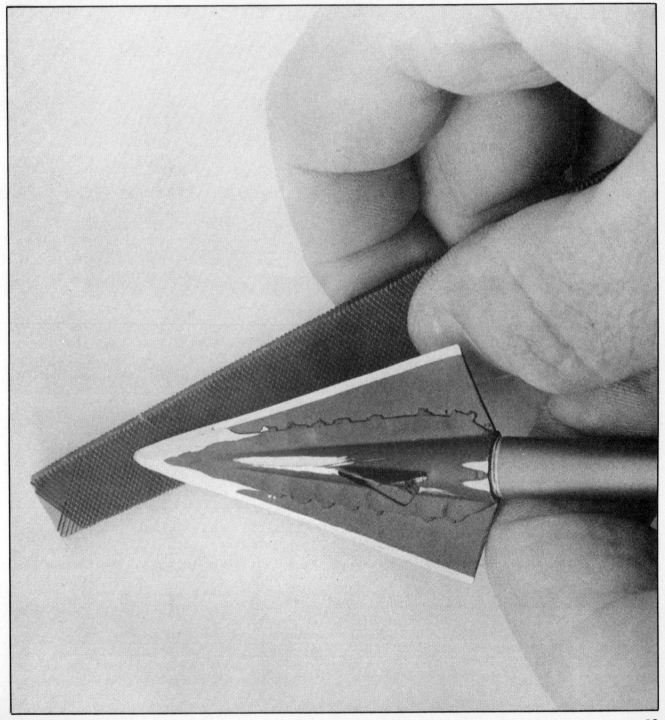

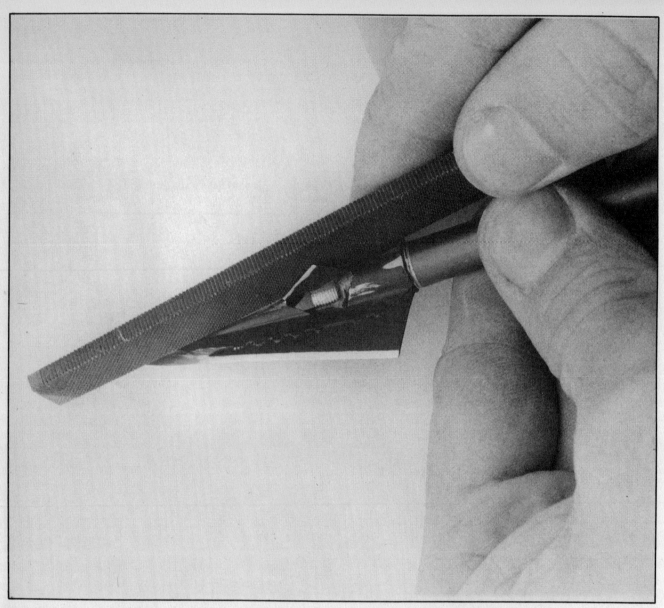

*The next step in the sharpening sequence is to file the secondary blades to the same angle as the main blades. In this step, one again uses the back of the ferrule as an angle guide. With practice, it becomes a simple effort.*

more sturdy and shock-resistant of the lot. Stay away from long, needle-nosed heads that tend to snap off, and also stay away from heads with thin, razor-blade-like blades that are also prone to break upon impact. It is a proven fact of physics that a broadhead three times longer than it is wide will penetrate a maximum amount, so longer, narrower heads than this don't help you one iota more. Similarly, a broadhead blade .050-inch thick penetrates every bit as well as one .015-inch thick, provided both are sharp. Choose a sturdy broadhead that will hold together in game for maximum results.

So-called "ripper blades" on broadheads are a solid waste of time — a pain to sharpen and a hindrance to penetration and bleeding in animals. These saw-tooth blades look wicked for sure, but the serious bowhunter uses a broadhead with smooth, shaving-sharp edges that slice off everything in their path and cause maximum tissue damage and blood loss in animals. Although some bowhunters debate the point, it is a proven fact that a smoothly honed, scalpel-sharp edge outperforms a jagged or even slightly ragged file-sharpened edge. Such a smooth edge penetrates best, causes no pain to an animal, promotes the most and the longest bleeding, and allows less chance of wound infection with marginal hits on animals that get away.

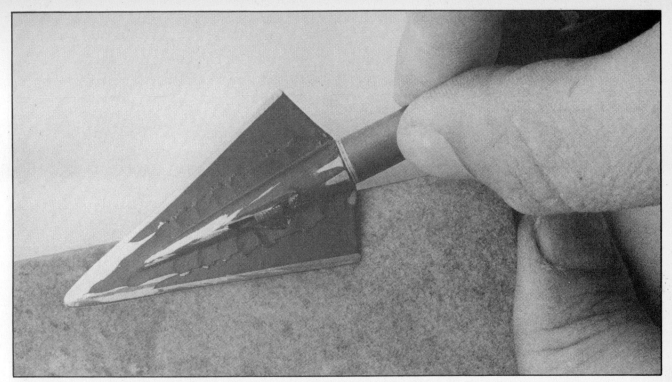

The bowhunter then carefully hones the main broadhead edges on the sides of the whetstone. However, extreme care must be taken during this step to maintain the original filing angle, if the ultimate in sharpness is desired.

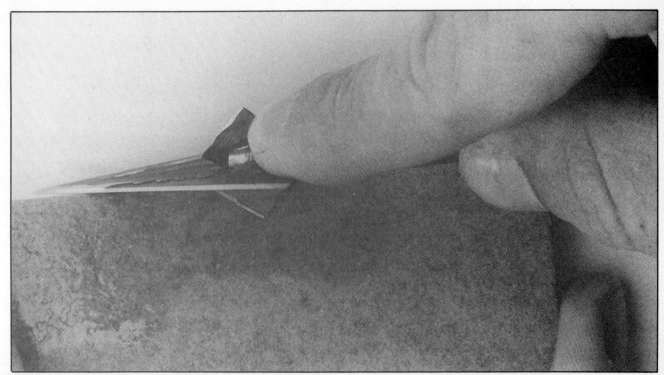

The secondary blades of the broadhead are honed as shown, taking care to retain the original blade angle. This will ensure the maximum sharpness of this edge, if done right. This sort of sharpening can be done afield, if needed.

Once all broadhead's edges are keen, strop them by dragging each side of each edge backwards along a block of wood to remove microscopic steel burrs.

There are several tests for checking the sharpness of a broadhead. If the edge slices medium-weight paper with ease, it is ready for hunting game.

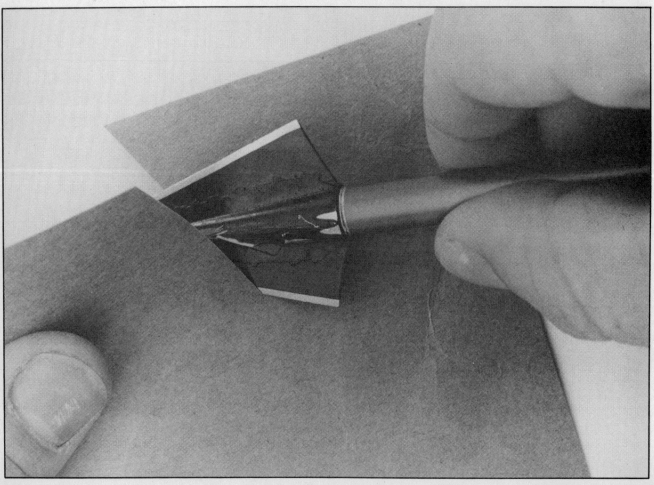

*Another simple test for checking the sharpness of a broadhead is to run every edge across a thumbnail. If the edge grabs the nail instead of sliding over it, the edge is sharp.*

*A bowhunter should never hunt with broadheads unless they are shaving sharp.* This is perhaps the single most important rule in hunting archery. If you can't shave hair easily with all blades on all your arrows, stay home and watch television. To hunt with a dull broadhead is a crime, a disservice to both the hunter and the game. An arrow that is dull does not penetrate deeply, does not cut cleanly to cause bleeding, and does not kill animals neatly unless it smacks a vital organ like the heart dead center. Never, but never hunt with dull broadheads.

There are two ways to ensure shaving-sharp broadhead edges. One is carefully sharpening them with file, stone, and strop (see the accompanying photo sequence on how to sharpen a broadhead). This method takes time, patience, and skill, which many bowhunters do not have. The other,

and much easier, way to keep broadheads sharp is buying top-quality factory-sharpened heads like Savora Super-S Swept-Wings. The best factory-sharpened broadheads feature quick blade interchangeability, shaving-sharp edges, easy screw-in attachment to arrows, and a rugged, pointed, streamlined design.

Broadhead blades should be inspected regularly on a hunt and touched up or replaced if they appear to be nicked or dull. They should be lightly oiled at the outset to prevent edge-damaging rust, and should be oiled periodically in damp or rainy weather. Treat your broadheads right and they'll treat you right.

**The Importance Of Consistent Arrowhead Weight**

Although the majority of hunting arrowheads weigh in

A good bowhunter checks the edges of each broadhead regularly during any trip afield to be certain they are always sharp enough for big game. This has meant continuing success for top trophy hunter Jim Dougherty.

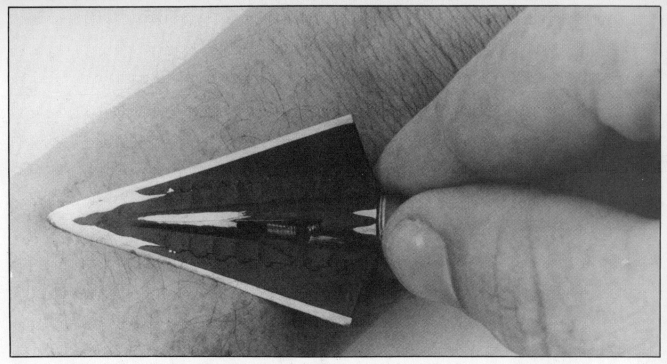

*Another check for sharpness of your broadhead is to find whether it will shave hair from an arm or leg easily. If so, it is ready for hunting. Check the entire length of each blade, then rehone any dull spots until they pass.*

the neighborhood of 125 grains, there are some notable exceptions to this rule. For example, the big, popular Black Diamond Delta broadhead glued to a standard 45-grain screw-in aluminum broadhead adapter weighs over 175 grains prior to sharpening. When properly sharpened, it weighs about 170 grains. In order to use such a broadhead and have other kinds of points hit the same place with careful bow tuning (see Chapter 7), these other points must also weigh close to 170 grains. The problem is, no manufacturer makes field points, blunts, or other common arrowheads weighing over 150 grains. As a result, the shooter using Black Diamond Deltas must create his own 170-grain field points by gluing old-style 125-grain field points to 45-grain screw-in adapters, and must slip 45-grain rubber blunts over 125-grain screw-in steel blunts to achieve the same point weight in a stump-shooting head. Similarly, bowhunters who prefer broadheads weighing 145 or 150 grains (a common broadhead weight range) should use commercial field points of the same weight. Freely interchanging arrowheads of different weights invariably produces wobbly arrow flight with some and maddening changes in point of impact.

It is extremely important to choose your hunting arrowheads with care and to match them to specific tasks at hand. The result will be good accuracy and pleasing performance on targets and various kinds of game.

*To create a hunting blunt of the same weight as a 170-grain broadhead, a bowhunter should slip a 45-grain rubber blunt over a 125-grain screw-in steel blunt. Matching weight of arrowheads is a must for maintaining consistent accuracy.*

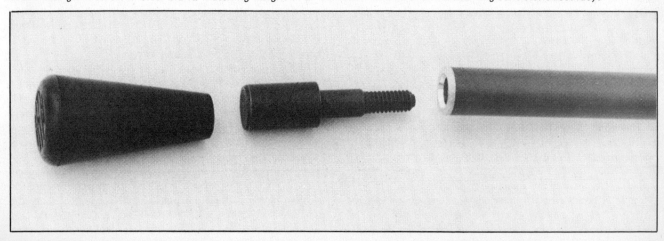

# CHAPTER 7

# PUTTING IT ALL TOGETHER

## Combining The Proper Tackle And The Proven Techniques Means Better Game-Getting

**A**FTER A BOWHUNTER has purchased his basic shooting gear, learned to shoot, fine-tuned his bow/arrow setup, and assembled other necessary equipment like an arrow quiver and practical hunting arrowheads, it is time to unite all this equipment and knowledge in one straight-shooting combination. Final preparation of the shooting combo is not difficult or time-consuming to carry out, but several steps must be taken to ensure maximum accuracy and bow/arrow performance.

The first thing to do is assemble the shooting unit exactly as you plan to hunt with it. Every item added to a bow and every thing changed about an arrow is apt to affect arrow flight characteristics, both the degree of arrow wobble, if any, and the exact point of arrow impact. For example, a bow without a bow quiver attached is likely to shoot differently and require a different arrow-rest/nocking-point tune and bowsight setting than

the same bow with quiver attached. Similarly, a hunting arrow thirty inches long will shoot differently than one twenty-nine inches long, and an arrow with feather fletching will shoot differently than one with plastic vanes. First decide what equipment you plan to use, then assemble it for a final tuning session on the range.

After an arrow quiver is installed on your bow, a shooting stabilizer is in place, and any similar modifications are made, you should add some sort of silencers to the bowstring to hush noisy string twang that might spook game. Such silencers cannot really be classified as shooting equipment because they do not enhance or detract from accuracy, but their added weight *can* slightly change the tune of a hunting bow. By far the best silencers I've used are so-called "catwhiskers" — clusters of thin rubber strands slipped between the filaments of a bowstring near each end of the string. These work equally well on compound and recurve strings. In addition, a hunter with a longbow or

*Above: Many types of effective rubber bowstring silencers are available. Author's favorite is cat-whisker type (far left), a cluster of thin rubber filaments slipped between the strands of the string of the hunting bow.*

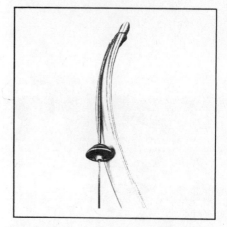

*Brush button prevents debris from jamming between limb and bowstring of recurve. It also dampens noise caused by the bowstring slapping against the bow during the shot.*

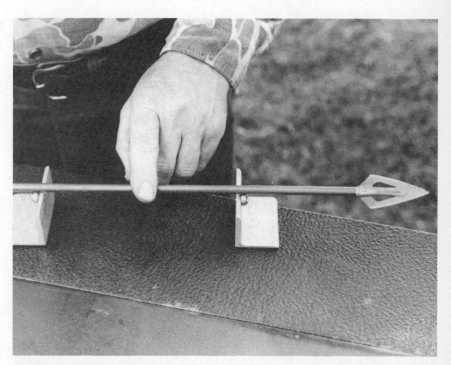

*Upper right: To check alignment of broadhead, shaft straightness on arrow rollers, balance arrow on the rollers. (Lower right) Spin shaft rapidly with a finger, watching for wobble along shaft and at tip of the broadhead. Nock straightness can be checked in virtually same fashion.*

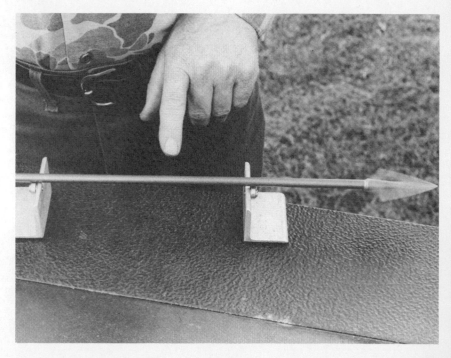

recurve bow should place a rubber "brush button" on the string adjacent to each limbtip to prevent twigs, grass, and similar debris from jamming between the bow and the limbtip. Such string adornment is necessary in bowhunting, and should be installed prior to final tuning of the shooting combination.

The nitpicking bowhunter also pays special attention to his arrows before trying to perfect the performance of his shooting combination. This includes making sure his arrow fletching is not nicked or tattered, rotating his arrow shafts on commercial or homemade rollers or rolling them across a table to make sure they are straight, and similarly spinning

arrows to check the straightness of nocks and arrowheads in relation to the shaft. A wobbly nock is a primary cause of poor accuracy and should be replaced at once.

A hunting broadhead with a point out of line with the shaft is also the kiss of death on accuracy, and should be reglued in better line with hot-melt cement (if the head is an old-style glue-on type) or screwed into another shaft with the hope that it will align better. In addition to rolling a shaft to check point alignment, a hunter can spin a broadhead-tipped arrow on the point of the head like a top to check broadhead alignment. If the arrow shaft wobbles at all where the shaft and broadhead meet, the

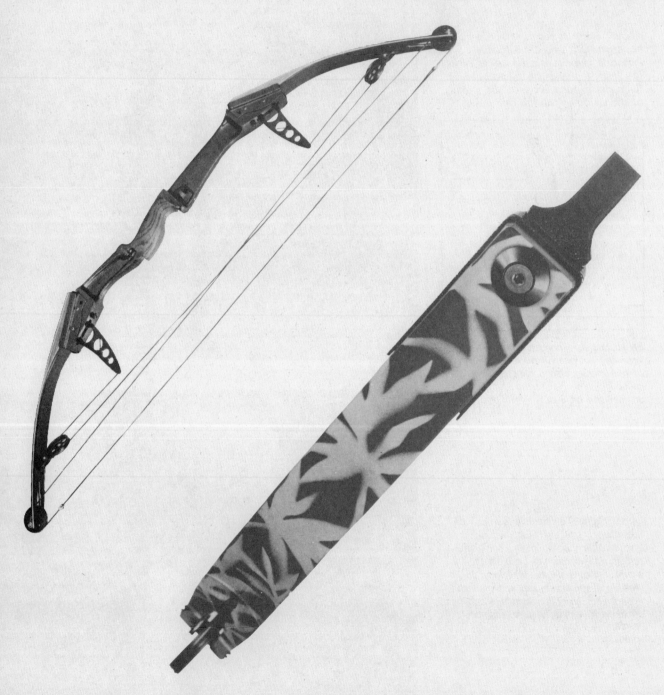

*A few commercially built hunting bows can be ordered with factory limb camouflage, including the Jennings Arrowstar. This particular model is available in both a slick-limb Hunter version and with a dull, leaf-pattern Camlimb.*

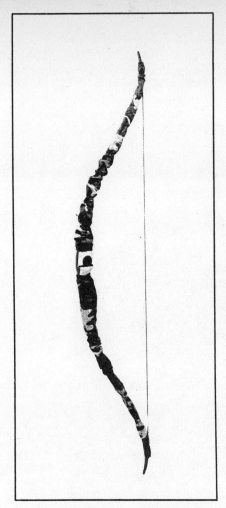

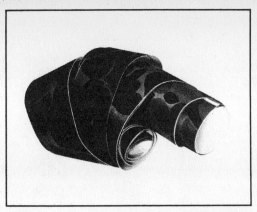

Camouflage tape that adheres to the surfaces of the hunting bow also can be utilized to break up the outline of bow during a hunt.

The shiny surfaces of a bow or even light-colored limbs can be hidden with bow-limb sleeves that are made of camouflage cloth marketed now.

Easiest and most practical method of camouflaging a hunting bow is spraying it with a pattern of contrasting, non-glare bow paints. This will camouflage nooks, crannies uniformly.

Author's favorite bow-paint pattern of wide, alternating black and light brown bands fooled this javelina taken at close range in Texas. The pattern also hides the bow from the more sharp-eyed deer, antelope, elk.

## Bowstring Selection Chart

| Draw Weight Of Bow | Number Of Dacron Strands |
|---|---|
| Up to 25 lbs. | 8 Strands |
| 25 to 35 lbs. | 10 Strands |
| 35 to 45 lbs. | 12 Strands |
| 45 to 55 lbs. | 14 Strands |
| 55 to 70 lbs. | 16 Strands |
| 70 to 85 lbs. | 18 Strands |

*When buying a spare bowstring, be sure to choose a string of proper length, strength to match your bow. These are made of several Dacron strands, must have sufficient strands to withstand regular shooting at a particular draw weight without possibly breaking. The chart serves as a guide to selection.*

head is not on straight. This technique is especially handy in the woods where rollers and flat tables are not behind every bush.

No two arrowheads screw into an arrow exactly the same way because of machining variations, and hunters using screw-in broadheads must juggle heads and shafts to find combinations which line up well. The only alternative is haphazardly slapping arrowheads on shafts and risking erratic arrow flight.

Once the bow is fully decked out and arrows are carefully inspected, it is time for a final bow/arrow tune-up. This entails shooting arrows with various kinds of hunting points, including field points, blunts, and your favorite broadhead. As mentioned in Chapter 6, all these arrowheads should be matched in weight to ensure the same point of impact.

As outlined in Chapter 4, you should shoot your bow at about twenty yards with a friend watching your arrows fly. It is best to begin shooting with broadheads because these are most critical to tune, and once tuned so they group well without wobble, it is highly likely that all other arrowheads of the same weight will hit the same place. If field points or other heads hit high, low, left, or right of broadheads, you must move your arrow rest and/or nocking point until groups move together. A little experimentation generally does the trick.

A hunting bow that shoots arrows quietly and accurately with a variety of arrowheads is pure joy to use. It can be sighted-in and left as is from then on — as long as the shooter doesn't change something about his equipment or his shooting style. Such a bow/arrow setup is almost ready to hunt with — almost.

First, however, the bow and all other shiny or light-colored bits of equipment must be carefully camouflaged to avoid the prying eyes of game. A few bows and shooting accessories come camouflaged from the factory, but most are left shiny to appeal to a customer's eye across the counter. The only shooting items that are always pre-camouflaged are first-quality dull-anodized aluminum hunting shafts.

Although camouflage tape and slip-over cloth bow-limb sleeves are sold by various archery companies, by far the best way to camouflage equipment is spraying it in a mottled pattern with two or three shades of commercial camouflage bow paint. This pattern should contrast to break up the outline of equipment. My favorite color scheme for most situations is an alternating pattern of black and light-brown bands. Prior to painting any bow, quiver, or other item, clean it thoroughly with rubbing alcohol and paper towels to ensure good adhesion of paint.

The only other equipment-setup necessity prior to heading afield is preparing at least one spare bowstring in case the original breaks or becomes badly frayed. All this simple step requires is replacing the original bowstring with a new one (with the aid of a quality bowstringer), letting the bow remain strung overnight to fully stretch the new string to length, and then placing a nocking point and string silencers on the new string to exactly match placement on the old string. This makes the strings interchangeable without noticeable effect on arrow flight.

At this point your shooting combination is entirely ready to hunt with, letting you turn your attention to other important matters like perfecting your ability to shoot in the field and learning to stalk within bow range of game.

# CHAPTER 8

# KNOWING THE RANGE

## Learning To Judge Distance Is A Prime Need For The Bowhunter

A WELL-TUNED bow and pinpoint shooting skill put an archer a long way toward hitting targets in the field. However, these requirements for shooting success alone are not enough to put game in the bag on a regular basis. A third ingredient also is critical to hitting targets and game in natural settings: the ability to determine the exact distance to the target.

A hunting arrow travels an incredibly arching path between the shooter and the target, a path that will blow any gun-shooter's mind. A medium-powered deer rifle will characteristically hit within six inches of the mark all the way out to three hundred yards, making range estimation in gun hunting a relatively insignificant factor.

By comparison, an average aluminum hunting arrow weighing around 500 grains and traveling about 200 feet per second (a snappy speed for even the fastest compound bows) drops off like a ping-pong ball after it leaves the bowstring. This dramatic arrow drop-off makes pinpoint range estimation a must for regular hits on targets and game.

The accompanying arrow trajectory data graphically shows just how critical range estimation is. The heavier the

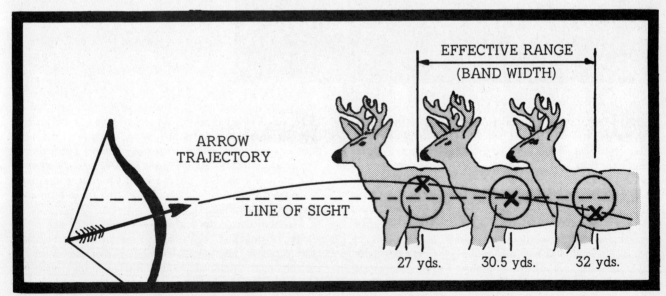

At a designated distance, a particular bow/arrow combination has a specific effective range. This range — or band width — becomes more narrow as distance to the target lengthens and the arrow trajectory becomes more arched. This is the primary factory which makes estimation of the range increasingly more critical as the length of shots increases.

*Author had to estimate distance to this prairie dog within one yard to make a solid hit on the animal at 45 yards. Pinpoint shooting at longer ranges will require plenty of practice or an accurate rangefinding device.*

arrow, the lighter the draw weight, and the less efficient the bow design, the slower an arrow travels and the more it drops. However, even a hard-shooting sixty-five-pound compound bow with lightweight 2117 aluminum arrows produces a trajectory guaranteed to frustrate any archer without the ability to tell how far away his targets happen to be. As the data shows, a misestimation of only six or seven yards at fifteen or twenty yards will produce a total miss on a small or medium-sized animal, and is likely to produce a crippling rather than a killing hit on a deer with an average chest depth of fifteen inches. The trajectory data also shows that range estimation becomes more and more critical as shooting distance increases and arrow speed diminishes. The same sixty-five-pound compound bow that allows a three or five-yard misestimation at twenty yards on

a deer-sized target produces an arrow drop of nearly a foot between forty and forty-five yards, requiring the bow-hunter to estimate within a yard, or so to hit a squirrel and within 2½ yards to solidly hit a deer with a dead-center hold on its sixteen-inch chest area. If a hunter is shooting a less powerful bow or heavier arrows, the range-estimation problem is magnified.

The ability to estimate range in the field is one of the most important skills any bowhunter can possess. Unfortunately, few hunters are even mediocre at estimating distance by eye on level ground, let alone in the deer woods where terrain is likely to be sloping, broken, or obscured by trees and undergrowth.

Accurately measuring distance by eye is definitely desirable, if an archer is capable of pulling it off, but tests

## Average Trajectories For Standard 29-Inch Aluminum Hunting Arrows

| Bow | Arrow Shaft Size | Total Arrow Weight (grs) | Arrow Velocity At Various Distances (fps) | | | | | | | | Trajectory For Various Sight-In Zeroes (in inches) | | | | | | | |
|---|---|---|---|---|---|---|---|---|---|---|---|---|---|---|---|---|---|---|
| | | | 10 Yds. | 15 Yds. | 20 Yds. | 25 Yds. | 30 Yds. | 35 Yds. | 40 Yds. | 45 Yds. | 10 Yds. | 15 Yds. | 20 Yds. | 25 Yds. | 30 Yds. | 35 Yds. | 40 Yds. | 45 Yds. |
| 45-lb. Recurve | 1918 | 522 | 162.8 | 162.0 | 161.3 | 160.6 | 159.5 | 159.0 | 158.8 | 158.3 | + 3.4 | 0 | - 6.3 | -16.2 | -29.6 | -46.4 | -66.8 | -91.0 |
| | | | | | | | | | | | +10.2 | +10.4 | + 7.2 | 0 | -9.2 | -22.7 | -39.7 | -60.2 |
| | | | | | | | | | | | +20.1 | +25.3 | +27.2 | +25.7 | +20.8 | +12.4 | 0 | -15.1 |
| 45-lb. Recurve | 2016 | 493 | 166.5 | 165.6 | 164.7 | 163.8 | 163.1 | 162.4 | 161.7 | 161.2 | + 3.1 | 0 | - 6.3 | -15.9 | -28.8 | -45.1 | -64.8 | -88.0 |
| | | | | | | | | | | | + 9.7 | + 9.9 | + 6.9 | 0 | - 8.9 | -21.7 | -38.0 | -57.8 |
| | | | | | | | | | | | +19.5 | +24.6 | +26.4 | +25.1 | +20.5 | +12.6 | 0 | -13.5 |
| 50-lb. Recurve | 2016 | 493 | 172.3 | 171.3 | 170.4 | 169.5 | 168.7 | 167.9 | 167.2 | 166.6 | + 3.2 | 0 | - 5.3 | -14.0 | -25.9 | -41.1 | -59.4 | -80.8 |
| | | | | | | | | | | | + 8.9 | + 9.0 | + 6.1 | 0 | - 8.7 | -20.9 | -36.2 | -54.7 |
| | | | | | | | | | | | +18.0 | +22.6 | +24.3 | +23.0 | +18.6 | +11.0 | 0 | -13.5 |
| 50-lb. Recurve | 2018 | 542 | 165.7 | 164.9 | 164.0 | 163.3 | 162.7 | 162.0 | 161.5 | 161.0 | + 3.4 | 0 | - 5.8 | -15.2 | -28.2 | -44.3 | -64.1 | -87.0 |
| | | | | | | | | | | | + 9.8 | + 9.9 | + 6.8 | 0 | - 9.2 | -22.2 | -38.6 | -58.6 |
| | | | | | | | | | | | +19.6 | +24.6 | +26.5 | +25.0 | +20.3 | +12.3 | 0 | -14.0 |
| 55-lb Recurve | 2018 | 542 | 176.5 | 175.6 | 174.7 | 173.9 | 173.2 | 172.4 | 171.8 | 171.2 | + 2.9 | 0 | - 5.3 | -13.8 | -25.1 | -39.4 | -56.8 | -77.3 |
| | | | | | | | | | | | + 8.6 | + 8.7 | + 5.9 | 0 | - 8.2 | -19.8 | 34.2 | -51.8 |
| | | | | | | | | | | | +17.0 | +21.4 | +23.0 | +21.7 | +17.5 | +10.4 | 0 | -13.0 |
| 55-lb. Recurve | 2117 | 535 | 177.3 | 176.3 | 175.4 | 174.5 | 173.7 | 172.9 | 172.2 | 171.5 | + 2.9 | 0 | - 5.2 | -13.5 | -24.8 | -39.0 | -56.2 | -76.5 |
| | | | | | | | | | | | + 8.5 | + 8.6 | + 6.0 | 0 | - 8.0 | -19.4 | -33.9 | -51.4 |
| | | | | | | | | | | | +17.0 | +21.4 | +23.0 | +21.7 | +17.6 | +10.5 | 0 | -12.5 |
| 55-lb. Compound | 1918 | 522 | 182.0 | 181.0 | 180.0 | 179.2 | 178.4 | 177.7 | 176.9 | 176.3 | + 2.7 | 0 | - 5.0 | -13.1 | -23.8 | -37.3 | -53.7 | -73.1 |
| | | | | | | | | | | | + 8.1 | + 8.3 | + 5.7 | 0 | - 7.5 | -18.3 | -32.0 | -48.4 |
| | | | | | | | | | | | +16.1 | +20.2 | +21.7 | +20.5 | +16.5 | + 9.8 | 0 | -12.2 |
| 55-lb. Compound | 2016 | 493 | 185.9 | 184.8 | 183.8 | 182.8 | 181.9 | 181.0 | 180.1 | 179.4 | + 2.8 | 0 | - 4.5 | -12.1 | -22.4 | -35.2 | -51.0 | -69.5 |
| | | | | | | | | | | | + 7.7 | + 7.9 | + 5.4 | 0 | - 7.3 | -17.7 | -30.7 | -46.7 |
| | | | | | | | | | | | +15.5 | +19.5 | +21.0 | +19.9 | +16.2 | + 9.8 | 0 | -11.3 |
| 60-lb. Compound | 2016 | 493 | 192.4 | 191.3 | 190.2 | 189.2 | 188.2 | 187.3 | 186.4 | 185.5 | + 2.5 | 0 | - 4.3 | -11.4 | -21.0 | -33.0 | -47.8 | -65.0 |
| | | | | | | | | | | | + 7.4 | + 7.5 | + 5.3 | 0 | - 6.5 | -16.0 | -78.3 | -43.0 |
| | | | | | | | | | | | +14.6 | +18.4 | +19.8 | +18.8 | +15.3 | + 9.4 | 0 | -10.2 |
| 60-lb. Compound | 2117 | 535 | 186.3 | 185.3 | 184.3 | 183.4 | 182.5 | 181.6 | 180.8 | 180.0 | + 2.8 | 0 | - 4.5 | -12.0 | -22.1 | -35.0 | -50.6 | -69.0 |
| | | | | | | | | | | | + 7.8 | + 7.9 | + 5.4 | 0 | - 7.2 | -17.5 | -30.4 | -46.3 |
| | | | | | | | | | | | +15.5 | +19.5 | +21.0 | +20.0 | +16.3 | + 9.9 | 0 | -10.9 |
| 65-lb. Compound | 2117 | 535 | 192.2 | 191.1 | 190.0 | 189.1 | 188.1 | 187.2 | 186.4 | 185.6 | + 2.5 | 0 | - 4.4 | -11.5 | -21.1 | -33.3 | -47.8 | -65.1 |
| | | | | | | | | | | | + 7.4 | + 7.5 | + 5.3 | 0 | - 6.6 | -16.2 | -28.3 | -43.1 |
| | | | | | | | | | | | +14.6 | +18.4 | +19.8 | +18.8 | +15.3 | + 9.4 | 0 | -10.2 |
| 65-lb. Compound | 2018 | 542 | 191.4 | 190.4 | 189.4 | 188.5 | 187.6 | 186.8 | 185.9 | 185.2 | + 2.5 | 0 | - 4.5 | -11.6 | -21.3 | -33.6 | -48.2 | -65.8 |
| | | | | | | | | | | | + 7.4 | + 7.5 | + 5.2 | 0 | - 6.7 | -16.5 | -28.8 | -43.7 |
| | | | | | | | | | | | +14.7 | +18.9 | +19.8 | +18.7 | +15.2 | + 9.2 | 0 | -10.5 |

# RANGEFINDER

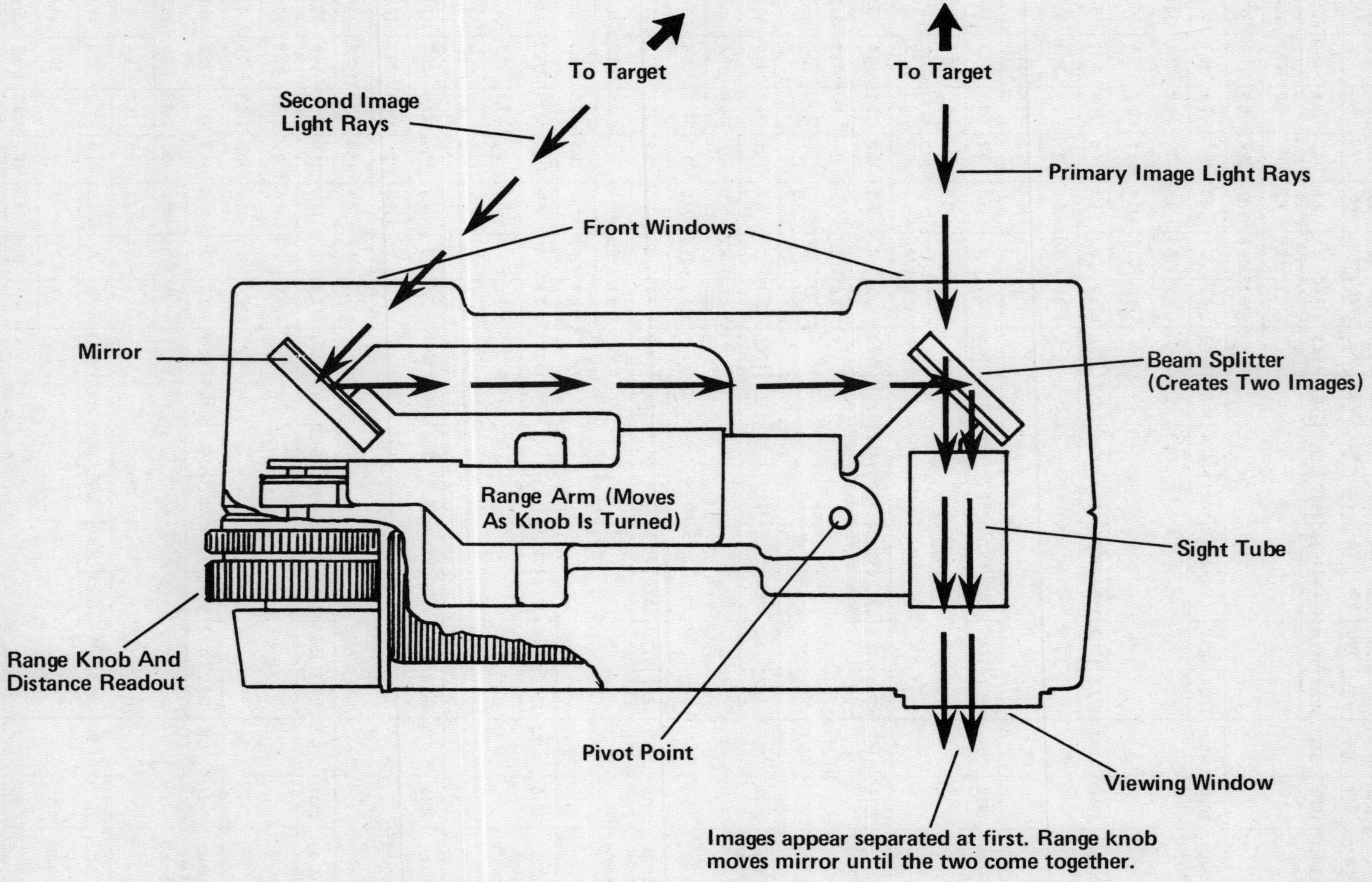

To Target

To Target

Primary Image Light Rays

Second Image Light Rays

Beam Splitter (Creates Two Images)

Sight Tube

Viewing Window

Images appear separated at first. Range knob moves mirror until the two come together.

Front Windows

Range Arm (Moves As Knob Is Turned)

Pivot Point

Mirror

Range Knob And Distance Readout

Illustration Courtesy Of Ranging, Inc.

*Left: The basic design of the rangefinder is relatively simple. (Above) A triangulating rangefinder takes double fix on a target, computes distance with turn of a range knob. When double image seen through viewing window blends into one, distance is read off range scale. Best units for bowhunting are accurate within ½ yard to 70 yards.*

by the U.S. military indicate that even rigorously trained observers of distance regularly misestimate range by seventeen percent or more.

This gross an error in range estimation will send an arrow far above or below a deer at all but the closest shooting ranges, resulting in shattered hopes after a careful stalk or wait on stand. A few bowhunters are relatively proficient at judging distance, but no one is even close to infallible.

Despite the odds against becoming consistently good, I strongly recommend that every bowhunter practice diligently at sharpening his ability to judge shooting range.

This can be accomplished both by regular shooting in the field (see Chapter 9) and by simply eyeballing distances and then pacing them off to see if your judgment is correct. The better a bowhunter is at this sort of thing, the better his chances of scoring with split-instant shots that do not allow the time to determine range by more surefire means.

Sharpening your ability to accurately eyeball shooting distance is quite important in bowhunting, but using some sort of accurate optical rangefinder is considerably more surefire.

Until recently there were no rangefinders commonly

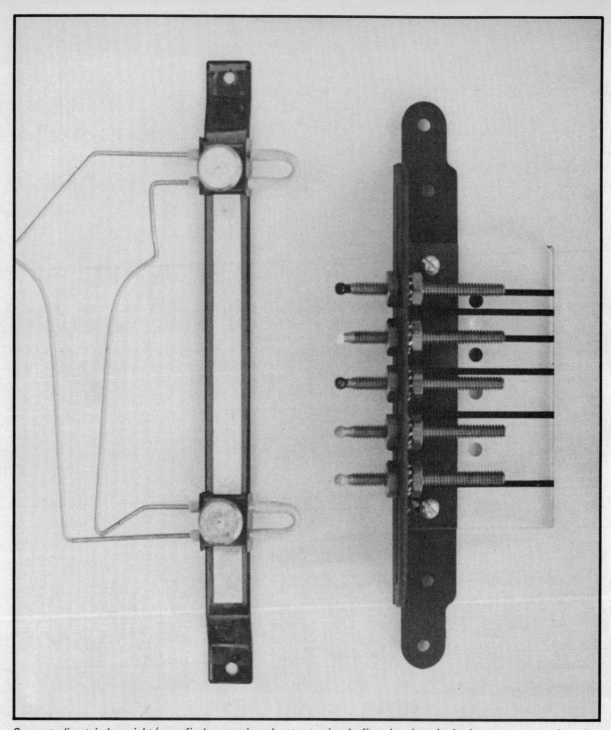

*Some stadimetric bowsight/rangefinders require a hunter to simply fit a deer lengthwise between converging wires, then let go with an arrow (left). Others require a hunter to fit a deer's body between horizontal bars, then aim with the proper sight pin which corresponds to the proper bar gap. Neither system works very well.*

available that were accurate enough to satisfy the bowhunter's pinpoint needs, but Ranging, Incorporated, now offers several dependable models that do the trick quickly and accurately. Learning to use an optical rangefinder takes just a few minutes, and pays off big whenever there is time to use this tool on nearby landmarks where game is likely to appear or on the animals themselves.

As mentioned in Chapter 1, a well-designed optical

rangefinder such as the Ranging Model 50 or the Ranging Sure Shot is far superior to more crude, less accurate rangefinding devices attached directly to a bowsight. A triangulating rangefinder like the Model 50 determines the range to any object with the simple whirl of a dial. When double images of the object being viewed come together, the hunter reads the range off a handy scale.

By contrast, a so-called stadimetric rangefinder attached to a bowsight requires the hunter to have a clear view of a broadside deer so he can visually fit that deer's body inside a box, ring or a set of stadia bars that corresponds to a particular yardage.

An obvious problem with such a system is the fact that different deer have slightly different body depths — which sometimes is enough alone to cause entire misses at longer shooting ranges. A hand-held, optical stadimetric rangefinder like the Ranging Sure Shot must be used in the same way as a rangefinder attached to a bowsight and embodies the same basic problems. However, it does not require the shooter to estimate range at full draw as muscles tighten up and threaten to ruin accuracy, and is therefore a much better bet.

A triangulating rangefinder is far superior to any stadimetric design because it can be used on any object of any size, not just an animal with the chest depth of a deer. Such a rangefinder allows a stand hunter to determine the range to nearby trees, rocks and other landmarks where game might appear; it also allows any hunter to determine the range to off-size critters like ground squirrels, woodchucks, javelina, moose, and the like.

A handy optical rangefinder on your belt and a well-practiced eye for estimating the range on extra quick shots are absolutely essential to consistent shooting success on game. Target archers generally know the exact distance of their shots and seldom consider how critical range estimation can be in hitting the mark.

However, every seasoned bowhunter knows that even an ever-so-slight error in range estimation results in a clean miss or a crippling hit no matter how accurate the bow or how perfect the shooting form.

The most powerful hunting bows available still cast arrows with extremely arching trajectories — a fact well worth remembering as you prepare for the moment of truth when the only thing between you and success is one accurate, properly estimated shot.

*Compact optical stadimetric rangefinder allows hunter to fit broadside deer between stadia bars without the strain of holding bow at full draw. Such rangefinders also allow finer, more consistent bracketing of animal.*

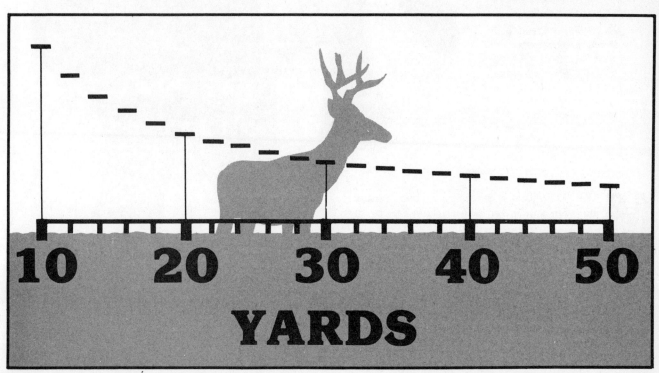

Deer shown above is 28 yards away.

# CHAPTER 9

# FINE TUNING YOUR SHOOTING SKILLS

## Knowing Your Tackle And How To Use It – From Every Angle – Can Mean Field Success!

*Consistently hitting such small, quick targets as a gray fox requires a good deal of serious practice.*

**M**AKE NO mistake. Becoming a good, versatile shot with bow-and-arrow gear is not easy by any means, although learning the basics and becoming proficient enough to start hunting is not all that difficult.

It takes the average person several years of steady bowhunting to really feel a mastery of this sport, even when these years are spent thoughtfully with total dedication. The nice thing is, the process of becoming a truly fine field shot in a variety of situations is pure fun, mainly because the challenge experienced and the shots missed only serve to make an archer try harder to excel. Nothing is fun that comes too easily; at least, not in hunting. A great deal of the skill any accomplished bowhunter has developed stems directly from experiences

104

One can practice shooting from odd, downward angles in his own backyard with the use of family stepladder.

*Knowing how to aim for shots at a downward angle pays dividends for a bowhunter, when he finds himself in terrain that is not of his own choosing. Versatility of this type is attained only through practice.*

on hunting trips. However, an archer can learn a great deal about shooting by secondary means that are also fun and do not penalize a missed shot with an empty freezer.

The place to begin fine-tuning your shooting skills is on the target range. Once you become a deadeye on bull's-eye targets, it is time to concentrate on targets without regular aiming spots. A bull's-eye target gives the shooter a psychological aiming edge, because he has a small, round area to hold his sight pin on. This edge is nonexistent in real-live hunting situations because animals usually have even-colored hides that make aiming at vital areas a guess-and-by-gosh maneuver for the inexperienced hunter.

Most good bowhunters are deadly on bull's-eye targets, but many excellent target archers are not worth a hoot on targets without aiming spots. It is best to become at least

partially prepared for shooting at game by practicing on the range to prevent unpleasant surprises later on.

A wide selection of commercial animal targets can be found at archery stores. These targets force a hunter to aim at vital areas without exact spots on which to line up visually. The average shooter's tight bull's-eye groups generally will widen considerably when he begins shooting at non-bull's-eye targets, but with practice these groups will shrink back to decent size.

Do-it-yourselfers are just as well served by a homemade target of cardboard, burlap or paper as by a commercial animal target, provided the target has no specific aiming spot. I am particularly fond of shooting at deer silhouettes roughly cut from large sheets of brown cardboard. Such silhouettes force a hunter to *pick a spot* on an animal to

*Author shot this nice Montana mule deer after a long sneak that placed him directly above bedded buck on the rocky ledge. An extra-low hold was used to skewer the animal through the chest area.*

shoot at, instead of aiming wildly at the entire deer.

This is the major key to hitting game with a bow after you have perfected your bull's-eye ability: *Locate the vital area on the animal and deliberately aim at it.* Specific vital areas in animals are discussed and illustrated in Chapter 15.

A versatile bowhunter learns to shoot at targets without aiming spots, and he also learns to shoot from positions other than the standard stance on flat ground described in Chapter 3. A hunter often is able to shoot at game from an upright, level stance, but just as often shots are sharply up, sharply down, or sharply to the side. Matters sometimes are even further complicated by overhanging branches or similar obstructions that force a hunter to kneel, sit and/or cant his bow to get off a shot. A hunter should anticipate such eventualities and practice shooting from oddball

positions on the range to better his chances of success.

Shooting sharply upward or downward is a major cause of missed shots in the field. Downward shooting is particularly common in bowhunting, because many deer hunters wait for animals in tree stands high above the ground. As a general rule, arrows fly considerably higher than normal when downward shots are taken, but fly somewhat higher than normal when upward shots are taken. How high arrows will hit depends on many things, including your bow/arrow setup, the distance of the shot and the angle above or below dead level at which you are shooting.

To anticipate and correct for shots taken at game below, you should shoot downward at a target from a stepladder, garage roof or another safe, easy-to-reach perch. Some

A wide selection of paper animal targets is available. The line from Martin Archery varies from small birds to bear, elk, deer, antelope. Shooting at such targets at unusual angles adds to the hunter's abilities.

Illustrations not shown to scale.

serious bowhunters actually erect tree stands in their backyards to make such shooting even more realistic.

When taking shots at targets above or below, you should always try to bend at the waist so your upper-body configuration and draw length remain the same as when you shoot on level ground.

A general rule of thumb on how to aim at targets above or below is as follows: shoot at targets according to the *level* distance they are away. For example, if a deer is fifteen yards from the base of your tree-stand tree and twenty-five yards away from you, you should aim as if the deer is only fifteen yards away. Similarly, a deer that strolls under your stand only five yards from the tree should be shot at as if it were five yards away, no matter how far the deer actually is from the front of your bow.

The foregoing shooting rule works accurately on downward shots, and also works well on relatively close upward shots. However, an arrow slows down rapidly when shot uphill and this tends to diminish and eventually cancel

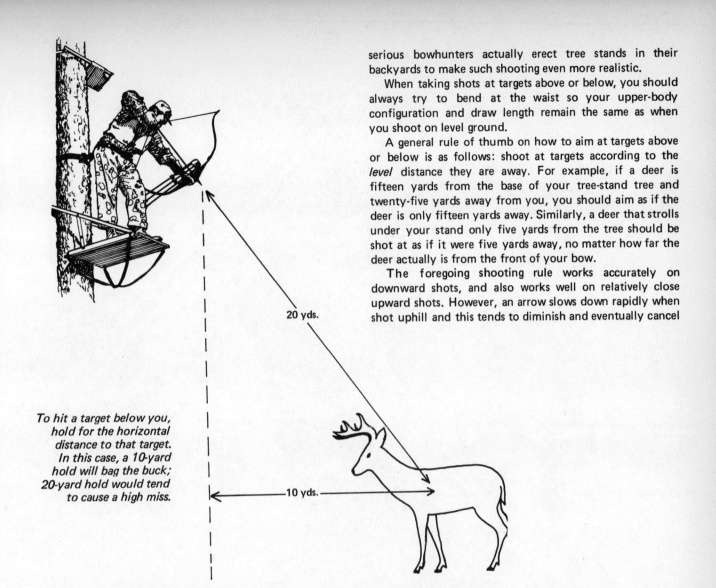

20 yds.

10 yds.

*To hit a target below you, hold for the horizontal distance to that target. In this case, a 10-yard hold will bag the buck; 20-yard hold would tend to cause a high miss.*

*Extensive shooting at dirt banks, other natural targets in the field offers ultimate practice prior to hunting season. To test out all of his equipment, bowhunter should wear same clothing he will wear on his hunt.*

The theory may not seem consistent, but short, upward shots at animals such as gray squirrels require that bowhunter utilize the same low holds that are utilized in downward shots. Small game such as this offers a special challenge.

out any necessary hold-under at ranges past thirty yards. Regular practice at different ranges and shooting angles will give you a good idea of how to aim.

Although a bowhunter should avoid awkward shooting positions whenever possible, he should devote a certain amount of practice to unusual positions that might be encountered afield. A little shooting practice while kneeling, sitting, twisting at the waist or sharply canting the bow will leave no surprises, if a shooter is called upon to make similar shots afield. Every serious bowhunter occasionally gets caught flatfooted and has to duck, twist or sag to let an arrow go. Practice at this sort of thing before season will put more game in the bag in the long run.

The final and perhaps the most productive way to fine-tune your shooting skills is regular practice in the field. Roving about the woods and shooting at natural targets like dirt banks, stumps, leaves and grass clumps is the best shooting practice next to actual hunting; it also is a solid kick in the pants when two or more friends get together and compete at targets an unknown distance away.

Such in-the-field shooting can be enjoyed anywhere away from people and buildings, and brings an archer's skills together as he shoots up, down, across ravines, under tree limbs and over the tops of bushes. It also lets him perfect his ability to use a rangefinder, string a second arrow quickly and do other things essential to regularly taking animals.

The most serious field-shooting practice should be done in the same clothes a hunter expects to wear on outings for deer and other game. In addition, he should take along binoculars, a day pack and any other gear he plans to carry in the field. This allows him to make sure all of his gear performs well and does not interfere with shooting. Many is the bowhunter who has become accurate on all sorts of targets, has practiced shooting in the field, yet has completely blown his best shot of the deer season because his bowstring bumped his brand-new hat during the draw, or because something else every bit as maddening and totally preventable has interfered with a clean shot.

Nothing can prepare a bowhunter completely for the pulse-pounding excitement of actually finding himself within bow range of an animal. All the preseason shooting in the world will not hold back the adrenaline and calm the nerves when a magnificent buck rolls his antlers methodically as he feeds on a bush in front of you. However, careful shooting before such an event will greatly improve your chances of aiming well at the vitals and scoring a clean, killing hit.

Fine-tune your shooting skills before season to ensure pleasant and successful outings later on!

# CHAPTER 10

# CARE & REPAIR OF TACKLE

## You Can Save Many A Dollar With Proper Care Or By Handling Your Own Fixing!

**M**ODERN ARCHERY equipment is relatively maintenance-free — much more so than it was a few years back. Durable materials like aluminum, fiberglass, plastic and stainless steel have revolutionized archery during the past decade or two, replacing the pain in the neck of worrying about yew wood and feathers with the enjoyment of toting about gear that is incredibly resistant to moisture, corrosive elements like blood and regular rough-and-tumble use. Despite the tough nature of modern archery equipment, a bowhunter should care for his gear wisely and know exactly what to do when this gear occasionally malfunctions. This is common-sense advice a thoughtful person applies to any well-made piece of equipment, be it automobile, lawnmower, gun or bow.

A quality bow will take a certain amount of abuse, but can be damaged almost instantly in a number of ways. *Never* dry shoot a bow; that is, never draw it and let go of the bowstring without an arrow on the string. This sends horrible vibrations through the bow limbs and places the wheels, cables and bowstring under considerable stress. Even if something does not break at the time of a dry fire, such an episode can lead to breakage of limbs, cables, wheels or handle riser at a later time. This rule applies to both compound and recurve bows.

Likewise, never allow any bow to become too hot to touch. The laminations in a quality bow's limbs and/or handle section are glued together with epoxy and can come

apart if this epoxy reaches temperatures above 200 degrees Fahrenheit.

The most common place where a hunting bow is likely to be ruined is in a hot car, especially under glass with the sun shining through. However, placing a bow near a hot campfire or laying it on a hot rock, car hood or similar super-heated support can also cause a bow to delaminate dramatically. Once laminations give way, a bow is completely ruined.

Laminated bow limbs should also be protected from sideways twist or overbending because both can warp or break a limb's inner core of wood. Twisted limbs usually result from careless use of a bowstringing tool and breaks from overbending are most common in compound bows when an archer draws back a bow to the let-off point and then draws even farther back with substantial force. Use a bowstringer with care according to manufacturer's directions and never deliberately overdraw a compound bow.

A modern bow's limbs retain their flex remarkably well, but a bow's limbs should always be relaxed before it is stored for long periods of time.

Actually, the best way to care for a recurve bow is to unstring it every evening after the hunting is over and leave it unstrung until just prior to the next hunting excursion. A compound bow's limbs are not under as much tension when strung as those of a recurve bow, so leaving a compound

*Recurve bow should be unstrung after every shooting session to prevent the bow limbs from developing a set.*

*Placing any bow under the window of a sunlit vehicle is a sure way to ruin the limbs completely, author states.*

strung most of the time is okay as long as it is regularly used.

Leaving any bow strung at hunting tension for long periods of time without using it is apt to cause a permanent set in the limbs — a set that reduces the bow's draw weight, slows arrow flight, and requires a retuning session to get arrows to fly properly once more. If you intend to put away your compound bow for a month or more, wind down the draw weight according to manufacturer's instructions.

A good-quality hunting bow normally is finished with water-resistant materials to prevent wooden parts from soaking up moisture. However, keep your bow as dry as possible at all times. The metal parts on a compound bow can rust if moisture is excessive, and too much regular water contact can eventually penetrate bow limbs and result in limb failure. Hunting in the rain is never a problem, but dry off your bow after each damp day is done. A bowhunter should periodically relubricate his bow's friction points as outlined in Chapter 2 to prevent rust, friction, and shooting noise. Once a year is often enough for the average bowhunter. Similarly, he should wax his bowstring to help prevent strands from fraying or breaking. With regular shooting, a bowstring should be waxed at least once a month for best results.

In addition, a bowstring's central serving section

eventually becomes worn where the arrow is nocked and/or where the bowstring slaps the armguard, requiring installation of another string or replacement of the serving on the original one. A simple serving tool sold at archery stores makes serving replacement a snap, but replacing the whole bowstring is almost as cheap in the long run. Suit yourself.

It is highly unwise to alter any bow by drilling holes in the handle riser, filing on the limbs, or otherwise changing the factory configuration. Such tampering can ruin a bow's shooting performance and/or result in breakage.

When storing any bow, always avoid setting it on a limb tip, because this can warp or twist a limb. Hang it across horizontal pegs or commercial bow clamps, lay it on its side or suspend it from the handle of a bow case or hang it vertically from a peg under a compound wheel. When transporting or storing a bow, it is a darn good idea to put it in a commercial case for this purpose to prevent damage caused by sudden impact with a hard object or scraping from something sharp. A soft, lightly padded case is fine for bow transport in an auto, but always use some sort of hard plastic or aluminum bow case when traveling by air.

Hunting arrows require more regular maintenance and repair than bows. An arrow that is shot repeatedly is subject to a certain amount of fletching damage — especially when feather fletching is used — and all other parts of the arrow are prone to become broken or bent during collisions with other arrows, rocks, bones and

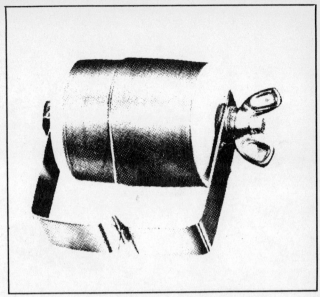

*An inexpensive serving tool should make replacement of a worn bowstring serving a relatively simple task.*

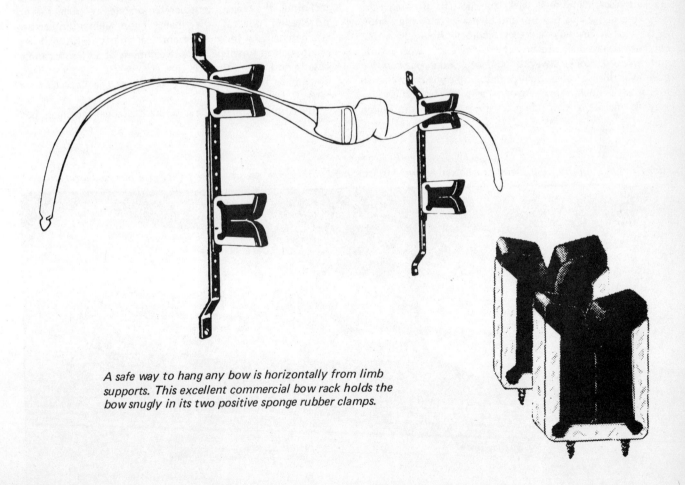

*A safe way to hang any bow is horizontally from limb supports. This excellent commercial bow rack holds the bow snugly in its two positive sponge rubber clamps.*

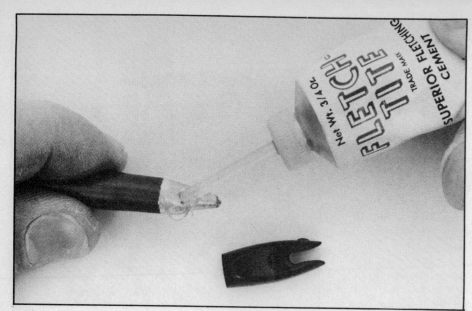

Cracked or crooked arrow nocks should be removed and replaced immediately. A quality fletching cement bonds the nocks to shafts.

similarly unyielding obstacles. In addition, hunting arrows require cleanup after they hit an animal and sharp broadheads require regular maintenance to make sure they are not nicked or rusty.

Let's begin at the back end of the arrow and work forward. A hunter should inspect arrow nocks frequently to make sure nocks have not become cracked or bent. A cracked nock can break when the bowstring is released, causing a dangerous dry fire and obviously blowing a shot. A bent nock severely degrades accuracy. Any nocks that become damaged should be cut away carefully with a knife and replaced. Nocks always should be glued in place with a thin, even film of good-quality fletching cement applied to the arrow's nock taper. Arrow shafts can be difficult or easy to maintain, depending on the material from which they are made. Good-quality aluminum shafts are the easiest to care for, scrubbing clean with ordinary soap and water and seldom bending unless an arrow smacks something extremely solid or rolls with a hard-hit animal.

When aluminum shafts do become bent, they can normally be straightened for a small fee at any archery store. The alternatives are straightening them by hand — a technique that takes considerable practice to perfect — or purchasing one of the many good aluminum arrow straighteners on the market and learning to use it well. As mentioned in Chapter 7, the straightness of an arrow can be determined by rolling it on commercial arrow rollers, homemade rollers, wooden V blocks or the flat top of a table.

By contrast, fiberglass arrows are also easy to clean, but

Today's aluminum hunting shafts can be safely and easily cleaned with warm, soapy water to remove dirt or blood.

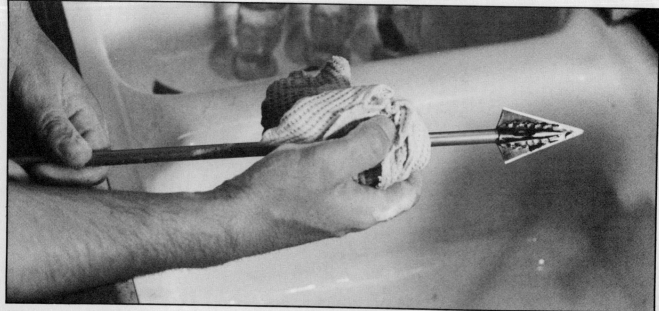

A flexible padded bow case provides excellent protection during storage, normal transportation in a vehicle.

*Matted feather fletching bounces back quickly to original shape when steamed carefully over the spout of a teapot.*

must be inspected periodically for dangerous cracks in the glass, which can cause an arrow to literally explode in the bow. Wooden shafts also can be washed, but must be dried immediately to retard warpage. If a fiberglass or wooden shaft develops a crack, it must be discarded. Wooden shafts that warp can sometimes be straightened by heating them slightly near a stove and massaging out bends with the hands.

Arrow fletching is prone to require periodic repair or replacement. Feathers are especially fragile, tending to tatter after lots of shots and wilt in moist conditions. Feathers that become bloody must be washed out in warm water and allowed to dry naturally. After completely dry, they will bounce back to their original shape if carefully steamed over the spout of a teapot.

Steaming also returns wet, wilted fletching to its original shape after it is allowed to dry. It can be a solid pain to keep fletching dry in wet weather — a major reason plastic vanes are so popular today — but feathers can be kept reasonably dry for a while by slipping a large plastic bag around them in a bow quiver and/or spraying them with hair spray or special silicone waterproofer.

Plastic fletching is virtually maintenance free, except that it needs to be washed with warm, soapy water after an arrow is recovered from an animal. Regular target shooting with plastic vanes usually results in a few ragged holes in vanes where other arrows have hit and passed through. These ragged areas can hiss obnoxiously through the air, and also can cause uneven air resistance that harms accuracy. To eliminate these problems without gluing on a new vane, the ragged area can simply be snipped away with a triangular scissor cut. A few small wedges missing from vanes do not seem to adversely affect arrow flight in the least.

When feather fletching becomes badly worn or when vanes become too torn or cut, it is time to refletch the arrow. This chore can be handled by most archery dealers, or the bowhunter can refletch arrows himself with a simple fletching jig and quality die-cut feathers or plastic vanes.

If you decide to fletch arrows yourself, carefully peel off old fletching with a knife, being sure not to cut the shaft of the arrow. Next, remove old glue from the shaft by scrubbing it with a paper towel soaked in acetone. Also be sure to scrub the fletching area of each shaft with warm water and Ajax cleanser to completely degrease the shaft and ensure a solid fletching bond.

*A liberal coating of ordinary hair spray from an aerosol can can be used as an aid to help feather fletching retain shape under damp conditions.*

Dry the shaft with a clean paper towel and avoid touching the fletching area of the shaft with the fingers. Wooden shafts do not need to be cleaned. If you are fletching with plastic vanes, be sure to clean the glue base of each vane with a paper towel or cotton swab soaked in acetone to remove the thin film of casting wax that coats all vanes.

Fletching should be installed so it spirals around the shaft in the same direction and to the same degree as the original fletching did. It should be glued down with a quality fletching cement like Bohning Fletch-Tite. After an arrow is fletched, an extra drop of glue should be dabbed at each end of each fletch to spot each fletch even more securely to the shaft and to prevent debris from wedging between the front end of a vane and the shaft.

As mentioned in Chapter 6, hunting broadheads should

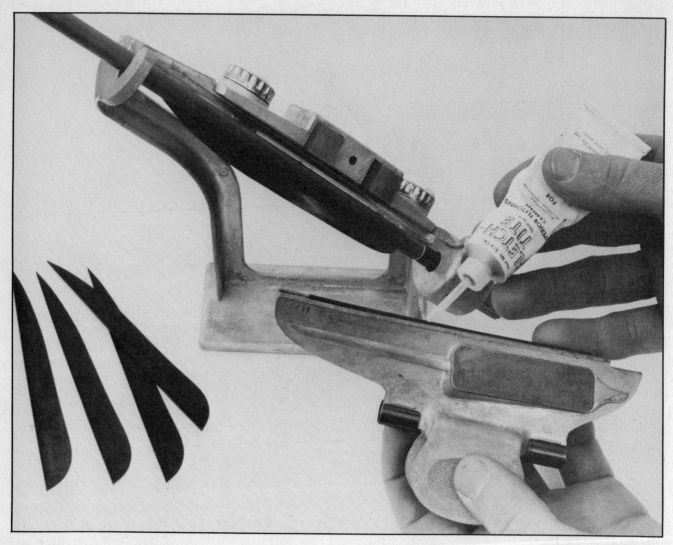

*Fletching arrows can be a snap with a simple fletching jig. The keys to success are thoroughly cleaning the shafts and vanes, then using a quality fletching cement to ensure a solid bond that will not loosen under field conditions.*

be oiled regularly to keep them free of rust. They also should be inspected after each shot to make sure they are not bent out of line. An out-of-line broadhead that goes unnoticed will generally steer an arrow badly off course — perhaps at the worst possible time on the biggest buck you've seen all year.

Simpler arrowheads like field points and blunts require no maintenance. However, any arrowhead design can cause a major problem, if it wedges too tightly in a tree or stump to allow easy removal. Several companies sell arrowhead removers to extract tightly wedged heads, but these sometimes bend a head and/or arrow out of shape during the removal process.

An easy way to salvage an arrow wedged deeply and tightly in wood is simply to unscrew the shaft from the arrowhead and leave the arrowhead where it is. If old-style glue-on arrowheads are used, a wedged head must be separated from a shaft by heating it up with a match or a cigarette lighter. Careful: don't start a forest fire in the process!

Arrows can be stored and transported in several ways. The easiest for a small quantity of arrows is simply leaving them in an arrow quiver. A variety of commercial arrow boxes are also available at archery stores, from inexpensive containers made of corrugated cardboard to elaborate designs made of plastic or aluminum.

When arrows with sharp broadheads are stored or moved about, these broadheads must be prevented from grating

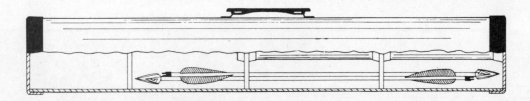

*A durable plastic tube is one popular container for storing and transporting arrows. The bowhunter can stuff arrows without heads into the simple tube, or clamp completely assembled arrows in the more elaborate setup illustrated.*

against other arrows or the sides of an arrow box. Some hunters wrap sharp broadheads in toilet paper, others put plastic tape over the edges, and still others sheath broadheads in commercial broadhead covers.

I feel that, with modern screw-out broadheads, it is far easier to keep broadheads separate from shafts except during a hunt. I press sharp broadheads into an oil-soaked block of styrofoam in rows when they are not in use, and transport them in a smaller oil-soaked block of styrofoam inside a large, leak-proof Tupperware container.

When traveling to a hunting area, I carry my shafts without arrowheads in a large plastic fishing-rod case. This case easily holds three dozen loose shafts without mashing down plastic fletching, and fully protects these shafts from bumps or abrasion. Once I reach my hunting area, I quickly assemble arrows and get down to business. To each his own.

Other archery equipment needs very little maintenance. The bow, quiver, and a few other items might need a camouflage paint touchup infrequently, but shooting glove, armguard, and most other gear require no special care.

The modern bowhunter is lucky indeed because archery equipment is more trouble-free than ever before in history. A minimum of preventive maintenance and infrequent, minor repairs will keep shooting gear in tip-top shape, allowing a bowhunter to concentrate his primary efforts on having a good time and hitting what he shoots at.

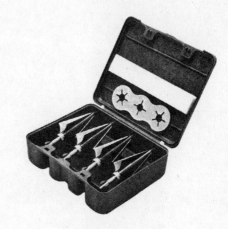

*Right (upper photo): A commercially made arrowhead box is practical for storing sharp hunting broadheads. (Lower photo): A plastic broadhead wrench allows safe and snug screw-attachment of your razor-keen hunting broadheads.*

# SECTION II:

# Introduction

# HUNTING EQUIPMENT AND TECHNIQUE

*Hanging a nice buck on the meat pole requires much more than simple shooting ability, as one hunting partner learned.*

A T LEAST half the bowhunting battle is won through the use of proper hunting equipment and the application of productive hunting technique. A few well-chosen hunting aids like clothing, binoculars, tree-stand gear, and similar items can make the critical difference between success and failure in the field, provided of course that these props are used sensibly by a well-seasoned outdoor enthusiast.

The importance of accurate bow-shooting never should be played down, but a genuinely skillful hunter can stack the odds in his favor even if the world is full of better shots than he. The nimrod who regularly sets up twenty-yard shots at deer and other species need not shoot quite as well as the fellow who has trouble getting within fifty yards of wary game.

Equally important to bowhunting success are knowing how and when to shoot at game, and what to do after a hit has been made. It is quite important for a hunter to possess raw shooting talent, but knowing how to apply this talent in the field is a whole 'nother matter. Similarly, making a good hit on an animal and making this hit pay off are two entirely different things. A well rounded hunter must be able to find game, close the gap to set up a shot, take his shot at the most opportune time, purposefully hit a vital area, follow up the hit to find the animal and care for his downed trophy skillfully and confidently. Only when all these skills have been mastered can an archer truly call himself a bowhunter as well.

A good case in point occurred several years ago on a bowhunt for Eastern whitetail deer. There were six of us in hunting camp — all decent archers and most experienced hunters. However, one of our group was on his first hunt with bow and arrow. This fellow happened to be a former national target archery champion, a no-nonsense technician who knew shooting equipment like the back of his hand. He made no bones about it, either, proclaiming over breakfast on the first morning out that this whitetail hunting ought to be a snap for one so skillful as himself.

Our cocky young companion received his first major jolt the next day as we all fanned out to scout the area and do a little preliminary hunting. The woods were cornflake dry, making fox squirrels sound like elephants as they hopped about in search of food. I immediately gave up on stillhunting and spent the morning hours looking for a profitable place to set up a tree stand for the remainder of the trip. I had found it by noon: a heavily used deer trail crossing a small creek a stone's throw from the edge of a cornfield. I jumped three deer while rummaging about, grinning as their white flags bobbed away through the trees. With luck, I figured, I'd have my tag filled in two or three days of sitting aloft. By dark, my stand was all set up and I was lounging around camp with four of my five hunting companions.

Late that evening our target-archer friend hobbled into camp with a scowl across his face, declaring he had walked

*Well-chosen hunting aids like binoculars and footwear can help the skilled bow-shooter stack the odds in his favor.*

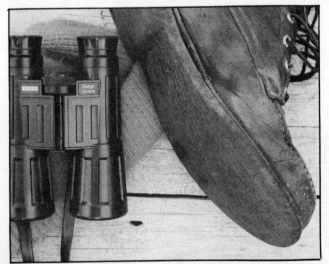

his legs to the knees without seeing one stationary deer. He bad-mouthed the area for a while, but finally confided that he was a plucky fellow and wasn't about to quit just yet. The rest of us said little, but from the twinkles in the eyes around the fire, I was sure the other veterans in the crowd had erected setups similar to my own.

The next evening, two nice whitetail bucks were hanging in camp, one of which I had nailed with a fifteen-yard shot through the spine. Our target-archer pal came in late again, and his customary scowl turned to a look of pure amazement as he gawked at the fat deer on the meat pole. It was his turn to say little that night, apparently mulling over the astonishing fact that deer had actually been taken.

The third evening another deer was hanging and our hot-shot friend asked for help. His blisters were sprouting blisters, he said, and there apparently was something about this hunting business he had failed to grasp.

The next morning I took him to my tree stand, still hanging above the creek crossing. I instructed him to stay aloft and remain perfectly still until a deer walked into view and passed his position to provide a shot quartering away. Only then was he to draw his bow and loose an arrow.

At noon our humbled companion shuffled into camp with his classic glum expression. He had hit a deer, he said, but the animal had run away. He had scrambled out of his stand to chase it, but by the time he reached the ground the woods were completely quiet and the critter had apparently left the country. He hadn't seen any blood on the ground, but he wasn't sure he'd looked in the right place, because the countryside looked different from the ground than it had from the tree. He gave the three of us in camp a half-pleading, half-disgusted look and tossed up his hands.

Thirty minutes later we were at the hit site. Five minutes after that one of us found a tiny spot of blood on a leafy trail leading into the trees. Ten minutes of hands-and-knees searching turned up a dozen more spots of blood along the same trail. This blood was a bright pink in color, indicating a probable lung hit. Two of us decided to follow the trail a ways at a steady walk — and nearly stepped on the deer within fifty yards of the tree stand. The arrow had skewered both lungs but had lodged low in the far shoulder to prevent a fast-bleeding exit hole.

It was good to see our deadeye target-archer friend smiling instead of frowning as he pumped our hands in genuine thanks. Today he's a first-class hunter as well as a mean hand with a bow; as good a hunter as I'd ever care to share a tent with. He's also considerably more modest now, because he knows how tough and how complex the hunting half of bowhunting happens to be.

Learning to be a good hunter with archery gear can be frustrating at times, but in the main it is a highly enjoyable endeavor. The basic hunting equipment discussed in Chapter 11 ensures a smooth, happy outdoor experience, and the basic hunting know-how offered in the rest of this book will provide a solid base for the process of becoming truly skillful at various forms of bowhunting.

From there, it is up to you to perfect your hunting ability through hours and hours of satisfying time in the field.

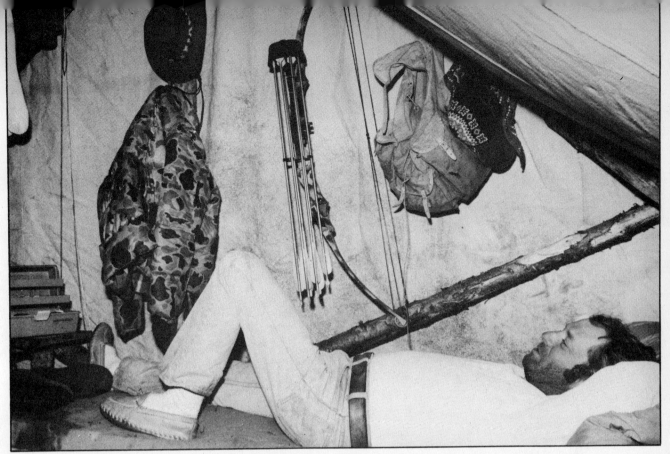

Opposite page: Author Adams used the proper camouflage clothing to stalk and then bag this record-sized blacktail with velvet antlers at twenty-five yards. The smile is well-earned! Above: A simple, well-chosen collection of hunting equipment and clothing gets the job done. As famed hunter Jim Dougherty learned, it's easily stored.

## CHAPTER 11

# THE NEEDS FOR HUNTING

## Without Going Overboard, There Is Definite Necessary Equipment

ASIDE FROM shooting equipment, an archer needs other important gear to make a bowhunt enjoyable and smoothly successful. Necessary hunting equipment varies from one bowhunter to another, depending upon the game he plans to hunt, the terrain encountered, his chosen hunting techniques, and his own personal rathers.

As a general rule, a hunter always should keep his in-the-field equipment to a simple, smoothly working minimum. Certain aids will improve a hunter's score

greatly, but an overabundance of gadgetry tends to hinder rather than help. The fellow who heads for the woods adorned like a Christmas tree with archery-shop goodies invariably makes more noise than a hunter with a few well chosen articles of gear and a bow-bender overloaded with equipment tends to flounder around in the presence of game as he tries to decide which little gizmos he actually needs. The result usually is frustration and failure.

The sensible, successful bowhunter selects his hunting equipment with extreme care, experimenting incessantly

Left: Conventional, Jones-style bowhunting cap hugs the head to avoid contact with bowstring, yet provides some protection from the elements. Below: A stocking cap with fold-down face mask provides maximum protection in cold weather. This wool model is also mottled to provide added concealment from game.

with a wide variety of aids in the off season, but ending up with only well tested, easy-to-use items when serious hunting seasons roll around.

## CLOTHING FOR THE BOWHUNTER

Every bowhunter should choose clothing that matches his particular style of hunting. Proper clothing from head to toe performs several important functions: it hides a hunter from game, functions quietly in the noisiest outdoor conditions, yields maximum comfort and protection from the elements and allows accurate shooting of a bow.

A bowhunter should carefully select a complement of clothing based on the following suggestions, bearing in mind that what he wears will have a decided effect on how successful he is in the field.

A wide variety of headgear can be seen in the bowhunting woods: from stocking caps, to bowl-type Jones-style hats, to simple bill caps, to wide-brimmed, camouflaged jungle hats. Choosing the proper chapeau is important to any bowhunter and no one hat design will work well in every situation.

Of primary importance when choosing any hat is whether it will interfere with a hunter's ability to draw and shoot his bow. Some archers' shooting styles severely limit their hat choice, because they draw a bowstring within an inch or two of their foreheads. Other shooters cock their heads at a different angle and/or anchor the string in a different place, allowing them to shoot the widest-brimmed hat in the world without accuracy-destroying interference with the bowstring.

If a bowstring bumps a hat, this invariably blows a hunter's shooting concentration and causes a miss or crippling hit — even if the target animal does not hear the collision of string and hat and depart like a turpentined tomcat.

*The type of headgear favored by bowhunters is subject to personal preference as much as anything, and it's not surprising to see variations from cowboy or wide-brimmed hats to scalp-hugging stocking caps in hunting camps today.*

If you tend to draw the bowstring close to your forehead, your hat options are few. The best bowhunting hats in such a case are either the stocking cap, which hugs the brow closely, or the Jones-style hat, which has a narrow, angled-down brim.

In addition to shooting ease, a hunter should consider other factors when choosing a hat. One is camouflage. A hat is not usually large enough to catch an animal's eye as long as it is in a color that blends closely with surrounding terrain. But, a plaid or conventional leaf-print hat blends better with terrain than a hat of one color and sometimes makes the critical difference with sharp-eyed critters like whitetail deer and wild turkey. Because I draw the string close to my brow, I normally wear a brown or green stocking cap when hunting game with average eyesight, but I sometimes don a leaf-print Jones-style hat if shots are likely to be close and the game being hunted is especially alert.

A mottled, multi-colored hat blends best with a wide variety of backgrounds and also tends to break up the outline of a hunter's head. However, I seldom worry excessively about using a multi-colored hat, unless game is likely to be encountered at under twenty yards.

Aside from being relatively camouflaged, a bowhunting hat must be quiet to wear. Many so-called bowhunting hats are ill-suited to bowhunting, because they are made of hard-surfaced materials that whine and squeal when they scrape across nearby brush or limbs. Prime offenders are some Jones-style camouflage hats and most jungle-style hats with wide brims. If a hat makes noise when fingernails are dragged across it, it is not a decent choice for hunting in heavy foliage.

Obviously, a bowhunting hat must provide protection from the elements. A stocking cap with an internal face mask is ideal for keeping a hunter's noggin warm, providing the ultimate protection from cold and precipitation when

Camouflage makeup helps to eliminate shine from oily skin or light complexion, and increases your chances.

*Thin, airy camouflage headnets like this one eliminate the need for makeup, and are favored by many especially during warmer fall days. Too, there's no cleanup time required as with the makeup. Again, personal preference dictates.*

conditions really turn grim. The stocking cap is my favorite all-around hunting hat, although it can be somewhat warm during summertime archery season.

I generally wear a wool stocking cap in cold or wet weather because wool is warm and remains warm even when it becomes soaked with water. In warmer weather, I prefer a cooler, loose-weave Orlon stocking cap instead.

A brimmed hat of some sort obviously provides superior face and neck protection from the sun and heavy rain or snow. The Jones-style hat is a compromise between the close-fitting stocking cap and hats with wider brims, providing more warmth and more compactness than many wide-brimmed designs and more protection from overhead elements than the stocking cap. If sun, rain, or snow is

likely where you plan to bowhunt, and if your shooting style allows you to wear it, you might want to use a quality bill cap, felt Western-style hat, or wide-brimmed jungle hat instead of more compact headgear. A wide-brimmed bowhunting hat has two disadvantages — the tendency to scrape nearby brush, and the tendency to catch wind and blow off — but it can be a godsend in certain situations.

My solution to the problem of hot, burning sun on the face or steady rainfall is a camouflage bill cap, turning it around backwards when I feel I might be close to game. The frontal bill does not snag foliage to the sides and protects my face from painful sunburn or a frontal attack of raindrops. Granted, my neck gets a little burned or wet at times, but life is full of compromises.

When choosing a bowhunting hat, always ask yourself the following questions. (1) Can you shoot your bow accurately with a particular hat design? (2) Is a particular hat comfortable to wear? (3) Is a hat of the proper color to fool the prying eyes of game? (4) Is a hat likely to protect you from sunlight, cold, and precipitation? If the answers are all affirmative, the hat should serve you well in the field.

A bowhunter's face is a fairly large, monotone area that can catch an animal's eye and scare it clear out of the country. Most bowhunters wear camouflage hats and camouflage clothing, but quite a few never stop to consider that their light, shiny complexions often stand out like sore thumbs against dark forest backgrounds. A Caucasian hunter strolling through the woods often appears to be waving a white flag if he has not taken pains to camouflage his face — a flag that alerts game with alarming frequency. A serious hunting archer takes pains to hide his face from the alert, hunter-wise animals he's after.

Even if you have a dark complexion or a swarthy tan, the natural oils in your skin are apt to shine like a mirror — especially as you work up a sweat while huffing and puffing over hill and dale. This face shine can spook game — even if the color of your face does not — necessitating careful camouflage to completely hide your mug.

There are two basic ways to camouflage your face prior to hunting with a bow. One is smearing some commercial or home-grown ingredient on your face to break up the color and cut the shine. Another is covering your face with a camouflage headnet. Both methods work well, but each has certain advantages, certain drawbacks.

Several kinds of commercial camouflage makeup are

*Below: Camouflage is most important for the upper portions of the body, since waist and legs often are hidden in brush. Opposite page: All game animals are color-blind, and this coyote was fooled at 15 yards by bowhunter attired in red-and-black plaid jacket with a bright red hat. He called in the unsuspecting varmint and zap!*

*Opposite page: This is a staged how-NOT-to-do-it photograph. Hunter is wearing light, solid-colored garments and you can see how well they stand out against the darker foliage normally found in forest. Even the blue jeans stand out, and game will give him wide berth. Above: The choice of fabric for hunting clothes should be considered, too. Soft wool or cotton makes no noise when scraped against branches or snagging undergrowth.*

available at archery stores, including ordinary camo makeup in woodsy greens, blacks, and browns and special makeup impregnated with insect repellent and/or odor-masking scent. Camouflage makeup is quite easy to apply, allows the hunter to camouflage hard-to-get-at places like his lower neck and hands, effectively breaks up the human shape of his face, and neatly cuts the telltale shine of complexion.

Camouflage makeup can present problems, too. It can be messy in hot weather, running as a hunter moves about and perspires. It is always a pain to remove, requiring a thorough scrub with soap and water. Camo makeup also tends to stain clothing if it is applied on the neck as well as the face. This is not to mention the strange looks people give a bowhunter complete with face camouflage as he eats breakfast at the local all-night cafe.

A few bowhunters of my acquaintance use charcoal or mud to camouflage their faces when hunting especially wary animals. Applying charcoal or mud to the face is more difficult than using commercial makeup, and these substances tend to be more messy and/or difficult to remove. I wouldn't recommend them to anybody given the low price of good-quality commercial camouflage face makeup.

Wearing a camouflage headnet makes a lot of sense for those hunters who can shoot well with such a net in place. I personally prefer a net instead of camouflage makeup because it can be instantly put on or removed without fuss or muss. However, a headnet interferes with some bowhunters' ability to anchor properly during a shot, making camouflage makeup a better route to take.

A camouflage headnet should have one eye slot instead of two eyeholes to prevent a strip of material between the eyes from obscuring an archer's vision as he looks sideways at the target during a shot. This net should extend downward over a hunter's collar to camouflage the neck as well as the face, and should fit snugly enough to prevent the net from flapping obnoxiously in a breeze and perhaps scaring nearby game in the process. A tight-fitting headnet can rub your nose raw over the course of a hunting day, so don't choose a net that fits too tightly.

In a pinch, an ordinary stocking-cap mask can be pulled down to cover your face during a critical stalk. However, such a mask can be excessively hot unless weather is on the nippy side.

I seldom wear any kind of face camouflage when hunting near-sighted game like wild boar, black bear, and javelina. However, my camo headnet is always in my pocket just in case I spot another legal species with keener eyeballs, or in case I expect an especially close-range encounter with my intended quarry. Even the poorest-eyed game will recognize a light, shiny mug if the range is short.

A serious hunting archer always pays special attention to his selection of shirts, jackets, and similar upper-body wear. A hunting shirt is a large item which must be quiet and

camouflaged to give a hunter an even shot at success.

When choosing a camouflage shirt or jacket, it is important to realize some of the essential ingredients in effective camouflage. These ingredients make the critical difference between bowhunting success and bowhunting failure.

All huntable animals are completely color-blind, seeing the world in black, white, and shades of gray. Many birds can see color well, however, including ducks, geese, and the wary wild turkey. A hunter must match his clothing to the species being hunted, worrying about color with creatures that see color and worrying about shades instead of colors with animals like deer, elk, and bear.

Except when hunting birds, a bowhunter's primary concern should be to break up his human outline with mottled clothing that closely matches areas he intends to

*Hunting partners Chuck Adams (left) and Jim Dougherty illustrate different shades of camouflage used in the same general hunting area. Adams wore dark duds to bowhunt goats in the dark-gray rocks well above camp. Dougherty donned lighter apparel to bowhunt the lighter-colored moose valley near camp. Match clothing to hunting situation always.*

hunt. In most cases, his upper body will be most visible to game because it will be above bushes, logs and other natural objects close to the ground. His upper body is likely to catch more attention, too, because the arms and shoulders are moved a lot as a hunter draws a bow to shoot, reaches for a backup arrow, raises binoculars to scan the countryside or performs a similar hunting function. As a result, the choice of a bowhunting shirt, jacket and/or vest is extremely important to success.

A bowhunting hat can be one medium color, because it is relatively small, but a shirt or jacket must be multi-colored as it covers a much larger part of the body. A multi-colored shirt or jacket will melt into many backgrounds with ease, while a monotone garment blends with *no* background except one that exactly matches.

In addition, a contrasty upper-body garment breaks up a bowhunter's human shape — a shape wary critters have learned to easily spot even if a hunter is completely motionless. A human looks precisely like a human to an animal unless that human is wearing a mottled outfit that blends with terrain and tends to break down the basic human shape.

A bowhunter should choose upper-body wear based on the general coloration of the area he plans to hunt. For example, an archer frequenting high deserts in southern California, Arizona or New Mexico will want to wear relatively light-colored camouflage that blends with these water-starved, light-colored areas. In contrast, a bowhunter stalking the dark-green thickets of Oregon, Washington, Alabama or Michigan will need to wear much darker clothing. Use your common sense when choosing basic upper-body colors.

*If you plan to use solid-colored trousers, ensure that cover will be sufficient to hide them. This archer is wearing dark-green pants, but the tall grass easily covers the trousers. Note importance of upper-body camouflage.*

*Complete head-to-toe camouflage is often desirable in bowhunting situations. This archer's knife sheath is even multi-colored, to conceal him and eliminate possible flash of reflected sunlight off slick, tanned leather.*

Contrary to popular belief, traditional leaf-print camouflage clothing is no better than the highly contrasty plaid clothing available at any department store. A deep-woods bowhunter will do quite well with a shirt or jacket covered with dark green and brown leaves against a lighter tan background, but he'll do every bit as well with an outfit of alternating dark and light squares of color. One of my favorite hunting jackets for relatively dark-colored areas is a black-and-red plaid hunting coat made of wool. This garment breaks up my outline quite well, virtually disappears against medium to dark-colored backgrounds and has successfully hidden me from dozens of big, smart trophy animals. The red in this coat will scare the bejeesus out of any self-respecting turkey, but it completely fools color-blind animals as long as I move slowly and follow other solid hunting procedures.

For lighter hunting backgrounds, a bowhunter must wear lighter-colored apparel, either commercial camouflage garments in light brown fall colors or light-colored, contrasty plaids. There's nothing mysterious about choosing a bowhunting shirt or jacket of a proper coloration; just be sure the overall garment matches the hue of surrounding terrain and breaks up your outline with sharply contrasting individual colors.

Aside from coloration, an upper-body garment must be soft-surfaced to ensure against game-spooking noise. Many otherwise acceptable shirts, jackets, and vests are poor choices for bowhunting simply because they have hard, noisy surfaces that telegraph the sounds of danger as a hunter moves through heavy cover, fidgets involuntarily on stand, or draws back to shoot his bow. The worst offenders are various camouflage garments made of ripstop nylon, 60/40 cloth, and other hard-weave fabrics that scrape foliage with little shrieks guaranteed to send keen-eared game stampeding toward the next county.

Many so-called bowhunting shirts and jackets are completely ill-suited to the sport, because they are made of stiff cotton that whines and crackles as it is worn. Some such garments soften up with repeated washings, but others do not. If you can create audible sound by dragging your fingernails across any shirt or jacket, the garment should be avoided no matter how good it looks.

Author carefully matched clothing to arrow this little meat buck. Dark plaid shirt matched scattered evergreen trees in area, and the lighter mottled pants blended with deadfall grass covering ground.

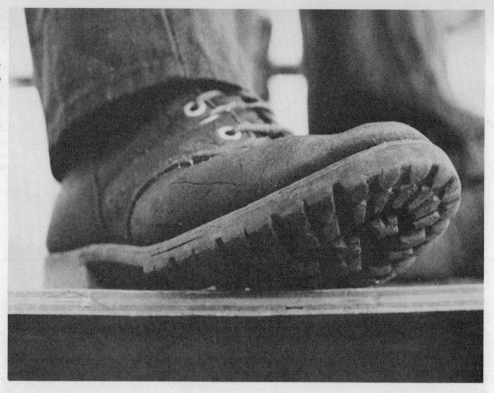

*Vibram-type lug soles are too noisy for sneaky stalking, but do provide solid grip on tree stand platform.*

The best bowhunting shirts and jackets are of wool or soft-weave cotton. Wool is the warmer of the two and remains warm even when wet. Cotton is a better choice in warm weather, but soaks up water and quickly becomes miserable anytime it rains. Take your pick.

Rubber raincoats, canvas jackets, and similar rain-shedding upper garments should never be used in bowhunting because they are noisy to move in and tend to

shine when wet. Wool is the ideal wet-weather fabric for bowhunting.

Many bowhunters do not worry about the kind of trousers they wear, but this mental lapse often results in ruined chances at game. Bowhunting pants always should blend reasonably well with the terrain being hunted so they don't stand out like a sore thumb. Because lower-body wear is often obscured by brush, a bowhunter in solid-colored pants can often score well on game. For instance, I often bowhunt with good success in ordinary old blue jeans, provided I am stalking or stillhunting in areas where I am most often obscured by bushes, rocks and similar cover from the waist on down. Similarly, one of my favorite bowhunting garments is a solid green pair of wool hunting trousers that are completely quiet in the heaviest brush and quite warm in damp and/or chilly hunting conditions.

Upper-body wear must be multi-colored because foliage at chest and head level is usually a mottled pattern of leaves, branches, sunlight, and shadows. However, colors lower to the ground are often more uniform — another reason solid-color pants can sometimes be worn with perfectly good results.

However, if a bowhunter is planning to spend time in an area where his lower body will easily be seen by game, he should by all means wear camouflage pants to improve his odds of success. These pants should fulfill the same basic coloration and noise requirements as bowhunting shirts and jackets. The selection of suitable camouflage bowhunting

*The best boot sole for stalking or walking is soft neoprene. Such a sole wears well, provides good traction, and gives when contacting twigs and other underfoot noisemakers.*

*Down-filled mitten provides ultimate protection from an icy bow grip, and can be instantly shed from bowstring draw hand to facilitate accurate shot. Model shown here is made specifically for bowhunting, but good-quality ski mittens can work every bit as well. Watch out for shiny vinyl that reflects.*

pants is considerably more limited than the selection of good shirts and jackets, but a few soft leaf-print cotton and plaid wool pants can be found at well-stocked sporting goods stores.

Most bowhunters do not wear the best form of footwear. For example, the vast majority of stalking and stillhunting bowhunters persist in wearing Vibram-soled boots, which are by far the noisiest choice for walking in any sort of terrain. Similarly, those hunters who have given some thought to quiet walking often wear tennis shoes or similar low-topped, soft-soled footwear that does not support the ankles adequately or give adequate protection from the elements.

Hard-soled Vibram boots are the favorite choice of serious hikers and gun hunters, which is probably the

reason many bowhunters automatically strap these on prior to heading for the woods. Such boots provide traction in a variety of terrain, gripping on wet rocks, steep hillsides and the like. However, Vibram soles are noisy to walk in, making them a bottom-of-the-barrel choice for any serious walking bowhunter.

Vibram-soled boots do come into their own in tree-stand hunting situations. These positive-gripping soles are safest when climbing trees and standing on small, elevated platforms; they minimize the chances of a dangerous slip or fall.

A much better bet for all-around bowhunting use is a well made boot with a soft neoprene sole. Such a sole gives with underfoot debris like leaves and branches, minimizing noise and allowing a hunter to feel his way along and detect

Calf-high rubber pacs are best when bowhunting in areas with standing water or excessively damp footing.

larger objects underfoot. A neoprene sole is almost as sure in mountain terrain as Vibram, is relatively safe in a tree stand and wears surprisingly well with heavy use.

Neoprene is dangerously slippery on ice or snow and any bowhunter expecting such footing is advised to switch to insulated rubber pacs with deep-grooved gripping soles. A rubber boot with shiny surfaces can be easily dulled for hunting with a light sandpaper rubdown. Rubber, calf-high pacs are also just the ticket for hunting in damp or downright wet conditions. Despite what manufacturers might claim, there is no such thing as a truly waterproof leather boot.

A wide variety of other footwear is used with more or less success by bowhunters around the country. One hunting buddy of mine swears by simple leather moccasins for sneaking after whitetail deer in the noisy fall woods; another wears old Hushpuppies, because they are cooler than calf-high boots and have soft, quiet rubber soles. However, for the vast majority of situations, a calf-high leather boot soled with neoprene cannot be beat for comfort and hunting practicality, performing well both on stand and on the move.

Every serious bowhunter occasionally encounters situations that require other kinds of clothing. For instance, the archer waiting out late-season whitetails in subzero weather must protect his hands from the cold as he sits patiently on stand. Ordinary finger gloves degrade bowshooting accuracy, but a toasty pair of down-filled ski mittens successfully fight the cold and can be quickly shed just prior to a shot.

Similarly, special camouflage problems require special solutions. The archer who finds himself hunting pronghorn antelope on flatlands blanketed by snow must don pure white to have a decent chance at these ultra-keen-eyed animals, and the hunter who goes after Rocky Mountain goats in their drab, uniformly gray habitat must wear special clothing that matches this unusual backdrop.

When considering any garment, a bowhunter should make sure it allows accurate shooting, provides decent comfort, ensures good camouflage, and prevents game-spooking noise. If any form of clothing meets these common-sense requirements, it should serve you well in the field.

## OTHER EQUIPMENT

There is a mistaken notion among some archers that binoculars are not necessary in bowhunting, because this is largely an ultra-close-range sport. Nothing could be farther from the truth.

A quality binocular is just as important in bowhunting as in any other form of hunting sport. The fact that bowhunters take shots at ranges under seventy-five yards

*Like most expert bowhunters, Jim Easton, president of Easton Aluminum, uses binoculars to locate far-off animals.*

*No matter the distance, binoculars can be useful in spotting small parts of well-concealed animals like this bedded buck. At moderate to long range, these antler tips mightn't be seen with naked eye. Below: Bota bag allows the the quiet, slosh-free transport of water, even after a fair amount of contents have been consumed by the bowhunter.*

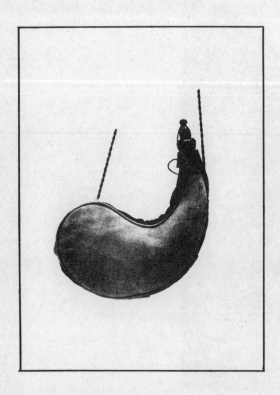

has nothing to do with whether or not binoculars are needed to improve an archer's chances of success on various kinds of animals.

The proper binocular will improve virtually anybody's enjoyment and success in the field. A good glass has several important applications. For one, it allows the bowhunter to scan the far-off countryside for animals he might not otherwise see. Once located, such distant animals can often be approached with a careful stalk into the wind.

A good binocular also allows a bowhunter to locate at relatively close range animals almost entirely hidden in heavy brush or trees. The peculiar curve of an amber antler-tip, the slight glow of a wet nose, or the unique texture of a small patch of deer hide might not be visible to the naked eye — even at ranges under fifty yards — but a clear, sharply focused binocular can help the bowhunter locate these bits and pieces of animals, allowing him to be ready when game steps into the open or presents a fleeting glimpse of a vital area.

Every really good bowhunter of my acquaintance feels naked without some sort of binocular, both stalking hunters and hunters who prefer to sit patiently on stand.

For some reason that escapes me, many modern bowhunters prefer tiny compact binoculars that fit neatly

*Expect tradeoffs when selecting between these two pair of binoculars. Middle-sized, rubber-coated model at left allows good magnification, light gathering and has wide field of view. It's heavier than ultra-compact glasses (below), but smaller model sacrifices in other three areas described.*

in the palm of the hand. Such glasses do provide the ultimate in carrying ease and convenient storage in a pocket, weighing less than fifteen ounces and measuring just slightly larger than a pack of cigarettes. However, lightweight and compact design are their only advantages. A small binocular sacrifices a great deal in light-gathering ability — a problem at dawn and dusk when most game is seen — and also severely limits a hunter's field of view.

In addition, a compact binocular's extremely light weight works to a hunter's disadvantage by accentuating hand jiggle caused by heartbeat, breathing and other natural body functions. On top of all these negative factors, an itty-bitty binocular normally has a magnification level of six power or less, which is below the ideal for the majority of hunting situations. In short, ultra-compact binoculars are not all they are cracked up to be.

Although seldom seen today, monoculars are sold by a few companies and embody all the disadvantages of a small binocular plus the added lack of clarity, light-gathering ability and field of view caused by one-eye viewing.

The best choice for bowhunting is a good-quality binocular weighing between fifteen and thirty ounces,

having a magnification between seven and ten power. Such a glass is light enough in weight for virtually anyone to carry in comfort on a neck strap, yet heavy enough and large enough to dampen hand jiggle, gather adequate light for viewing in dim conditions and provide a large field of view to facilitate searching for hidden or faraway game.

By far the best bowhunting binoculars are so-called armored glasses which are completely encased in rubber to dampen noise and eliminate metallic glare. The glasses I

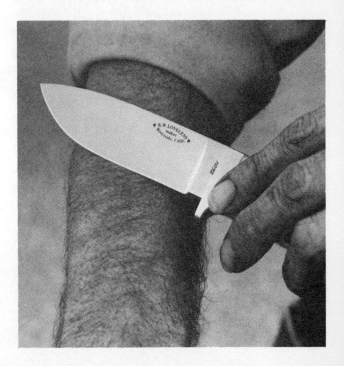

*A drop-point knife blade like this design from R.W. Loveless is the most practical for bowhunting. It provides a sturdy pointed tip and curving blade ideal for cutting, skinning.*

*Buck Stop Lure Company is the nation's largest supplier of top-quality bowhunting scents. Among their most popular odor-masking fragrances are Acorn, Wild Grape, and Apple. How to apply them is discussed in text.*

most often use weigh only twenty ounces, are covered with green rubber, and give me a sharp eight-power view.

A second pair I'm also partial to weighs a bit more, but gives a ten-power view for glassing distant hillsides in search of trophy game. Any binocular over ten-power accentuates hand jiggle to the point where eye strain results from long-term viewing. Stick to mid-sized glasses in the seven- to ten-power range and you won't go wrong.

A bowhunter who plans to move about in dry terrain needs to carry some sort of water container. Unfortunately, an ordinary rigid-wall canteen is not a good choice for bowhunting, because once it becomes partially empty the water sloshes about noisily. This sound can scare away nearby game.

The best kind of water container for a bowhunter on the go is a flexible water bag, sometimes called a bota bag. Such a container collapses as water is consumed, allowing no air pockets in the bag to cause noisy splash. Bota bags are made of canvas, leather and/or rubber are available through archery shops and general sporting goods stores.

Obviously, a hunter on stand can use any sort of water container he desires. Regular old GI canteens are fine, as are larger round, flat-sided models.

I've found that one of those clear plastic, liter-sized

*Many bowhunters apply odor-masking scent directly to their clothing. It's much tidier, though, to use a scent pad.*

Although a meat saw is necessary for cutting an animal in half lengthwise, this task is normally tackled at home. In most instances, a bowhunter can perform all field chores with small, sharp hunting knife, as discussed.

*The author used odor-masking scent to help him stalk within solid bow range of this huge, 35-inch California Spanish goat. Heavy heads are especially wary and call for all aids one can employ.*

bottles that originally contained a soft drink makes an excellent and extremely inexpensive bowhunting canteen. Such a container can be carried in any backpack, provides ample water under average weather conditions and is flexible enough to be manually collapsed as the water is used up to prevent game-spooking slosh caused by air pockets in the bottle.

Every bowhunter should carry a hunting knife for field-dressing and skinning big game. Such a knife also is handy around camp, serving in every capacity from potato peeler to rope cutter to steak knife to limb pruner around a stand.

Many hunting archers make the mistake of carrying a knife too large and too bulky for the needs at hand. A three-inch blade is adequate for field dressing, skinning and quartering the biggest animals like moose and elk.

Knife choice is a highly personal matter, but in my opinion, the best bowhunting knife is a three-inch folding model carried on the belt in a small, sturdy leather sheath that snaps securely shut at the top. Such a knife should have a sturdy drop-point blade made of high-carbon stainless steel which holds an edge and resists corrosion even when wet or bloody. The handle should be a combination of the same stainless steel and a tough, moisture-proof and blood-proof material like Micarta, plastic, or dense hardwood. Several top-name knife manufacturers offer hunting knives that fit this basic description.

Incidentally, a bowhunter can field dress an animal successfully with a sharp hunting broadhead, if he has lost or forgotten his hunting knife on a particular outing. The process is considerably slower than with a knife, but saves an animal like a deer from certain spoilage by cooling out the carcass.

Many hunters carry meat saws at all times, either in belt sheaths or hunting backpacks. Such saws normally are not necessary, because most field processes required on a big-game animal can be carried out with a sharp hunting knife. This includes cutting an animal in half to simplify transport to camp or the nearest road. A meat saw is necessary when quartering a large animal like an elk or caribou to facilitate transport, because the spine must be sawed in two lengthwise during the quartering process.

A flashlight is an extremely important item to every bowhunter. Such a light helps a hunter make his way to a productive area before daylight and eliminates potential problems if he doesn't make it back to camp before dark. I often walk out of the woods after dark with the aid of a flashlight, because until it is too dark to see, I have nothing on my mind but trying to find an animal. A quality flashlight also is an absolute must for trailing hard-hit animals when weather is too warm to wait till morning to follow up a shot.

I've used just about every kind of flashlight offered to mankind and most varieties are not worth the powder to blow them up. Many's the time I have struggled out of heavy forests after dark with a cheap flashlight that flickered, sputtered, then gave up the ghost.

After several years of smacking second-rate lights against trees and rocks to keep them working, I finally bought a first-rate two-D-cell Kel-Lite which I've been using without an instant of trouble for over six years. This and similar black, heavy-wall, aircraft-aluminum flashlights are manufactured primarily for police officers and are worth every penny of their relatively high price tags. Such flashlights cannot be smashed, are not affected by moisture

*Potent animal lures such as those offered by Buck Stop and Baker can greatly improve a bowhunter's success on rutting. deer. These are intended primarily for the still or stationary hunter, as bucks will come looking for the doe.*

and feature solid-state switches which are not prone to failure. I carry my light in a handy commercial belt sheath along my right side.

Another flashlight option to consider is a bow flashlight which screws directly into the stabilizer hole in the front of a bow's handle riser. Such a flashlight is sold by several outfits and provides a handy source of nighttime light plus the accuracy-enhancing frontal weight of a normal shooting stabilizer.

As will be discussed in Chapter 12, a bowhunter must be extremely careful to avoid letting wary animals detect his human odor. In addition, there are times when a particular odor will actually attract that animal within bow range. For these reasons, the majority of serious bowhunters use one or more varieties of odor-masking scent or animal lure to help them set up decent shots at game.

A wide array of odor-masking scents are currently sold at archery stores — scents designed to at least partially cover a hunter's game-spooking body odor. The average animal can smell a hunter at half a mile or more when the wind is blowing from hunter to animal, making successful hunting with archery gear virtually impossible if breezes are blowing the wrong way.

Every knowledgeable archer hunts into the wind or in a cross-wind direction, but air currents are never completely stable and often switch direction. Odor-masking scent is good insurance in case the hunter cannot completely control wind direction and an air current suddenly fans the back of his neck.

Some of the more popular odor-masking scents on today's market include acorn, apple, wild grape, and skunk. These and others are generally sold in liquid form in small plastic squeeze bottles; they are applied either directly to a hunter's clothing or to a separate absorbent scent pad pinned to a hunter's shirt or pants.

*Above: A frameless, camouflage-print day pack is one answer to a bowhunter's equipment-carrying needs. Right: Compact, leaf-print fanny pack provides ample space for small bowhunting items like spare bowstring, bowstringing tool, and razor-sharp replacement broadheads.*

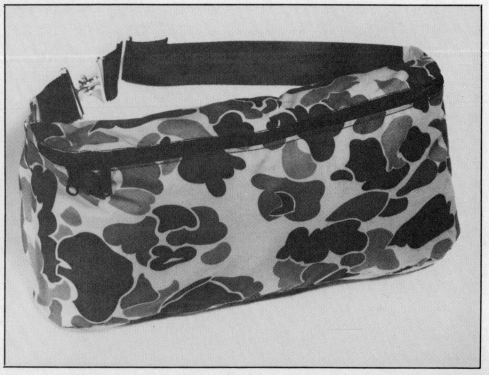

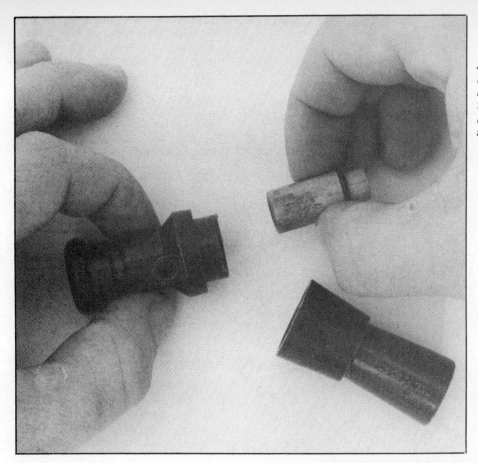

A mouth-blown, dying-rabbit call is used to lure in hungry predators like foxes and coyotes. Convenient three-piece model shown here takes reeds that imitate different rabbit species. Practice with the calls.

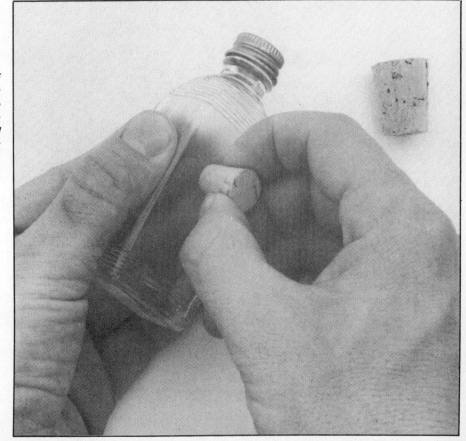

A homemade squeaker call consists of a flat-sided vanilla bottle and a wet cork. In expert hands, this simple predator call will produce the sounds of frightened rats, mice, birds and similar critters. Corks of different sizes produce different tones in use.

Author often uses regular backpack frame and lower pack sack for serious bowhunting in remote areas. He used such a rig to carry lunch, flashlight and survival gear up 2500-foot peak, then bagged record Rocky Mountain goat after a long stalk, and packed head and hide back down to camp in a single day. He was one tired hunter!

*Small hip pouch might hold all of the gear an archer needs for a single day of bowhunting. It needn't be camouflaged, since it's small, but this is something for you to decide.*

A hunter always should match the odor-masking scent to the area he plans to hunt. For example, wild grape scent is entirely out of place in the high mountains, because no wild grapes grow there. Much better choices for mountain hunting are acorn scent or skunk scent, as both acorns and skunks are prevalent in many high-country settings.

Potent-smelling odor-masking scents like those sold by Buck Stop and Baker Manufacturing will improve a bowhunter's odds of scoring on game. Even if these scents do not completely fool an animal, they are prone to confuse the critter long enough to allow a shot.

Animal lures of various sorts are commonly used by bowhunters as well to both hide human odor and attract nearby game. The most common animal lure for bowhunting is doe-in-heat scent, sometimes called sex scent. This liquid concoction smells exactly like a whitetail doe in heat and consistently draws in rutting bucks when properly used. Doe-in-heat scent normally is squirted liberally near a blind or at the base of a tree stand, allowing the archer to wait for a wild-eyed buck to saunter into range.

One of the most effective ways to bowhunt certain species is calling them into range with mouth-blown or electronic calls. Prime candidates for calling are predators like foxes, coyotes and bobcats, because such animals are suckers for any noise that sounds like a scared or wounded prey species such as a rabbit or bird. A wide variety of commercial mouth-blown calls and cassette tapes are sold today that duplicate the squeals of frightened rabbits, the squeaks of startled rats, etc. Most work well when employed properly.

Other commercial calls also benefit bowhunters after specific species. Among these are bugles that duplicate the multiple-note squeals of bull elk, horns that mimic the mournful moans of cow moose in heat, deer calls to produce the bleat of a frightened fawn, calls that sound like lovesick or lonely turkeys. These and similar calls should be investigated by a bowhunter, because they can be used to lure a normally wary trophy within point-blank range.

Every bowhunter should accumulate a complement of calls to match the kinds of hunting he most prefers to do.

An on-the-go bowhunter normally owns at least one equipment pack to carry essential in-the-field gear. A gun hunter usually goes afield without a pack, but an archer needs to carry things like a spare bowstring, bow-stringing tool, extra broadheads, odor-masking scent and oil to prevent broadhead rust on a heavily moist or rainy day. Some sort of out-of-the-way pack is a much better place to carry all this equipment than trouser and shirt pockets.

The most common bowhunting packs are frameless day packs and so-called "fanny packs" which ride directly above the hips. A bowhunter should check out available packs at local stores, choosing a model that is comfortable, of the right size to carry his personal gear, yet sufficiently quiet and camouflaged to avoid the possibility of spooking game.

Because frameless backpacks and fanny packs are positioned behind the body, these can be made of hard-weave nylon or canvas-like materials without the strong possibility of causing game-spooking noise. The primary concern should be that they are not excessively light in color. The best option is buying one of the many leaf-print packs available these days, especially in a backpack; such a pack is large enough to catch an animal's eye if it is one color and fails to blend exactly with a particular background.

The serious big-game bowhunter should consider buying a stout backpack with an aluminum or magnesium frame. Long treks afield make such a pack ideal, because more gear can be carried in comfort and game can be lashed to the pack for easier transport out of the woods.

My favorite setup for serious bowhunting in remote areas is a medium-sized aluminum backpack frame with two separate pack sacks attached. The top sack is used to carry clothes, food, and similar items into a remote wilderness camp. The lower pack carries day-to-day hunting items like water, lunch, et cetera. Once I reach a remote campsite, I remove the top pack and leave it in camp, allowing ample room above the lower pack to lash down an animal's cape, head, and edible meat for a long pack out. The frame is sprayed a dull green and I can carry it all day without discomfort or interference with sitting, walking or shooting my bow.

The zippered game pouch in some top-quality wool jackets allows storage of ample gear for a day-long stroll about the woods. My favorite hunting jacket for cold weather is an old red-and-black plaid Woolrich Stag Jacket, a design with a roomy game pouch in back accessible from the side through a zippered opening. This setup allows me to carry a lunch, spare bowstring, water bag, elk bugle and other necessary gear without the mild hassle of pulling on a separate pack. It also makes for ultra-quiet stalking because the game pouch is enclosed by noiseless wool instead of the normal nylon or canvas used in various sorts of backpack sacks.

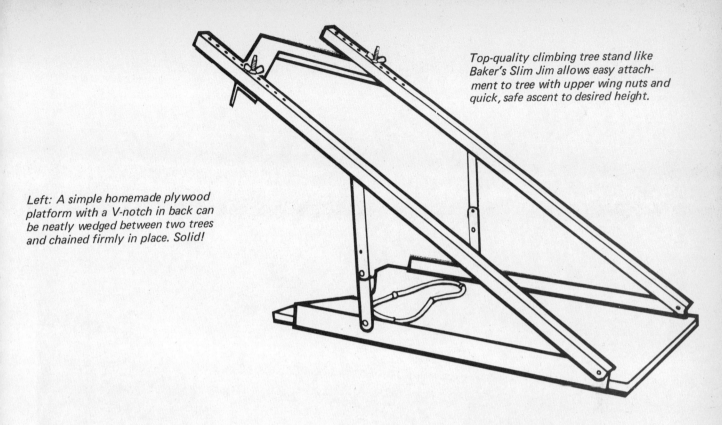

Top-quality climbing tree stand like Baker's Slim Jim allows easy attachment to tree with upper wing nuts and quick, safe ascent to desired height.

Left: A simple homemade plywood platform with a V-notch in back can be neatly wedged between two trees and chained firmly in place. Solid!

## TREE STANDS AND BLINDS

Aside from the gear an archer carries all day on his person, many bowhunters invest in a whole 'nother set of hunting equipment that lets them ambush game instead of actively approaching it.

A tree stand is any elevated platform that allows an archer to overlook an area where game is likely to appear. Tree stands afford a superior view of surrounding terrain, while placing a hunter above an animal's direct line of sight and smell. These advantages have made bowhunting from tree stands a favorite sport with thousands of dedicated archers.

Homemade tree stand design is as diverse as the bowhunters who erect these do-it-yourself contraptions.

Custom tree stands vary from small, simple plywood platforms notched at the rear and chained to trees to elaborate tree houses built around two or more trees with sturdy side rails and plywood or plank floors.

The hunter's imagination is the only limiting factor when such stands are being designed and erected and some pretty elaborate setups grace productive game areas around the country.

For example, one friend enjoys baiting black bears under roomy tree stands. Several of his stands are designed to be slept in at night so he can waylay bears at the crack of dawn without fear of scaring them away by stumbling to a blind in the predawn darkness. One of his huge tree houses is furnished with a cot, a wood-burning stove and elaborate

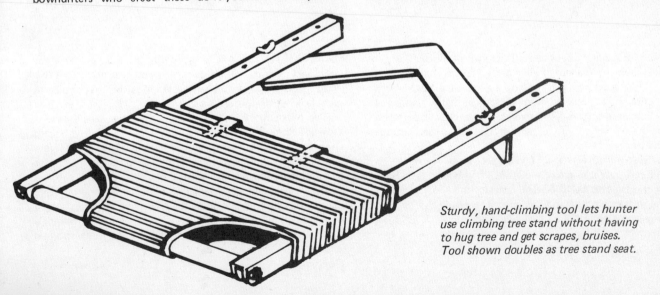

Sturdy, hand-climbing tool lets hunter use climbing tree stand without having to hug tree and get scrapes, bruises. Tool shown doubles as tree stand seat.

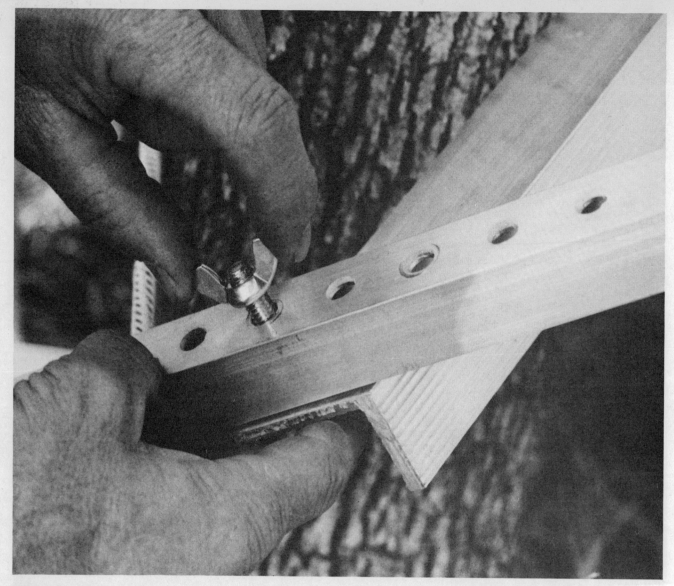

The best climbing tree stands, author feels, feature light sturdy aluminum construction and quick attachment to a tree with stout bolts and wing nuts. The aluminum used for these can support even the heaviest bowhunter. Right: When done properly, inch-worming up a straight-trunked tree with a climbing stand and hand-climbing tool is quick.

shelving for canned goods and other kinds of food.

Although permanent tree stands can be handy if a hunter has access to private land or knows a public area well enough to ensure that game will hang around a particular stand from year to year, a portable tree stand embodies many more advantages for the average bowhunter.

A permanent stand on public land normally is considered public domain and quite a few bowhunters have spent the time to build a stand only to find another archer sitting in it come opening morning. The result can be hurt feelings and a potential exchange of fists.

Likewise, many private landowners view permanent tree

houses as eyesores, yet allow polite bowhunters to erect temporary stands which are removed immediately after season is over. A portable tree stand is the best choice in most bowhunting situations.

The best commercial tree stands are so-called climbers — stands that can be inched up any fairly small, straight-trunked tree with a little muscle power and energy. Although climbing tree stands at one time required a hunter to hug a tree trunk as he hoisted the stand upward with his feet, the best contemporary climbing stands incorporate a hand-climbing tool that grips the tree above a hunter's head and lets him muscle his way upward by gripping a comfortable aluminum handle bar. This prevents strained

*Left: Tree stand safety belt snugs about both tree and hunter to ensure safety in case of misstep or slip.*

*Besides safety, the tree stand safety belt offers bowhunter extra steadiness as he bends at waist to shoot down.*

muscles or scraped skin associated with hugging a tree directly during climbing. Once the tree stand is inch-wormed to a desired height, the hand-climbing tool can be used as a tree-stand seat which eases the muscles during long waits for game.

Hand-climbing a straight-trunked tree goes as follows. The climber slips his toes under toe straps attached to the stand, allowing him to lift the stand upward with his feet. The stand should be bolted around the tree at this point so the platform angles somewhat upward, because as a hunter climbs, tree diameter gets smaller and the platform will level out. A level stand platform to begin with will result in a dangerous, downward-slanting platform once a desired height is reached.

Next, the hunter slides the hand-climbing tool (also bolted around the tree) as far above his head as possible, then pulls down on this tool to lock it firmly into the tree.

The next step is bending the knees sharply while pulling down on the hand-climbing tool, a move which slides the

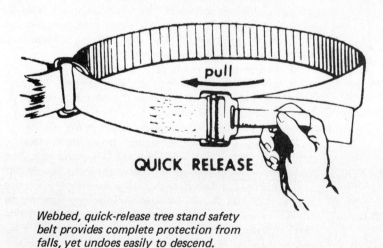

*Webbed, quick-release tree stand safety belt provides complete protection from falls, yet undoes easily to descend.*

*Compact wire thumb-ring saw is ideal for removing small limbs that impede hunter's upward progress with stand.*

*Simple screw-in tree stand steps (below) provide fairly safe access to an elevated platform, author says.*

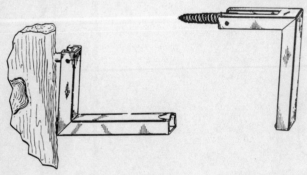

stand platform a couple of feet skyward. The hunter then eases his weight back on the stand platform, slides the hand climber upward again, and repeats the inch-worming procedure. An experienced hand-climbing bowhunter can ascend a straight-trunked pine or oak without branches like a nimble tree squirrel.

When buying a portable tree stand, a hunter should look for certain marks of excellence. For one, the stand platform should be large enough for comfort, preferably at least 16x20 inches in size. Also, the platform should be made of durable indoor-outdoor plywood which will not bend, break or become slippery when wet. A stand should have a strong but lightweight frame made of aluminum — a frame assembled with stout bolts and wing nuts that can be removed and replaced quickly when affixing a stand to a tree or removing it after a hunt is done.

On top of these structural considerations, a tree stand must have positive gripping blades that prevent the stand from suddenly sliding to the ground with the hunter on it. If you expect and demand these tree-stand qualities, erecting and using it will be a safe, enjoyable experience.

A serious tree-stand bowhunter needs some standing accessories that ensure stand-hunting safety and ease. The foremost of these is a good-quality tree-stand safety belt that saves the hunter's hide should he accidentally slip and fall. Such a belt should be a webbed, quick-release model similar to an automobile seat belt — a model with one section that cinches snugly around a hunter's middle, another section that cinches snugly around the tree, while a central extension section between the two allows a certain amount of freedom to move about a stand.

A hoist rope allows a safe climb to tree stand. Once archer is safely aloft, he can pull up his bow, day pack and other gear tied below. Easy!

*A commercial bow rack leaves hunter's hands free aloft, but nestles bow and arrow within quick, easy reach (right). This rubber-coated model snaps to side rail of a climbing tree stand.*

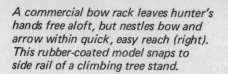

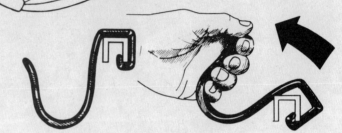

*Fold-down seat is practical addition to any climbing tree stand. This one from Baker attaches with two bolts and features handy under-pouch for storing small bowhunting items you must have.*

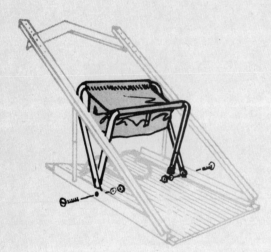

*Backpacking tree stand with handmade or commercially made straps allows safest, most comfortable transport during long or rugged trips to suitable hunting sites.*

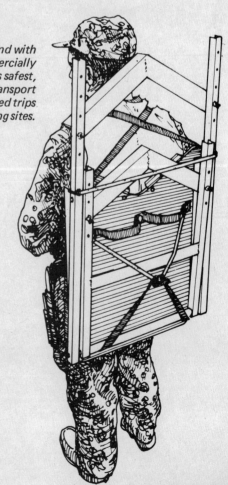

Never use a common rope as a tree-stand safety belt. Such a rope can cinch about a hunter's waist during a fall, cutting off breath, possibly breaking ribs, perhaps making escape from the rope difficult or impossible.

Another tree-stand accessory of importance is a limb saw to lop off small branches that interfere with an upward climb to a desired tree-stand height. A favorite with hunters is the simple, compact, yet effective wire sportsman's thumb-ring saw, a flexible tool that makes quick work of small limbs and easily rolls up into shirt-pocket size.

A hoist rope is essential in tree-stand hunting to pull up bow, day pack and other equipment after the hunter reaches a desired height and fastens his safety belt. It is dangerous to attempt any climb with bowhunting gear in your hand. Any medium-diameter rope will work as a hoist rope, provided it is thirty to forty feet long. My personal favorite is a length of quarter-inch braided nylon rope.

A hoist rope can come in handy in another situation, too. Occasionally a hunter finds an ideal tree-stand tree with a crooked trunk or too many large limbs to allow the conventional use of a climbing tree stand. In such a case, he

Rope ladder allows quick ascent and descent to tree stand or ground without hassle of installing steps.

can tie the rope to his climbing stand, climb the tree hand over hand, then hoist up the stand on the rope and bolt it around the tree at a desired height.

A tree stand to be left in place for several days requires a rope ladder or tree-stand steps to allow quick, easy ascent and descent. I prefer a rope ladder, because it is safe and requires no installation except tying it topside. A ladder or tree-stand steps also allow a hunter to bail out of his stand silently if he sees a distant animal and wishes to make a stalk.

Four other items are commonly used by tree-stand hunters:

One is a simple plastic jug with an airtight cap to be used as a urinal and/or ashtray while aloft. Answering nature's call over the side of a stand or flicking tobacco ashes into space will alert all downwind animals that danger lurks nearby.

Most hand-climbing tools double as tree-stand seats, but the hunter using a stand without a hand climber should buy some sort of sturdy, reasonably comfortable seat for his stand. A few of the better tree stands come complete with folding stools bolted directly to tree-stand platforms.

A tree-stand seat ensures waiting comfort and non-wobbly muscles when the time comes to take a shot. It also lowers a hunter's center of gravity on a stand as he waits for game, making him less likely to lose his balance and fall.

Another muscle-saver is some sort of bow rack attached directly to a tree stand or to the tree itself. Holding a bow

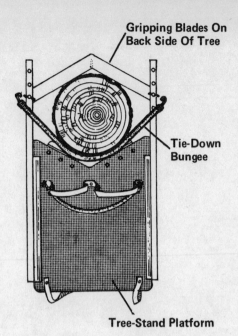

**Gripping Blades On Back Side Of Tree**

**Tie-Down Bungee**

**Tree-Stand Platform**

*Important safety feature standard on Baker stands is tie-down bungee that firmly holds gripping blades against tree once the stand is positioned at the desired hunting height.*

for hours on end can be a solid pain, a pain that is not necessary if a bow is nestled in a rack within easy reach.

Lastly, a bowhunter who plans to erect a stand some distance away from a road is best advised to pack in his portable stand with the aid of commercial backpack straps. This leaves his hands perfectly free to carry a bow and to steady himself against falls in rugged terrain.

The foregoing tree-stand equipment and other more specialized items are sold by a number of companies. A pleasant look through a major tree-stand catalog like the one published by Baker Manufacturing will open your eyes to what is currently available to serious tree-stand bowhunters.

Although in many instances a bowhunter can take a ground stand quite effectively by simply backing up against a stump, tree, or bush, there are times when some sort of ground blind can be very useful to completely hide a hunter

*Baker's Ground Blind is first-quality design, consisting of sharpened aluminum stakes and durable camouflage fabric. Several sizes and color patterns are available for selection.*

*Nylon-web spare arm with rigid metal core attaches to bowhunter's belt and provides handy hook on which to hang bow when both hands are needed. Right: Rangefinder is efficiently toted in a waterproof belt pouch.*

*An alternative to commercial ground blind is to use the real thing — a clump of brush near game location you've scouted.*

## SAMPLE IN-THE-FIELD EQUIPMENT CHECKLIST

| | |
|---|---|
| Underwear | Six Replacement Broadheads |
| Socks | Spare Bowstring |
| Camouflage Tee Shirt | Bowstringing Tool |
| Camouflage Shirt | Snakebite Kit |
| Camouflage Pants | Canteen |
| Belt With Dull Buckle | Binoculars |
| Neoprene-Soled Boots | Toilet Paper |
| Camouflage Hat | Pocket Watch |
| Wool Jacket | Hunting License |
| Hunting Bow | Deer Tag |
| Arrows In Quiver | Lunch |
| Finger Tab | Butane Cigarette Lighter |
| Armguard | Compass |
| Powder Pouch | Map Of Hunting Area |
| Rangefinder | Small File |
| Hunting Knife | Odor-Masking Scent |
| Frameless Backpack | Small Varmint Call |
| Flashlight | Spare Arm For Belt |
| Camouflage Headnet | Goose-Down Mittens |

from the probing eyes of game. Notable examples include bowhunting pronghorn antelope in flat prairie country and wild turkeys in relatively open grassland with scattered oaks.

An artificial blind enclosure is in some ways a handicap to a bowhunter, because he must draw his bow down low, then ease upward quite a ways before taking a shot. However, in some instances such a tactic is the only chance a hunter has to get within bow range of game in the first place.

Like tree stands, homemade ground blinds vary considerably. The most sophisticated are made of chicken wire or similar stiff meshing interwoven with natural foliage. The crudest are simple holes kicked in the brush. A hunter with an imagination can always fashion some sort of natural ground blind if the need arises.

A better bet is having a commercial camouflage-net blind handy in case you want to take a stand on the ground. Many commercial ground blinds are sold these days, from fragile, impractical painted cardboard enclosures to durable, easy-to-transport blinds made of fabric supported by

sharpened aluminum stakes. When not in use, such blinds can be rolled up tight for compact storage.

As is the case with shooting equipment, archery stores and general sporting goods stores are jam-packed with items "guaranteed" to improve your score on game. Some of these are very beneficial; others are total, laughable flops.

Experimentation and common sense are the keys to finding valuable hunting aids. For every profitable equipment find a hunter makes, he is likely to discard a dozen interesting but impractical inventions.

Examples of bowhunting accessories I personally rely on are a handy zippered belt pouch for my bowhunting rangefinder and a hooked gizmo called a "spare arm" which also attaches to my belt. The rangefinder pouch rides on my right hip, the spare arm on my left. When using binoculars, rangefinder, or anything else that ties up both hands as I stand, I hook the middle of my bowstring or the bow grip in the spare arm hook on my belt and let my bow hang out of the way until my hands are free once more.

These and similar simple but practical aids might help improve your bowhunting sport as well.

*What better proof of the effectiveness of a belt-mounted spare arm can there be? Author often uses one when glassing potential game-holding areas, where rock-solid, two-hand grip is required for an accurate scanning.*

# CHAPTER 12
# BASICS OF SUCCESSFUL BOWHUNTING

## You Have To Be Smarter Than The Game You're Hunting

**B**OWHUNTING is relatively easy to describe, but extremely difficult to carry out. In a nutshell, all a bowhunter has to do to be successful is to find game, penetrate his quarry's defenses, then make a clean, killing shot. If the archer can somehow get within twenty or thirty yards without being detected, draw his bow without being seen, and place an arrow exactly on the money, he has met the challenge with flying colors.

The big problem with bowhunting is the game being hunted. If an animal were like a stump, all the bowhunter would have to do would be to stroll within solid range, then blow the critter out of its socks.

Fortunately, bowhunting is never that easy or that boring. A modern game species like a deer, bear, elk, wild turkey or equally desirable creature is a fine-tuned defense machine programmed to detect and avoid human danger

*A deer is a fine-tuned survival machine that uses ears, eyes and nose to detect and avoid danger.*

Consistently successful bowhunters like well-known Jim Dougherty have mastered basics of getting close to animals. Dougherty took this record caribou from a well-placed blind.

*The author bagged this nice pronghorn antelope at less than twenty-five yards. Getting this close to a sharp-eyed antelope requires the careful use of camouflage and existing cover, the latter a bit scanty at this locale.*

with ease. The archer who has developed the skill and the patience to take alert animals and birds consistently can be proud of his ability, because he has mastered the most difficult hunting challenge of all.

Every game species has a three-pronged system of defense which an archer must carefully attempt to penetrate. This defense system consists of the eyes, ears and nose. A hunter should determine first how alert these senses are in the particular species he's after, then formulate a sensible game plan for thwarting these senses and making a clean, dead-center shot in a vital area.

Every game species has a different balance of protective senses. Some, like the whitetail deer and the elk, have uniformly sharp senses that give the hunter no advantage at

all. A mature whitetail with some survival experience is one tough cookie to take, because this animal has sharp eyeballs, a sensitive nose and ears set to detect the slightest sound of danger. The fellow who regularly arrows an animal equipped with such survival equipment has developed his own outdoor ability fully.

In contrast, the majority of animals and birds have one or more weak links in their chain of survival senses. A wild boar is a highly intelligent animal with a first-rate nose, but this critter's mediocre ears and poor eyesight allow a hunter to sneak within bow range with relative ease as long as the wind is blowing in the right direction and the target animal stays put during the stalk.

On the other hand, the pronghorn antelope has a poor

*Some animals have sensory deficiencies that work to the hunter's advantage. For example, the wild boar has extremely poor eyesight, allowing a reasonably quiet hunter to sneak close from a downwind position. Pork chops, anyone?*

nose and so-so ears, but possesses one of the best sets of eyes in the entire animal kingdom. The bowhunter after this particular species must concentrate primarily on staying out of sight to give himself a decent chance at success.

After a bowhunter has made a determination about the senses of the creature he plans to hunt, the next step is learning something about the habits possessed by that creature. Every kind of game has a peculiar temperament and set of living habits — a personality which determines a bowhunter's strategy and the eventual outcome of a hunting excursion. For example, the whitetail deer is one of America's most nervous animals, a tightly coiled spring ready to leap away at the slightest hint of danger. By

contrast, the mule deer is far more docile in nature, prone to hesitate and ogle a hunter after hearing or seeing what he thinks might be danger. This particular comparison of temperament gives the whitetail a clear victory when it comes to difficulty to bowhunt.

However, comparing the same two species in another category gives the muley a decided survival advantage. The mule deer is a highly unpredictable beast wandering a large home territory at random. In contrast, a person often can set his watch by a whitetail's movement patterns within this animal's small home territory. A bowhunter after mule deer usually must spot animals from a distance and make tedious stalks over noisy ground, whereas the archer after whitetails can often sit by a well used game trail and be assured of a shot at under twenty yards. The hunter attempting to ambush a mule deer from a stand might wait several weeks without so much as one glimpse of a close-range deer.

Knowledge of other habits can also prove vital to success on particular animals. For example, blacktail deer often move about throughout the day in spite of afternoon temperatures that soar above 90 degrees Fahrenheit. In contrast, black bears seldom move from heavy cover except at first and last light of day. The bowhunter without these tidbits of habit information can waste a lot of time and energy which could have been applied to nailing a fine, fat trophy.

The accompanying chart showing the traits of common big-game species should give any bowhunter a base to work from when planning a strategy for taking a particular kind of trophy. From there, his basic hunting skills and shooting ability coupled with the ability of his quarry and good old-fashioned luck will determine the outcome of his efforts.

How to apply a particular hunting strategy to a particular species is discussed thoroughly in Chapters 13 and 14. However, no matter what the strategy employed, a bowhunter must know some facts about how to avoid an animal's three basic defense systems — the eyes, the ears and the nose. The following tips will stand any bowhunter in good stead as he moves about on foot or waits patiently on stand.

Any species of game has at least mediocre eyesight and many have peepers as good or better than those of the human hunter. A bowhunter always should take pains to avoid the eyes of the game he's after, knowing full well that failure to do so will scare hell out of his targets and result in failure to set up a decent shot.

Even the dim-eyed little javelina will run like a scalded dog if a bowhunter gets careless at close range and moves too quickly or fails to exercise proper camouflage precautions. More keen-eyed species like elk, mountain goats, and mule deer require the utmost camouflage care at

*Because mule deer are unpredictable open-country animals, they are generally spotted from afar and stalked instead of hunted from a stand (below). Blacktail deer are known to move about during warm midday hours, a trait the smart bowhunter can exploit. This fine-racked buck is on full alert in this photo (opposite page), and is difficult to arrow.*

*This bristle-backed javelina is afflicted with the poor eyesight of his swine brethren, but will spot unwary bowhunter at close range. His erect ears and alert nostrils indicate he's detected something awry close by!*

all ranges, and one little slip will send these animals packing in the twinkle of an eye.

The first step to avoiding an animal's eyes is dressing in proper camouflage and making sure all hunting and shooting gear is equally tough to see. Basic camouflage precautions have been discussed, but the careful hunter goes much further in his effort to remain hidden at all times.

For one thing, he always moves with the speed of a snail whenever the chance exists that game might see him and flee. A quick movement is most likely to catch the eye of any animal, while an infinitely slow movement might go unnoticed even when a creature is staring directly at the archer. Patience and painstaking care of movement are major keys to avoiding an animal's eyes.

A bowhunter always should use his head to make the best camouflage use of existing terrain. An archer never should allow himself to be seen on a skyline because the resulting human silhouette will make him stand out starkly no matter how well camouflaged his clothing and equipment happen to be. This rule is equally true if a hunter is on foot or sitting in an elevated stand. Always make sure a rock, tree, bush or hillside is behind you to obscure your human shape in case game looks your way.

Similarly, a bowhunter should take special pains never to walk in the sunlight with a background of deep shadow or walk in the shadows when a sunlit hillside looms behind. Such sharp contrasts make a hunter leap at the eye of an animal, scaring it badly, unless it is nearly blind and senile to boot.

Whenever possible, a bowhunter should keep solid objects between him and his quarry to completely eliminate the chances of being seen. For instance, stalking a bedded deer on a hillside is considerably easier if a hunter can drop out of sight in a ravine that runs behind the animal instead of easing down a ridgetop in plain view.

Thwarting the eyes of game requires sensible use of camouflage, plus the common sense to stay completely out of sight whenever possible.

It also requires some knowledge about the peripheral abilities of a particular animal's eyes. Most prey species like deer, antelope and elk have eyes set to the sides of their heads to let them see both forward and to the sides. A hunter who attempts to move on a broadside deer will receive a rude awakening when the animal tosses its head and bounds away in terror. Unless facing nearly straight away, any animal with side-mounted eyes can detect nearby danger with ease.

By contrast, certain species like black bear, bobcats, and coyotes have eyes set to the front of the head and have no better side vision than you or I. A bowhunter can take movement liberties with such creatures he'd never get away with when hunting animals with more expansive peripheral ability.

A bowhunter always should capitalize on special situations that work against an animal's eyesight. For example, if a hunter has the chance to stalk an animal with the sun low behind his back, he always should do so, because the bright sun is as hard for an animal to look into as it is for a human. Similarly, a heavy fog can help a bowhunter greatly, because it cuts visibility and lets him stillhunt closer to game before he can possibly be seen.

Keen-eared species such as deer require a bowhunter to be as quiet as a dandelion puff as he moves along, sits on stand or draws his bow to shoot. Virtually any animal is put off by loud, obviously human noises like the slamming

## SENSE ACUTENESS OF COMMON GAME SPECIES

| Game Species | Senses | | |
|---|---|---|---|
| | Eyes | Ears | Nose |
| Black Bear | Fair | Fair | Excellent |
| Blacktail Deer | Excellent | Excellent | Excellent |
| Brown/Grizzly Bear | Poor | Poor | Excellent |
| Caribou | Excellent | Fair | Good |
| Elk | Excellent | Excellent | Excellent |
| Javelina | Poor | Fair | Excellent |
| Moose | Fair | Good | Excellent |
| Mountain Sheep | Excellent | Fair | Good |
| Mule Deer | Excellent | Excellent | Excellent |
| Pronghorn | Excellent | Fair | Fair |
| Rocky Mountain Goat | Excellent | Fair | Good |
| Whitetail Deer | Excellent | Excellent | Excellent |
| Wild Boar | Poor | Fair | Excellent |
| Wild Turkey | Excellent | Excellent | None |

*Although not noted for its intelligence or in-the-field wariness, the open-country caribou has excellent eyesight. This factor alone makes him difficult to stalk, especially when coupled with the barren, treeless terrain.*

Although a simple, elevated seat blind is okay for gun hunting at long distances, the bowhunter who's similarly perched will scare game out of their skins! Here, author demonstrates the high visibility of skylined hunter on such stand.

*Animals with side-mounted eyes can easily see movement to the sides and slightly behind. Both of these deer would instantly spot a moving bowhunter, hence the need for stalking only when animal's eyes are shielded.*

of a car door, talking, or a loud cough or sneeze. Avoiding such noises is a common-sense procedure with any decent hunter, whether he uses a gun or a bow.

Less obvious forms of noise also can spoil a bowhunter's best-laid plans. As discussed in the previous chapter, the slightest scrape of clothing against brush can scare game into the next county. The barely audible jingle of loose change in a pocket, the click of a butane cigarette lighter, or the slight thump of a boot sole against a tree-stand platform are all enough to alert and probably frighten wary game away.

Every bit as bad are noises associated with drawing and shooting a bow. An arrow that scrapes noisily across an ill-suited arrow rest or is dropped accidentally off the rest onto a bow's handle riser is enough to freak out the creature being drawn on. The bowhunter must be sensitive to any noise his clothing or equipment is apt to make and

to do his best to prevent this noise from occurring when game is able to hear.

A hunter on stand has the least problem with making noise, because his hunting method allows him to stand or sit motionlessly in wait of game. A hunter on the move has considerably more to worry about, constantly avoiding noisy foliage as he slips along and constantly concerned about noises made underfoot.

The keys to walking in relative silence are moving slowly and picking your movement route with care. Virtually any kind of terrain can be negotiated in near silence if a hunter is wearing soft-soled footwear, takes the time to choose the quietest route available and moves slowly enough to eliminate disturbing sounds. Even if he has to stoop and brush leaves, twigs and/or other debris out of the way between steps, the hunter can slip along silently if he'll take the time to perform the steps necessary for silent walking. Most

*Proper bowhunting camouflage makes the waiting archer all but invisible to the excellent eyesight of deer.*

movement noise is caused by impatience and the inability to slow down sufficiently to turn a heavy-soled crunch into a light-soled whisper.

What game is doing at a particular time is extremely critical to whether that game hears the hunter. Stalking within bow range of a bedded animal is by far the toughest chore any hunter can tackle, because his quarry is motionless with ears cupped to detect the tiniest sound. On the other hand, the same animal feeding with its head buried in a bush is making considerable noise on its own as well as crunching its jaws and thus further dulling its sense of hearing.

The smart bowhunter considers such factors and attempts to move on game when conditions are least likely to give him away. It is often best to leave a bedded animal alone until it gets up and begins feeding, then to begin a stalk with a knowledge that the trophy is preoccupied and making plenty of noise on its own.

Most animals trust their sense of smell more completely than any other single mechanism of defense. A deer that hears a strange noise may linger about to double-check its suspicions with another sense and a deer that sees something suspicious also may doubt what it has seen. Indeed, one bowhunter of my acquaintance contends that an animal almost always double-checks one sense with another before running away in fear. This sometimes may

Your success ratio will diminish if the properly dressed bowhunter walks into sunlight with shadows behind, as proven in this photo.

177

be true when a creature detects danger with eyes or ears, but it is never true when danger is detected with the nose.

The smell of a human is apparently dreadful and unmistakable to any animal with a good nose, for I never once have seen an animal linger about after the wind has blown from a hunter to that animal. The reaction is always the same — a mad dash for safety without a second's hesitation. When game smells the hunter, game is gone in a flash.

A bowhunter has two basic means of keeping wary animals from smelling him. The first is simply doing his darndest not to let the wind blow from him toward an animal. This is sometimes much easier said than done, but the careful archer who at least realizes how critical wind direction can be has a definite leg up on the nimrod who wanders haphazardly about the woods.

No matter what the hunting method being used, one of the bowhunter's primary considerations should be the direction of prevailing breezes.

A stand hunter always should take a stand on the downwind side of areas where game is likely to appear, especially when he's on the ground instead of in a tree. A tree stand fifteen to thirty feet above the ground normally places the hunter in upper-air currents that waft his smell away high above the noses of deer and similar animals. However, a tree-stand hunter also should set up downwind of animal approach routes whenever possible to avoid the chance of being smelled on unusual downdrafts.

A bowhunter should take particular care when approaching a stand so he doesn't leave a scent trail that spooks away animals. A sharp-nosed animal such as a deer can smell the scent put down by a hunter's feet as a bird dog smells the scent of a running pheasant.

On many occasions, I have experimented with deer and wild pigs in the off-season to see just how well they could smell trails laid down with my feet. The pigs are the keener-nosed of the two and a hunter can ruin his chances by walking along the wrong route when going to his stand.

*Below: Animals like deer have an extremely sharp sense of hearing. When their big, cupped ears spring tensely forward, you know you've made too much noise. Opposite page: A bowhunter moving through heavy brush must wear super-soft clothing and move like a snail to avoid the sensitive ears of game. Otherwise, he'll be detected.*

*Author Adams arrowed this enormous European wild boar after a long, tedious stalk (left). He kept the wind in his face at all times, and this is major ingredient in success.*

**Wind carries man scent above and beyond deer.**

*A tree stand normally puts the bowhunter up where upper air currents carry his scent aloft, away from wary game animals.*

A typical example is a test I conducted awhile back. I knew where about fifty wild hogs were feeding before daylight on an open flat and I deliberately walked across two main trails from this feeding ground to the brushy canyon where the pigs had been bedding during midday hours. I then walked to a higher point downwind from the hogs to wait for daylight to break.

About an hour later the animals began filtering through the trees toward me in waves of three to fifteen. Most followed the two trails I had crossed earlier, and every single hog stopped, snorted, then took off like a short-legged racehorse the instant it reached my scent trail. Even two hours later, the last stragglers heading for bedding cover reacted exactly the same way. I've encountered similar results with experiments on deer.

Obviously, a hunter should approach a stand as many hours as possible before game is likely to appear to allow his scent to fade out along his approach route. In addition, he should pick a route to his stand that does not cross areas where animals are likely to move later on.

An added precaution I'd strongly suggest is squirting some odor-masking scent like acorn, wild grape, or skunk on the soles of your shoes prior to moving in to your stand. This procedure helps to destroy the human scent you lay down when walking along.

As mentioned in the previous chapter, a hunter also is well advised to use odor-masking scent or deer lure on his

*A bedded animal like this fine old blacktail is extremely difficult to stalk successfully because he's motionless, alert for the tiniest sounds. Whiling away the midday hours in this cool spot, he won't often be caught in daylight.*

upper body to cover his game-spooking odor. An added precaution for the stand hunter is squirting some extra scent on bushes near his stand and on the trunk of the tree in which a tree stand is located. One never can be sure when the breezes will shift unexpectedly or when the odd animal will pop up in an unexpected area, but he can exercise precautions to turn such eventualities into at least possible shots at success.

The bowhunter moving along on his two hind legs has a different set of wind worries than the hunter on stand. He doesn't have the concern of masking the trail laid down by his feet, but he must constantly monitor the wind and always move directly into it or at least in a cross-wind direction.

There are several solid ways for a walking hunter to keep tabs on breeze direction. One is tapping a powder pouch and watching which way the talc floats away. Another is lighting a butane cigarette lighter, noting which way the flame leans in air currents. A third method is filtering a little fine dust through the fingers at chest level and watching which way it floats as it settles toward the ground. A fourth way is tying a fine nylon thread to the upper tip of your bow and checking this sensitive wind sock on a regular basis.

Which breeze determiner you use is strictly a matter of personal preference. I've tried them all, and they all get the job done in the slightest air currents.

The more experienced a bowhunter and the more he knows about a particular hunting area, the more skillful he is likely to be about using the wind to his advantage. For example, one area I hunt has a strong south wind before sunrise and after sundown, and a strong north wind during the rest of the day. The one exception is a deep canyon in the middle of this area — a canyon with over half a dozen predictable wind directions depending upon the side ravine being hunted. These predictable wind patterns have helped me take deer on many occasions, but until I learned the area the winds messed me over more often than they helped me out. There's no substitute for knowing a hunting area intimately when it comes to doping the wind.

*The strong, barnyard odor of the elk is easily distinguished by experienced hunters at over one hundred yards distance. If you smell them, you can make plans to proceed with stealthy stalk, or remain vigilant and let them come to you. Opposite page: The experienced bowhunter will periodically check wind direction by dropping a small handful of dust from about chest level. Keep wind in your face while stalking, or you'll be detected.*

*Opposite page: One key to successful bowhunting from tree stand is to keep body movement to a minimum, and stop noise. Note flash off this archer's belt buckle! Above: Use all of your senses, including smell. The Spanish goat found in California and on other preserves has a strong, unpleasant odor that will give away his presence.*

Knowing the game you hunt and learning to avoid an animal's defense senses are keys to bowhunting success. So is using your own senses and brain to good advantage. The human animal is a hunting machine developed over thousands of years — a machine with sharp eyes, good ears, and a fair nose designed to detect prey species in a wide variety of circumstances.

Many modern bowhunters spend the bulk of their time in cities and other environments which constantly bombard their senses with a barrage of sights, sounds, and smells. The overall effect is a dulling of these senses and a reduced awareness of the surrounding world. A bowhunter who wants to be successful must train himself to become aware of little things in the woods, sharpening his senses to detect the slightest clues to the presence of game.

A beginning bowhunter is apt to charge about the woods at much too fast a pace, neglecting the need to look, listen and smell for the game that lives there. I always have trouble slowing down and becoming aware of the little things around me on the first few days of a bowhunt because I lead a fast-paced, often frantic modern lifestyle full of obnoxious sights, smells and sounds. However, I've trained myself to calm down, slow down and once more use my God-given senses within a few days afield so I can perform as the well-developed predator that I am.

At his best, an expert bowhunter is incredibly alert and completely focused on the task at hand. The slightest crackle of a twig, the slightest shuffle of a hoof against the forest floor, the slightest movement of an ear flicking flies or the slightest odor of a nearby animal is picked up by this fine-tuned hunter. Without using his own senses in such fashion to detect game in the first place, a bowhunter has no chance to go ahead and make a successful try at penetrating the animal's own ears, eyes, and nose.

Anybody can understand how important his eyes and his ears can be in hunting game, but many may be confused about how a hunter can use his nose to good advantage. Don't kid yourself. Your nose is not nearly as well developed as that of a deer, elk or wild pig, but it can detect animal clues if you learn to use it. For example, the elk and the wild hog both have distinctive barnyard-like odors that can be smelled at a hundred yards or more. The javelina lets off a skunk-like smell from the musk gland atop its back — a solid clue to the whereabouts of this heavy-cover animal. In addition, almost any animal has a musty odor when its fur is wet. This odor is recognized easily by a tuned-in, experienced hunting archer. Use your nose as well as your other senses to improve your score on game.

Anyone can sharpen his bowhunting senses if he works at it. The major key to doing this is slowing down and taking the time to really soak up your surroundings instead of charging through them willy-nilly. The best bowhunters become a part of nature whenever they enter the woods — not intruders completely out of touch with their surroundings. The result is not only consistent success on game — it is also an ever deepening respect and appreciation for the out-of-doors and the creatures that live there.

## CHAPTER 13

Antelope water in the same places with regularity, and the smart bowhunter will capitalize on this where legal.

# TAKE A STAND!

**A**MBUSHING GAME from a stand is one of the most productive methods of hunting with a bow. Hunting on stand allows the archer to wait without the worry of creating noise or game-spooking movement. Because the stand hunter lets game come to him, his job is relatively simple once he has found a productive hunting area and has taken pains to erect a stand in a place that will yield decent shots. Stand hunting is in many ways a complex art, but can be a relaxing and fairly easy method of putting game in the bag.

Stand hunting can be effective on the majority of huntable American species, provided the hunter has the know-how to wait in a place where the odds are high of getting a close-range shot. A few unpredictable species like blacktail deer and mule deer are virtually impossible to stand hunt with consistent results, but most other species have discernible movement patterns that make them vulnerable to the observant and dedicated bowhunter.

The most easily stand-hunted species are those that faithfully follow regular daily routines. Among the animals that fit this category are whitetail deer and pronghorn antelope. Such kinds of game live in relatively small home

186

# Here Are Dos And Don'ts For Successfully Out-Waiting Game

territories and feed, water, and bed within these territories at specific times and specific places. The avid bowhunter can figure out these habit patterns by a number of means prior to setting up an ambush — a highly rewarding experience in and of itself.

A sportsman should pay close attention to various forms of animal sign when initially searching for a general area to take a stand. The best time to scout for sign is during midday when animals are tucked away in bedding areas. At this time a hunter can rummage about without spooking up-and-about game and perhaps causing animals to alter their normal daily routine.

Tracks and droppings are the primary signs a hunter should look for in a known game area, although quite a few other clues to animal movement are also important if a hunter knows what to seek. The most dependable movers like whitetail deer invariably beat out trails that are faithfully followed — trails tattooed with fresh, well-defined tracks. Similarly, the mud around waterholes where pronghorns quench their thirst at least once a day is

*Whitetail deer are natural candidates for the tree stand deer hunter, because of their predictable movement patterns. Author nailed this buck from stand near feeding area.*

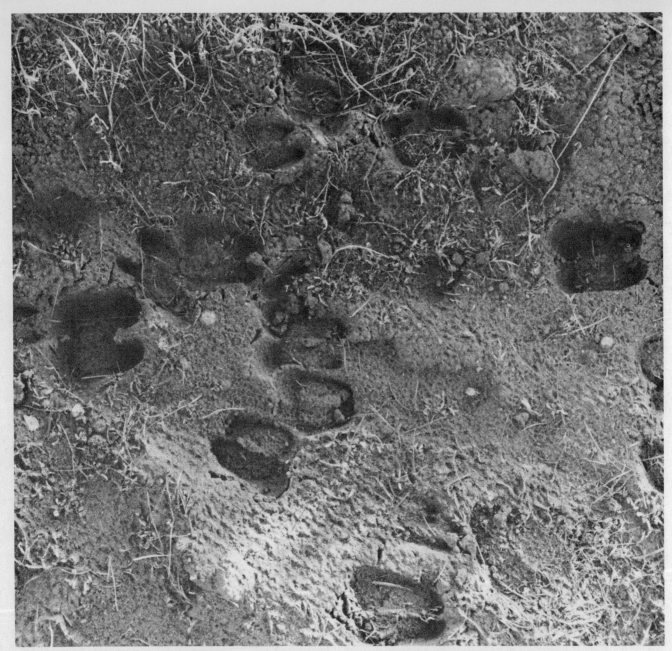

Game trails tattooed with fresh tracks mark prime places to take a bowhunting stand. The only other thing a bowhunter must determine is when animals are likely to pass by so he can be ready and waiting for action.

pock-marked with the hoofprints of these animals. Alfalfa fields and similar feeding areas for deer are the primary places droppings are found, although a fair quantity of soft, fresh dung along a deer trail marks it as a veritable animal highway.

Once a hunter has located fresh animal sign, the next step is observing the general area through binoculars from afar or actually erecting a tree stand or ground blind and spending several hours field testing various hunting locations prior to archery season.

Most of us have acquired knowledge about game in our favorite hunting areas strictly by the seats of our pants, muddling around for a few years and eventually learning a particular critter's habits in the school of hard knocks. However, the wiser way to go is doing some homework in addition to actually going afield. This speeds the process of learning to anticipate animal movements and greatly reduces the amount of time an archer needs to spend observing game before each season because he already has good ideas about where animals are likely to be at particular times of day, when they are likely to move, and where the best ambush points are likely to be located.

There is not room in the pages of this book to expand on the habits of all major species regularly bowhunted in North America. However, any library contains a wealth of outdoor lore both in books and back issues of popular outdoor magazines. The would-be bowhunter who pores over such fact-filled material will learn that whitetails prefer heavy daytime bedding cover, that they feed near brushy edges during evening, nighttime and early morning, that they normally water in the same place at least once a day, et cetera. Such facts are vital to interpreting sign and laying a successful ambush with a minimum of trial-and-error effort.

Looking for tracks and droppings is elementary work. In time, a developing woodsman picks up on more subtle but valuable information about the movement patterns of game. Rubs where rutting deer, moose or elk have battered their antlers against trees, scrapes where these same animals have pawed out shallow depressions to urinate in an attempt to attract females in heat, hair scraped off against a rough-barked tree along a regularly used path and a broken-down cattle fence where large animals like elk have bulled their way through are a few common clues to the whereabouts of animals. The list goes on and on.

Reading terrain is just as effective as reading sign when it comes to locating productive places to take a stand. Animals, like people, tend to travel along the course of least resistance, skirting heavy brush instead of wallowing through it and crossing a ridge through a saddle instead of climbing over higher ground. Even if sign is not abundant in such areas, stands placed here can produce well, especially on animals with more random movement patterns.

Whitetail deer and pronghorn antelope are the exception to the rule when it comes to following certain rigid routines within a fairly small home territory. Most other animals like

*Elusive, largely nocturnal animals like black bear betray their presence with tracks. A fresh snowfall made this bear track easy to spot (right).*

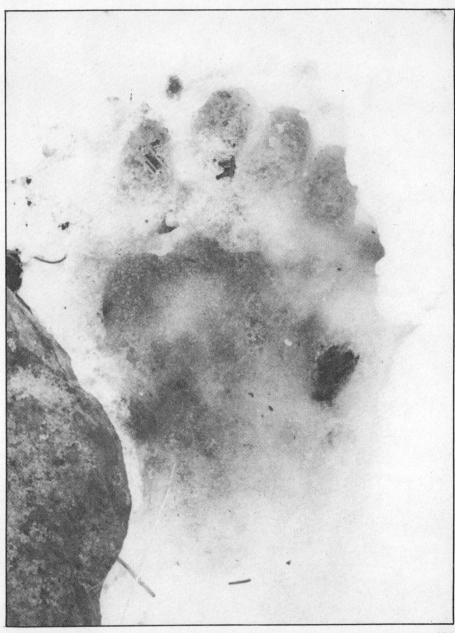

Observing a game area with binoculars can tell a bowhunter how animals move at dawn and dusk without disturbing them. This scouting procedure is especially effective on farmland whitetail deer. Ask permission first!

*The soft mud around a waterhole is an open book to the expert bowhunter who can read what the animals have written. It's also a clear indicator as to the types of animals frequenting the area — you could be surprised by the variety.*

black bear, elk, moose, blacktail deer, mule deer, Rocky Mountain goat and others have larger territories and more complex movement patterns — if there happen to be patterns at all. Virtually all of these species can be ambushed from stands, but for consistent success a hunter must look at the complete puzzle with care and spend considerable time scouting his intended hunting area. By puzzle, I mean *all* the clues that might help in properly locating a stand, including various forms of sign and an ultra-close study of terrain.

Here's an example. My favorite method of bowhunting mule deer is spotting animals from afar, planning a stalk into the wind, and then carefully closing the gap. This method works well, because I have a basically sneaky nature, because I enjoy walking far more than sitting tight for hours on end, and because I can generally hit what I shoot at out to seventy or seventy-five yards if stalking won't let me get any closer.

However, a mule deer can be taken at close range from a stand if the hunter has the time, patience and know-how to pull it off. First, he must find an area with a heavy concentration of deer. Second, he must cover lots of ground (if he is physically able) to pinpoint areas with an especially heavy littering of tracks, droppings, and other

A broken-down fence where a game trail crosses is a sure sign of elk activity in areas where both elk and deer are present. Deer jump over fences, while elk often bull their way through them (above). Opposite page: A fresh elk rub indicates that a rutting bull is probably lurking not far away. Keep ears peeled for bellowed challenges.

sign. Third, he must study terrain to locate places where deer are apt to pass when moving between bed and water, water and food, bed and food, et cetera. And fourth, he must watch the area for several days with binoculars to reinforce his notions about where deer are most likely to be at different times of the day.

From here, the bowhunter makes his best guess at a stand location and plants his fanny to wait. He may have to wait several days before an animal strolls into range, but it will probably happen eventually if he has placed his stand in a practical spot that hides his body, carries scent harmlessly away, and allows a decent shot once the animal is within solid bow range. Mule deer cannot be *consistently* taken on stand like whitetails — especially particular trophy animals — but stand hunting is a decent technique if carefully and patiently employed.

Knowing a particular kind of animal's habits well can work to a bowhunter's advantage in another way as he searches about for the ultimate place to take a stand. In many areas, bowhunting pressure is heavy enough to push animals out of their original range or make them severely alter the way they move within this range. Scouting animals carefully before season can be a total waste of time if these animals change their habits on opening day as nimrods tramp the woods, laugh and shout, tear up the landscape with dune buggies and motorcycles and proceed to behave the way some people's children are prone to act. However, the really tuned-in hunter anticipates the human factor and uses it to good advantage.

Take the blacktail deer in my native California, for example. These animals are largely unpredictable, but in a few of the public areas where I bowhunt, the unpredictable

Chewed-up prickly pear cactus is a clear sign that javelina frequent the area. No sense hunting the midget porkers in places where they aren't!

Opposite page: Don't assume the area is hot for game if you find shed antlers like the elk antler author is holding. They aren't surefire indicators with migratory animals like elk and muleys.

blacktails temporarily become quite predictable as they migrate away from hard-hunted areas after opening day. During the first week of bow season, a smart bowhunter in a well placed tree stand has his pick of nice blacktail bucks that are using convenient escape trails to relocate from five to fifteen miles to areas less congested with camo-clad bow-benders.

Realizing that enough bowhunting pressure might move animals can get your trophy, and it can also prevent the hair-tearing frustration of spending days on end in scouting only to find yourself back on square one as your well-scouted area is emptied of animals on opening day.

Let's say you have thoroughly scouted a particular game area and have found one or more specific spots where a stand is likely to pay off. The next step is deciding what sort of stand to take — ground blind, tree stand, or another — and exactly where to put it.

Deciding what kind of stand to take should be based on three major factors — the alertness level of the animal being hunted, the lay of the land, and the length of time the stand location is apt to be productive.

An extremely alert animal like a deer, elk or pronghorn requires perfect camouflage for decent results — either a ground blind, a tree stand or a natural setup of bushes and terrain that hides a well-dressed hunting archer. In contrast, an animal with a deficiency such as the near-sighted wild

## SIGN COMMONLY LEFT BY BIG-GAME ANIMALS

| Species of Game | Important Sign |
|---|---|
| Black Bear | Tracks, piles of dung, torn-up stumps and logs, hair scraped off on rough-barked trees |
| Blacktail Deer | Tracks, droppings, bedding depressions, shed antlers, used trails |
| Brown/Grizzly Bear | Tracks, piles of dung, freshly fed-on carcasses of other big game |
| Caribou | Tracks, droppings, heavily used migration trails, shed antlers in wintering areas |
| Elk | Tracks, droppings, regularly used trails, broken-down fences at trail crossings, bedding depressions, shed antlers, rubs and scrapes during rut |
| Javelina | Tracks, droppings, chewed-up prickly pear cactus, rooting marks in soft soil, peculiar musky odor in heavily used areas |
| Moose | Tracks, droppings, bedding depressions, shed antlers, rubs and scrapes during rut. |
| Mountain Sheep | Tracks, droppings, well-cut trails across steep slopes, bedding depressions |
| Mule Deer | Tracks, droppings, bedding depressions, shed antlers, antler rubs on trees |
| Pronghorn | Tracks near waterholes, shed horn shells in heavily used areas |
| Rocky Mountain Goat | Tracks in non-rocky areas, droppings, well-cut trails across steep slopes, white hair rubbed off on rocks near trails |
| Whitetail Deer | Tracks, droppings, heavily used trails, bedding depressions in thickets, shed antlers, rubs and scrapes during rut |
| Wild Boar | Tracks, piles of dung, rooting marks in grassy areas, wallowing depressions in wet mud |

*Left: A large saddle in a high ridge provides a natural pass for game. A bowhunter who first studies track patterns in such a place can set up successful ambushes on a regular basis. Above: Chart tells sign to expect for game animals.*

*Although generally unpredictable, a blacktail buck like the author's nice trophy can sometimes be waylaid as it flees heavy opening-day bowhunting pressure along established migration trails.*

pig can be ambushed more leisurely by simply leaning motionlessly against a tree or sitting in front of a bush.

The lay of the land has a great deal to do with where a stand ought to be placed. Common sense should be your major guide. If there are no trees, a tree stand is obviously out of the question. If rocks, logs and bushes are arranged a particular way, a natural blind might be formed with minimal effort. If foliage is scanty, a commercial ground blind might be just the ticket.

When deciding on blind placement, you should always have the camouflage and wind direction suggestions in Chapter 12 firmly in mind. You should also try to develop a setup that allows easy shooting at an unalarmed animal. It is fine and dandy to sit quietly and have a monstrous trophy come tripping within ten or fifteen yards. However, if the critter is looking your way all the while, how on earth can you draw and take a shot? My favorite blind setup gives me a clear view of areas where game might materialize, yet requires animals to either walk past before I draw my bow or disappear behind cover for at least a few seconds before they pop out again in solid bow range. In either case, I can ready myself and draw without being seen, leaving only one well placed shot between me and a trophy on the meat pole.

*Natural cover can form an adequate blind, provided the bowhunter is dressed to blend with foliage.*

The length of time a stand is apt to be productive is a consideration every bowhunter must roll around in his mind before he lays an ambush. With animals like whitetail deer, which live their entire lives within one square mile, a permanent tree house overlooking a year-round water source is an excellent way to go. Such a blind will be consistently productive year in and year out.

By contrast, building a permanent stand near an elk meadow with regular feeding activity would be a solid mistake, because elk often use one area for a week or two, then relocate and never use that area again. A better bet after locating elk would be to erect a portable climbing tree stand that can be taken down and easily backpacked to another area where elk have temporarily set up housekeeping.

Again, an intimate knowledge of the game you hunt is especially important if you decide to bowhunt from a stand.

In situations where animal activity is likely to be extremely short-lived, I prefer to dispense with conventional stand equipment and use natural, existing cover to help me lay an ambush. For example, I once

*This buck had to pass behind a large oak tree while following a well-used deer trail — a situation tailor-made for drawing a hunting bow without being seen. You can find such spots.*

*There are occasions in which bowhunter can make use of natural elements for his stand. But...*

arrowed a black bear after finding a deer the animal was feeding on and taking a stand near the rotting carcass that very night. My blind was a four-foot-deep hole backed by the dirt-clogged roots of a fallen pine tree. The hole completely hid two-thirds of my body, and the mass of roots broke the outline of my chest, arms, and head. The bear came sauntering in just before dark, a nice, cinnamon-colored specimen with a large white blaze across his chest. One careful shot at twenty yards laced both lungs for a quick, clean kill.

Another time, I shot a nice Montana whitetail from the top of a haystack as the animal moseyed past to munch on the leavings in a freshly harvested grainfield. A couple of weeks later not one deer could be seen in the area because rains had ruined the grain and because an alfalfa field a quarter-mile away provided tender, fresh sprouts to eat.

A word of caution here. Any time you take a natural stand, be extremely careful not to get yourself into situations where you can fall and/or cut yourself severely with a broadhead. Solid commercial tree stands are safe to use, but haystacks, tree limbs and other inviting elevated stands can be shaky and potentially dangerous perches,

*...be sure it will support you! This nimrod was beaned by bale, but luckily unhurt.*

especially if a hunter does not have conventional safety gear like a hoist rope or tree-stand safety belt. Several bowhunters are hurt each year from falls out of trees, off stacks of hay, out of windmills beside stock pounds, etc. Watch your step and use your noggin at all times.

Although the majority of bowhunters take stands to ambush animals along natural movement routes, stands can also be used with good effect when game is somehow lured within range of the hunter.

Perhaps the most common application of stands in luring animals occurs during the whitetail deer rut, an event that often overlaps archery hunting seasons. At this time of year — which varies from area to area — a potent doe-in-heat scent sprinkled near a stand will suck in amorous bucks like honey draws flies. This circumstance is also discussed in Chapter 11.

Actually, many game animals can be lured to a stand if the hunter knows what he's doing. Where legal, a well-placed bait will regularly attract black bear, wild pigs, and other sharp-nosed carrion eaters. A baiting bowhunter usually sits in a tree stand or ground blind, and often enjoys shots at fifteen yards or less.

*A sharp-toothed predator like the red fox can often be lured to a mouth-blown dying-rabbit call.*

*Many kinds of large and small game can be baited within shooting range of a stand. This camp robber — a feathered, north-country pest — was shot after it swooped down on a baitpile of table scraps. Make sure baiting is legal.*

*Pronghorn antelope can sometimes be "flagged" into bow range with a white handkerchief waved above grass or brush. These animals are extremely curious by nature, and often walk right up to such a flag if hunter's hidden.*

Calling is another common bowhunting technique that requires a hunter to carefully take a stand. A wide variety of game can be called into bow range, including wild turkey, elk, deer, moose and various predators like foxes and coyotes. Coaxing a tom turkey to the lovelorn yelp of a hen, a bull elk to the bugle of a rival bull, or a coyote to the terror-filled shriek of a dying jackrabbit is an extremely exciting method of hunting, and a very effective method as well if the archer takes a stand that successfully hides him from alert, searching eyes.

Although calling game is often a spontaneous hunting technique used when a receptive animal appears or makes nearby noise, the ideal stand to take when calling is not a hastily kicked hole in the brush. Because any called creature is zeroed in on the source of the sound being made, a hunter must be completely hidden to give him a decent chance at success. A suitable tree stand or ground blind provides the ideal cover, but if a hunter needs to call on the spur of the moment — if a bull elk suddenly tunes up in a nearby thicket, or if a coyote suddenly slinks out of a nearby brushpile, as examples — this hunter should carefully plant himself in front of outline-breaking cover and hope his body camouflage is good enough to do the trick.

Note: Whenever taking a stand in natural cover, never sit on stand behind cover like a bush or stump on the theory that this cover will hide you well. It is far better to stay in front of cover so you can see clearly without having to bob your head and shoot clearly without potential bow or arrow interference. If your clothing is camouflaged and your face properly concealed, you should blend in relatively well with whatever backdrop you choose.

Taking a stand is a highly effective bowhunting method when properly employed. A smart, versatile nimrod learns as much about stand hunting as he possibly can and uses this information whenever he has the chance. The results are extreme satisfaction and consistent success on all sorts of huntable game.

An archer on foot can take most kinds of game on a regular basis, provided he uses proper camouflage clothing and exercises patience at all times.

## CHAPTER 14

# ALL ABOUT

ALTHOUGH BOWHUNTING from a stand is an easier, less complicated way to bag game, the skillful foot hunter will experience greater thrills and greater challenge in his effort to move within bow range of wary animals. In addition, a fellow who has truly mastered the art of hunting on his two hind legs is a more versatile and a more consistently deadly predator than any stand hunter; he has a chance to strike with success virtually any time he detects the presence of game.

There is nothing easy about bowhunting on foot, which is probably the main reason the majority of archers prefer to sit on stand. The foot hunter must be in relatively good physical condition, must be alert as new terrain rolls into view and must use his brain continually to plan walking strategy that matches the constantly changing terrain. This is an active, intense sport that separates the experts from the neophytes.

There is unique satisfaction associated with being able to spot a squirrel, javelina, deer or moose and sneak in close

no matter what the terrain or what the animal happens to be doing. Such confidence is developed only over years of hunting experience, but such confidence can be justified completely if an archer has worked hard enough to fully master himself plus the ins and outs of nature and the wary game that lives there.

Stand hunting is a highly effective method on certain species, but skillful hunting on foot is a more universally productive endeavor. It is also a more spontaneous adventure, requiring no preseason trail scouting or stand building to ensure meat in the freezer.

An expert foot hunter with a bow in his fist can enter any game-rich area with the good chance of taking the animal or bird he is after. The same cannot be said of a hunter who feels hamstrung without a tree stand or blind to settle down in. Every year, hundreds of eastern whitetail deer hunters head west to sample the joys of bowhunting elk, mule deer, Rocky Mountain goat, caribou, moose and other unpredictable Western big game. They are shocked

# HUNTING
# ON FOOT

severely when they realize the hard way that these animals are not easily ambushed from a stand.

The bowhunter without walking skill and without a week or more to watch mule deer, mountain goats, Spanish goats or similar quarry will experience total frustration as he either bumbles about the countryside on foot or attempts to wait out animals that never show up. Were a hunter stubborn and naive enough, he might sit unsuccessfully the whole season in one spot, as animals regularly appeared within five hundred yards of his stand.

By contrast, the capable sneaking bowhunter would throw a stalk on the first desirable animal he saw and run a reasonably good chance of creeping into range. A skillful foot hunter is far more versatile than any stand-only hunter, able to take a stand if the situation dictates, but also able to roll with the punches and bail out of his stand, if a distant animal lingers around or to give up standing entirely if conditions require steady movement on foot.

Although bowhunting on foot is a complex and taxing pastime, there is absolutely nothing magic about taking animals in this way. The hunter must pay strict attention to the tips in Chapter 12 on how to penetrate an animal's defenses and how to use his own senses, concentrating on moving slowly in the presence of game to make darn sure he does not slip up and allow himself to be seen, heard, or smelled.

Also abundantly important is the hunter's ability to spot, hear and smell animals before they locate him, an ability that requires patience, slow movement, and concentration, but no magical or mysterious ingredients. A skillful foot hunter has developed his talents through plenty of thoughtful time afield — a feat anyone with average abilities can duplicate if he works at it on a continuing basis.

Although bowhunting on foot is more difficult than sitting on a stand, a well developed foot hunter is operating under no handicap at all as he attempts to take game in this way. The mental and physical energy expended when stalking, stillhunting, jumpshooting or otherwise trying for game on the ground is far greater than that expended by someone sitting in one spot, but a good foot hunter will take as much or more game than a good stand hunter in the same hunting area.

There are notable exceptions which must be recognized

*Below: Unpredictable, open-country animals like the Rocky Mountain goat are best bowhunted on foot instead of from a stand. Opposite page: A stalk over wide-open terrain produced this fat, middle-sized muley meat buck for author Adams. Careful hunting on foot often pays off on game species without set feeding, bedding, and movement patterns.*

*The author took this big whitetail buck from a stand after deciding the woods were much too dry for bowhunting on foot. A flexible archer adapts to individual situations, hunting on foot when this method is best and hunting from a stand if foot hunting is out of the question because of noisy footing or other negative walking factors.*

here. When the footing is virtually impossible to negotiate quietly, as in the dry autumn whitetail woods, or when the terrain offers no cover at all, as on table-flat antelope plains, an avid foot hunter is far better off taking a stand in a potentially productive area. Part of consistent success at bowhunting is knowing when to pass on a particular hunting technique — even if it is your favorite — and wisely employ another.

A major reason for perfecting your foot-hunting skills should be the intense satisfaction that comes from pulling off this especially difficult method of taking game. One friend of mine bowhunted deer for years from tree stands with excellent success, gradually becoming bored with the long waits in the air and the easy ten or fifteen-yard shots that invariably resulted. The turning point of his bowhunting career came one day when he spotted a nice

whitetail buck feeding two hundred yards away, silently climbed out of his tree stand, and managed to stalk within thirty yards of the animal without being detected. He missed the shot clean, possibly because he never had shot at a deer that far away before, but he was so thrilled by the whole experience that he sold his tree stand and took to sneaking about the woods instead. He bags just as many deer today as he ever did and says he enjoys bowhunting ten times as much. He also says he'll never take a stand again no matter what the situation.

Being a practical sort of fellow, I firmly believe a bowhunter should employ the tactic which nets him the most reward. If I feel I have as good a chance sneaking around as sitting on stand, I'll generally put on my walking shoes. However, if a stand makes more sense in a particular situation I'll be the first one to sit tight and wait. As I've

*Above: A walking bowhunter must be skillful at penetrating the fine-honed senses of all sorts of game, including wary varmints like the big-eared jackrabbit. Below: In addition, a sneaking archer should use his own senses to detect game before game detects him and flees. There are three deer in this photo — can you find them all?*

*Above: The use of binoculars is quite important in stillhunting, allowing the archer to spot small parts of animals in heavy cover that might be overlooked by the naked eye. Opposite page: Some unusual trophies can be taken incidentally while sneaking along. The author nailed this big rattlesnake with a ten-yard shot while stillhunting.*

said before, a bowhunter should be flexible, rolling with the punches and constantly changing his strategy to make sure his game tag is filled before the season is over.

Several basic foot-hunting methods are normally employed by bowhunters. A seasoned hunter knows when to use each to good advantage, matching a specific method to a specific set of hunting circumstances.

Stillhunting is a walking technique used in areas with heavy or semi-heavy cover. It is especially effective when topography is too flat to allow a good, consistent view of distant terrain where animals might be moving about.

This particular bowhunting strategy requires more mental concentration than any other, and also requires the

quietest, most perfectly camouflaged clothing for best results.

The stillhunting archer moves slowly through a likely game area, picking his route with care to find the quietest footing, staying away from noisy brush and trees, maintaining excellent concealment, and keeping the prevailing breezes more or less in his face. The general procedure is taking a step or two, stopping to peer carefully around, then moving a step or two more.

Stillhunting is blind hunting, with game likely to be nearby at all times but not likely to be seen until it is already within solid bow range. As a result, the stillhunter must never drop his guard, always assuming a deer is behind

the next bush and constantly trying to see that deer before that deer sees him.

This can be a mentally draining bowhunting method, but it is effective in areas with high densities of animals inhabiting heavy cover. The major key to stillhunting success is never to become impatient, even if game has not been sighted for hours. An archer who becomes disgusted and charges ahead will spook most animals in the area without even knowing it; those he does walk within range of will see him before he sees them, making a shot next to impossible as they either bound away or eyeball him intently with muscles bunched to flee before he gets the bowstring back even halfway to his face.

Because stillhunting is a heavy-cover activity, the archer using this tactic should wear especially soft-surfaced clothing to dampen scrapes against foliage to an inaudible whisper. My favorite stillhunting outfit in all but the warmest weather consists of head-to-ankle wool because nothing else is quite as quiet in brush and trees.

As mentioned, camouflage must be especially complete because shots often present themselves at point-blank range which lets an animal spot the slightest human clue. Needless to say, footwear must be soled with neoprene or an equally soft, quiet walking material.

Because a good stillhunter moves with the speed of cold syrup, he always should wear a potent odor-masking scent to cover human odor drifting away from his position when breezes cease entirely or when they swirl unpredictably in heavy cover. He should check breezes regularly with the powder in a powder pouch, the flame of a cigarette lighter, or another means discussed in Chapter 12.

Quality binoculars are extremely important in stillhunting, because they help the archer scrutinize objects screened by brush that might turn out to be parts of

*Opposite page: A stalking bowhunter lets his eyes do most of the walking, carefully glassing surrounding terrain for animals he might be able to creep up on. Below: The moose is one of many animals that can often be spotted from a distance, then stalked successfully with extreme caution after an approach route has been decided upon.*

*Open-country animals like caribou are sometimes seen in areas where stalking is next to impossible. In such cases, the bowhunter can only wait for animals to move — either that, or go find some other trophies to stalk instead.*

animals. Even at twenty-five or thirty yards, the human eye alone cannot always identify small parts of an animal that are easily recognized when magnified seven or eight times through clear, well-focused field glasses.

Animals commonly stillhunted include whitetail deer, blacktail deer, elk, black bear, javelina, wild boar and moose. Obviously, this technique can be applied only to species preferring semi-dense cover which allows quiet, steady walking and provides a short-range view.

The best time to stillhunt game is during a light drizzle or when fog is dense enough to load up on foliage and drip to the ground. Both situations give the archer an edge, because the moisture makes footing silent, covers most sounds with the patter of water drops and also tends to obscure an animal's view of a slow-moving hunter. The nimrod in such a situation cannot normally hear an animal, either, but he can use his eyes to good advantage.

Although stillhunting is the most intensely demanding of bowhunting sports, stalking is probably the most interesting and exciting for serious bowhunters. This method can be used in any hunting area that provides a good view of surrounding terrain and also provides ample sneaking cover in the form of brush, trees, and broken landscape. Stalking is a particularly fruitful technique in mountain or foothill country with ridges or peaks which can be used as vantage points to survey nearby real estate.

The stalking bowhunter first moves into a likely hunting area and takes a prominent position with a view, then lets his eyes do most of the walking until a sneakable animal is spotted. It is not uncommon for a good stalker to sit for hours on the same vantage point with his eyes glued to binoculars, sweeping visible game terrain over and over in search of feeding, watering, or resting animals. First-rate binoculars are extremely important in this particular form

*To prevent serious injury, always keep arrows safely tucked away in your arrow quiver whenever you negotiate rugged terrain. Veterans like Jim Dougherty (above with bow) know how dangerous an exposed broadhead can be during a fall.*

of bowhunting, probably more so than in any other phase of hunting with archery equipment.

Once a bowhunter spots an animal from afar, the next step is deciding whether or not he wants to try a stalk. The serious trophy hunter's first consideration will be whether the animal is good enough to warrant the effort. In contrast, a less persnickety archer won't worry about the size of antlers or horns, if present at all, and will make his decision based on the length and the difficulty of the stalk.

If a hunter finds an animal he wants to approach, he must survey the landscape between him and the animal to determine if a feasible approach route exists. Although a skillful, physically fit bowhunter can stalk the vast majority of animals he sees, there are times when a successful sneak within range is next to impossible because of factors beyond his control. For example, if an animal is bedded on a wide-open slope with the wind at its back and its eyes

surveying every inch of ground for one hundred yards in front and to the sides, the bowhunter who attempts an approach will be a sunk duck for sure. The only way to avoid the animal's eyes in such a situation is from directly behind, but the wind cancels out this approach route completely.

Normally, however, the stalking hunter can plan a potentially successful approach on an animal based on wind direction, concealing terrain, the presence of other animals in the area, and similar factors. It is solid fun to locate an animal, then try to solve the problem of sneaking within bow range. Once a plan is devised, the next step is executing the sneak as quickly and unobtrusively as possible.

Unlike stillhunting, stalking does not always require slow, monotonous movement through game country. As a matter of fact, a stalker often can move at breakneck speed

on an animal until he approaches within a hundred or so yards, dropping into a deep ravine, staying in heavy trees or otherwise completely hiding himself until he can move into position for a slow, final approach. Because wind direction can switch during an extended period of time, and because the target animal might decide to move substantially if left too long, a speedy initial approach is often a must for a decent chance of making a stalk pay off.

Caution: Whenever moving rapidly over rough terrain, always keep all hunting arrows in your bow quiver to prevent the possibility of being severely cut during a fall.

Once the bowhunter moves into hearing and/or seeing position of an animal, he must slow down to a creep and execute the final stalk with the same painstaking care exercised in stillhunting. The stalker has a decided advantage over the stillhunter, however, because he knows

at least approximately where his target animal is likely to be.

Aside from the normal hazards associated with trying to approach any animal, the stalker must be especially alert for other animals in his path that might spoil his stalk. Weaseling through a maze of animals to get at one particular trophy is never easy, but can be accomplished if the hunter thinks before he moves, exercises considerable patience, and manages to have Lady Luck on his side. What he must *never* do is yield to the temptation to rivet his whole attention on the target animal and fail to be alert for other game in the area. The result of such an oversight is often a snort followed by the thundering hooves of a completely overlooked animal that was standing, feeding or bedded along the hunter's approach path.

Animals most often stalked include the mule deer,

*Different hunting methods work best in different situations. Opposite page: Jumpshooting is a fine way to bag tight-sticking jackrabbits in grassy country, and is also excellent practice for jumpshooting big game in heavy cover. Below: Stalking is often the best method on deer in semi-open terrain with quiet footing, provided the archer pays close attention to* all *deer in the area to avoid detection as he weasels in for the kill.*

*Opposite page: The number of bowhunters needed for a successful drive varies considerably from area to area and situation to situation. Famous archer Joe Johnston (foreground), two partners, and the author were enough to drive wild boar on one successful bowhunt in California. Above: Another often-used boar-hunting method is baying up a hog with the help of a well-seasoned, hard-driving dog like a hound or this German shorthair pointer.*

open-country elk, pronghorn antelope, moose, Rocky Mountain goat, wild sheep, caribou and various exotic animals such as Spanish goats, mouflon sheep, and the like.

Small animals like woodchucks, ground squirrels and jackrabbits are often vulnerable to this technique as well.

Stalking is a complex and extremely interesting sport, a sport that builds excitement to fever pitch as a hunter draws nearer and nearer to the animal he wants to bag. It requires more raw stamina than any other form of bowhunting because stalks often cover several miles across rough, broken terrain.

Jumpshooting is a very specialized and seldom-used bowhunting technique. This particular method should never be employed if another bowhunting approach is possible, mainly because the shooting is difficult if a shot presents itself at all.

This technique is used when big-game animals like deer are sticking tight in heavy cover during all daylight hours. Such a situation occurs occasionally when weather gets exceptionally warm, when the moon is full and animals are feeding only at night or when hunting pressure has forced game to lie low during daylight hours.

In such a case, all a hunter can do is ease along in stillhunting fashion near heavy bedding cover with the hope that animals will spring up and run away in view.

Jumpshooting can be an effective technique on tight-sticking big game in heavy cover, provided the archer has trained himself to shoot well on close, moving targets. An ideal form of shooting practice for this particular bowhunting method is jumping jackrabbits or cottontails in thick cover and snap-shooting arrows at them as they speed away. An archer who deliberately practices such shooting can become surprisingly good at it, developing a feel and a sense of timing only regular shooting can perfect.

The same skills involved in jumpshooting are used in shooting at other moving targets like flying birds and swimming fish. It is usually a good idea to refrain from shooting at running big game because of the increased risk of crippling hits, but a good jumpshot with a bow can take game when everyone else is hanging his head in frustration.

In a few ultra-dense hunting areas such as those found along seacoasts and in the Deep South, driving is the only feasible method of moving whitetail deer, blacktail deer and similar animals within range of bowhunters. Driving is really a combination of foot hunting and stand hunting, with several archers moving through heavy cover toward other archers posted in tree stands or ground blinds. When properly executed, a bowhunting drive can produce decent shots for the archers on stand, and occasionally yielding shots for the walkers as well.

Driving obviously requires several hunters working according to a carefully formulated plan. Exactly how many archers are needed varies depending on the terrain, but five is normally a practical minimum. Drive hunters must know a particular patch of cover well to anticipate which routes pushed animals are likely to take when drivers move through in a particular direction. Armed with this knowledge, two or more bowhunters can move in silently to cover these escape routes, alert for the quick shot that might present itself.

To be successful, drivers must stillhunt quietly along, allowing animals to sneak away instead of pushing these animals past standers at breakneck speed. By moving slowly and carefully, stillhunters sometimes push animals to each other as well.

Even when animals are driven properly, they are completely alert and extremely difficult for a shot. A hunter must snap-shoot a driven animal as it runs away or draw when natural cover blocks off the animal's eyes. In either case, shooting is apt to be a tricky proposition.

Hound hunting such species as black bear, wild boar and mountain lion is a highly rewarding sport often requiring strenuous hiking to keep up with dogs and reach a treed or bayed animal. I've taken several nice trophies in this manner and thoroughly enjoy the hound music of the chase and the thrill of seeing an animal treed or bayed within a few short yards.

Nonetheless, nobody with widespread outdoor experience would dream of calling such activity a bowhunt. The shooting is often tricky on animals stopped by hounds: tree limbs block a clear shot, a shot is sharply upward or an animal is moving about on the ground with dogs and/or natural cover in the way. However, the actual hunting is done by the dogs — not by the archer — and the shooting is often a fish-in-a-barrel proposition.

I make no apology for hunting behind hounds with a bow in my hand, but I'd never pretend this was a bowhunting activity. Except in rare instances, a trophy treed or bayed by hounds is a gonner regardless of what shooting tool is used be it bow, handgun, muzzleloader or high-powered rifle.

No matter what technique is used, bowhunting on foot can be enjoyable, invigorating, and highly productive. It generally requires more mental intensity and razor-sharp skill than hunting on stand, but the rewards make this extra difficulty seem minor by comparison.

*Opposite page: An animal like the black bear makes an interesting, exciting trophy, but shooting such an animal from a tree is usually no large task for a good shot with a bow. Below: treeing game with the help of hounds is a rewarding sport, but the fun comes from watching and hearing the dogs — not from actually hunting with a bow.*

Knowing the exact distance to game can make the critical different between shooting success and failure. Chuck Adams used an optical rangefinder to get the range on this nice-sized, butter-fat five-point bull elk.

# CHAPTER 15

# THE HOW OF SHOOTING AT GAME

## ...With Notes On Where And When!

SHOOTING AT game is a quick, relatively simple event. However, the outcome of many days of pre-season preparation and long hours of ticklish hunting hinge on this short-lived performance of muscles, eyes, and brain. If the hunter draws his bow at the proper time and places an arrow in the proper spot, the next few hours will be packed with smiles, handshakes and a generally happy time. If he does one little thing wrong from the time he contemplates taking a shot until the arrow reaches his target, the outcome will be at best worrisome and at worst a complete and lingering disappointment.

The complicated chore of getting within bow range of a living target is difficult enough, but actually hitting that target is often more difficult still. The problems an archer must cope with are deciding how close is close enough, accurately estimating the range to the target, knowing when to draw to ensure a decent shot at the vitals, somehow drawing an arrow wihtout being seen or heard, then carefully placing that arrow in a quick-kill zone of the anatomy.

Additional things the bowhunter must concentrate on when taking a shot are where he thinks the arrow has actually hit, where the animal goes after being hit and how to get a second shot if taking such a shot seems immediately necessary.

The first things a bowhunter must decide when he finds himself within close range of an animal have to do with the distance to that animal. First, exactly how far away is the animal? And second, is the animal close enough to provide a reasonably good chance of a killing hit?

The smart tree-stand or ground-stand hunter makes a point of knowing exact distances to nearby landmarks where game is likely to appear. This is made easy with a handy, belt-carried optical rangefinder. The stalking or stillhunting archer also takes frequent distance readings on prominent landmarks ahead, especially when he believes a deer or similar trophy is lurking nearby. In addition, a bowhunter with a rangefinder can often take a reading directly off an animal if the creature is stationary and unable to see the movement involved in taking such a reading.

In some circumstances, a foot-hunting archer must estimate the distance to game by eye, a procedure every nimrod should practice in case he cannot use an optical rangefinder, because there is no time or the animal is apt to spot the necessary movement.

Once a bowhunter knows the distance to his trophy, the next thing he must decide is whether or not the shot is close enough for comfort. Every practiced archer knows his accurate shooting limits on targets, but other factors besides target capability often enter the picture in field shooting.

Is the wind blowing hard enough to drift the arrow off target between you and the animal? Is the animal tensed up and likely to move before the arrow reaches it? Are you winded from a stiff climb or jittery enough from the excitement of seeing game to shorten your normal effective shooting distance? Or is your body position too awkward to allow an accurate shot at the shooting distance facing you? These and other questions should be considered by a bowhunter before he ever raises his bow to shoot.

If there is any doubt about whether you are capable of pulling off a particular shot, it is often best to refrain from shooting and try to get closer or otherwise improve your chances of success. For example, if you are stalking a deer and have a marginal chance at maximum range, it is best to pass up the chance if you think you can set up a closer shot with some more careful sneaking. However, an experienced woodsman will sometimes take a marginal shot if he knows the odds of getting a better one are slim.

I sometimes take low-percentage shots when stalking unpredictable animals like elk or sitting in a tree stand where the only two options open are taking the shot or passing it up. As discussed later in this chapter, a truly sharp broadhead will kill an animal with virtually any solid hit, making long-distance or low-percentage shooting perfectly acceptable despite the ignorant claims of some that such shooting often results in wasted animals.

In the final analysis, there is no rock-solid rule to follow when deciding whether or not to take a particular shot that presents itself. The hunter must simply weigh the factors involved, then make a subjective decision about whether to

*Hitting an ultra-small target like a ground squirrel's head requires well-practiced shooting ability. However, such a shot can be made if a bowhunter knows the range, knows his shooting limitations, and takes the shot with confidence.*

hold off in hopes of a better shot, pass up the animal entirely and wait for another, or shoot as carefully and confidently as possible and hope for the best. When making this judgment, there is simply no substitute for lots of field experience and a thorough knowledge of your own capabilities and weaknesses.

Let's assume you've managed to get within bow range of an animal or bird and have decided to take a shot as soon as possible. The next step is picking the best instant to draw, anchor and aim your bow.

If the target is relaxed and likely to stay within range for a while — bedded, feeding or lounging around — then you probably have some time to play with. However, it is always best to take the first good shooting opportunity that presents itself because the longer you wait, the better the chance that factors like wind, other hunters, or nearby animals will spoil the chance entirely.

You should consider two factors when looking for the perfect opportunity to shoot. One is your own ability to shoot well; the other is the ability of your target to see or hear you draw your bow.

If you are breathing hard or have your feet tangled when

*Left: A bowhunter must carefully time his draw on deer and similarly alert critters to make sure they do not see the movement and bolt away before the sights can be settled on the target and the shot smoothly taken.*

game is before you, by all means take the time to calm down or reposition your body for the shot. Only move when it is perfectly safe to do so; impatience at this point is an absolute no-no. Once you are composed to take the shot, scrutinize the target animal carefully and go for the first decent shooting opportunity.

On keen-eyed species like deer and elk, a hunter never should draw his bow unless his target's eyes are obscured by brush, trees or similar obstacles or unless the animal is facing almost directly away. Being aware of and avoiding an animal's peripheral vision is discussed in detail in Chapter 12.

If an animal is relaxed and likely to give you the shot you want eventually, wait the situation out. Even if the creature is bedded facing you within good bow range with eyes peeled for danger, it makes perfect sense to wait even if the wait lasts several hours. The animal will rise presently and mill around, giving you the one perfect chance you need.

If there seems to be no hope of getting an ideal shot at game, a hunter must make the best of a bad situation. For example, an animal within good range that is alerted and boring holes through you with its eyes will not calm down again, so the best you can do is draw slowly and smoothly, hoping the animal stays put until the arrow is on its way. I have shot several animals in this manner, nailing them as they stood transfixed or hitting them as they turned to run. In either case, solid hits put them in the bag as surely as animals I have taken under less stressful circumstances.

No matter what the shooting situation, knowing where to aim on an animal is extremely important to success. Every wild creature has certain vital zones that promote near-instant death when hit with a sharp hunting arrow. A hunter should know how to reach these zones from several angles to make the most of shooting opportunities that present themselves. In addition, several more marginal areas also can be hit with positive results if a bowhunter knows where he has hit and proceeds correctly from there. A thorough knowledge of animal anatomy is an important ingredient for consistent success on game.

A hunter should be concerned about where he places his shots on big, tough-to-drop animals like deer, bear and elk, but he also should place his shots with care on other game as well. Even a two-pound ground squirrel can wriggle down its hole if hit in the paunch instead of the lungs, while other tenacious game like jackrabbits, woodchucks, coyotes, and wild turkeys also require pinpoint shots for positive results. The following discussion of where to hit animals applies primarily to big game like deer, but never shoot at *any* game haphazardly; always pick a vital zone and aim at the center of this zone with painstaking care.

If possible, the ideal place to aim at any animal or bird is the vital chest cavity. This cavity rides in the forward one-third of the body and houses lungs, heart and major arteries leading away from the heart. A hit here normally results in extremely quick death, although a fluke hit that passes through the chest and misses all vital organs can take somewhat longer to do its work.

The center of the chest cavity is the best place to aim on any animal because a hit here will slice through one or both lungs for a fast kill. A near miss usually will drop the animal, too, because the spine and aortic artery are above, the heart is below and the liver is behind. If possible, aim for the lungs on any animal if you think you can get an arrow into them. The only time this may not be possible is if an animal is facing directly away, although a powerful hunting bow is capable of punching an arrow into the lungs on a deer-sized animal from this angle, if it isn't slowed by impact with heavy bones in the rear.

*Although a bowhunter should wait for a decent opportunity to draw his bow and shoot, he should always take the first acceptable chance that presents itself. Otherwise, the animal might decide to walk away, ruining the setup entirely.*

*If possible, a bowhunter should wait until a deer has its head behind a solid obstacle before drawing his bow to shoot. However, a deer that looks directly away cannot see drawing movement, either — something to remember if there are no bushes, rocks, or trees nearby to shield an animal's searching eyes.*

A solid lung hit normally produces death within ten seconds or less. An arrow entering the lungs from the side or slightly behind usually makes a dull, watermelon plunk as it penetrates, especially if it slices off a rib on the way. A big-game animal's reaction when hit here varies, depending on the animal and the circumstance, but the most common reaction is a frantic run with body held low to the ground, feet stretching strongly to maintain maximum speed. A deer or similar animal hit through the lungs with an arrow can run fifty to two hundred yards before it drops — a distance easily covered in ten seconds or less by a charging four-footed animal. As a result, there is no reason to be alarmed should you hit an animal through the lung area and it runs completely out of sight.

A common misconception is that most animals hit with an arrow die from loss of blood. This is true enough with arrow hits in arteries and veins, but a normal hit in a place like the lungs causes vital functions to cease and kills for other reasons. In the case of the lung hit, an animal suffocates from lack of oxygen because its air center has

been entirely taken out. Lung-shot animals bleed like all arrow-shot game, but this blood loss has little to do with the cause of death.

The blood left behind from a lung hit is bright in color — often pinkish in cast — and prone to be frothy because it is full of air. Contrary to popular belief, lung-hit animals often leave little or no blood on the ground as they race away, so don't assume you've made a poor hit just because you can't find blood to follow. An animal shot anywhere in the middle upper chest sometimes bleeds internally, especially when the arrowhead fails to exit or when it exits through the paunch.

Another factor that sometimes makes a lung hit difficult to blood-trail is the fast clip at which the animal leaves the scene. Even if the animal is dropping fair amounts of blood, a speedy exit from the area does not leave much blood in any one spot.

Bowhunters seldom aim at the heart because this organ lies so low in the chest cavity, and because it is often at least partially covered by an animal's leg bones.

Sometimes a bowhunter gets caught flat-footed by an alert animal, and must either take a shot then and there or forever hold his peace. The wild boar in this photo was alerted by a non-bowhunting guide's light-colored shirt, and the archer with him lost the animal because he didn't shoot at once (both hunters appear as out-of-focus blobs at right).

Nevertheless, heart hits are a common occurrence in the bowhunting woods because archers often hit slightly lower than where they've aimed or shoot down through the lungs from a tree stand to hit the heart incidentally as the arrow is leaving the body.

Regardless of why an arrow hits the heart, this shot placement is a solid winner because it completely stops the blood pump and immobilizes the animal's entire circulatory system. The result is a death every bit as quick as that with a lung hit — sometimes quicker — because the animal passes out from lack of oxygen flowing to the brain.

An animal's reaction to a heart hit is almost always frantic. I've seen deer rear up like stallions, kick backward like mules and perform other interesting gyrations after an arrow smacked into the heart. The thump of a heart hit is often louder than that of a lung hit because bones often are nicked as the arrow penetrates flesh.

After being hit and leaping involuntarily, a heart-shot animal runs in a blind, frantic attempt to escape. If anything, this run is even more desperate than that resulting from a lung hit. Again, a heart-shot deer is often found a full 150 or two hundred yards from the point where it was hit.

The blood left by a heart hit is deep red in color. Unless the arrow has reached the heart from above or behind and failed to exit the body, the resulting blood trail usually is easy to follow because blood is spilling from a wound low in the chest instead of being trapped inside.

A hit in the spine is another common occurrence when bowhunting big game because an arrow goes high of the mark or because a hunter is shooting almost directly downward at an animal from an elevated stand.

A solid spine hit with a reasonably heavy arrow from a relatively fast-shooting bow is always an instant winner, knocking the animal down in its tracks as the broadhead crushes bone and discombobulates the entire central nervous system.

An arrow makes a loud crack when it hits the spine — a sound similar to that of a hardball thrown against a sidewalk. Another sound commonly associated with such a hit is the involuntary racket made by the poleaxed animal. Deer, elk, wild sheep, pronghorns and other antlered or horned species normally bleat when hit in the spine; meat eaters such as bears and coyotes tend to growl.

It is often necessary to finish spine-hit animals with a second shot through the lungs. Such animals cannot get

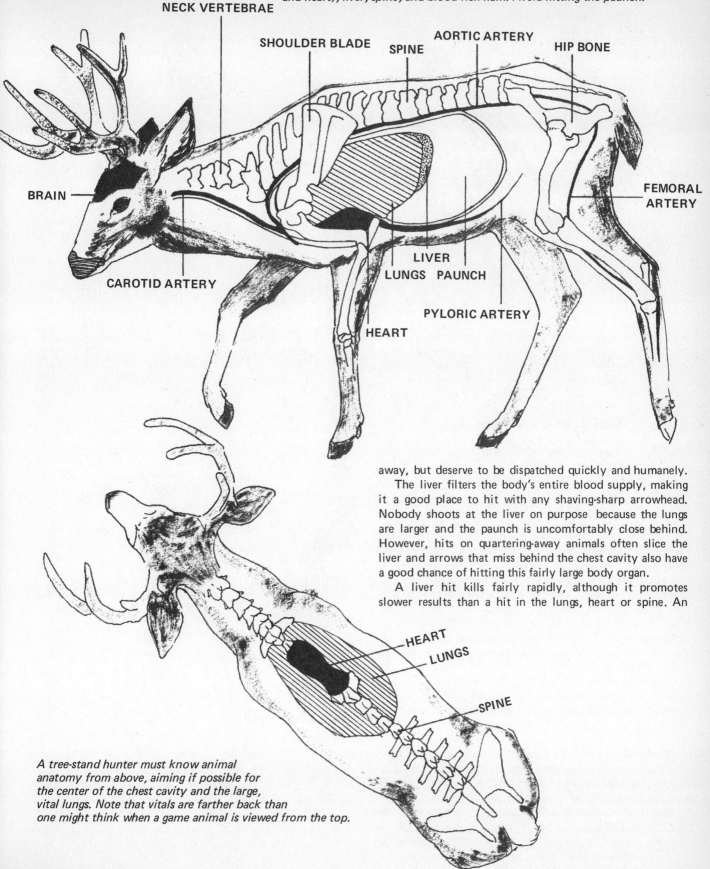

*A deer or similar big-game animal exposes several vital hit zones when broadside to the hunter. Such zones include the chest cavity (lungs and heart), liver, spine, and blood-rich ham. Avoid hitting the paunch.*

NECK VERTEBRAE

SHOULDER BLADE

SPINE

AORTIC ARTERY

HIP BONE

BRAIN

FEMORAL ARTERY

CAROTID ARTERY

LIVER

LUNGS

PAUNCH

PYLORIC ARTERY

HEART

HEART

LUNGS

SPINE

*A tree-stand hunter must know animal anatomy from above, aiming if possible for the center of the chest cavity and the large, vital lungs. Note that vitals are farther back than one might think when a game animal is viewed from the top.*

away, but deserve to be dispatched quickly and humanely.

The liver filters the body's entire blood supply, making it a good place to hit with any shaving-sharp arrowhead. Nobody shoots at the liver on purpose because the lungs are larger and the paunch is uncomfortably close behind. However, hits on quartering-away animals often slice the liver and arrows that miss behind the chest cavity also have a good chance of hitting this fairly large body organ.

A liver hit kills fairly rapidly, although it promotes slower results than a hit in the lungs, heart or spine. An

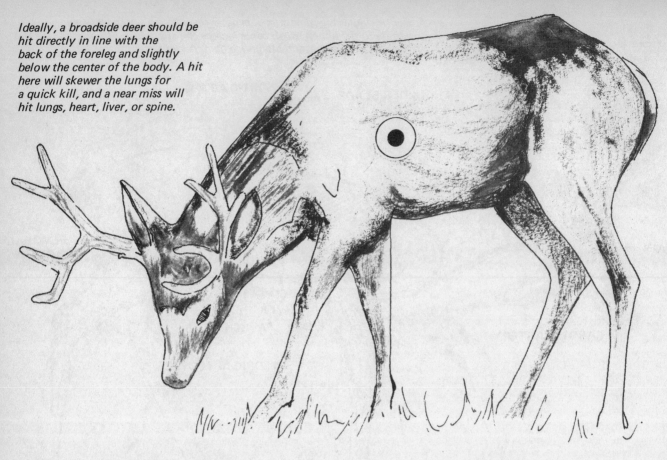

*Ideally, a broadside deer should be hit directly in line with the back of the foreleg and slightly below the center of the body. A hit here will skewer the lungs for a quick kill, and a near miss will hit lungs, heart, liver, or spine.*

*An angling-away animal presents the very best shot because vital tissue is hit with almost any arrow placement. Aim for the far shoulder for a lung hit via the paunch; a hit farther back will catch the ham for a fast kill.*

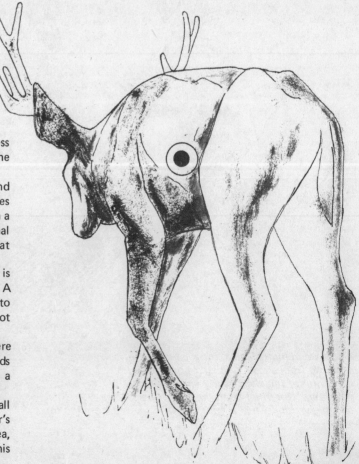

animal so hit dies from massive bleeding; the process usually takes from one to ten minutes, depending on the size of the animal and the exact location of the hit.

Because the liver is entirely outside the chest cavity and well away from major bones, such a hit often produces little or no sound at all. An arrow that hits the liver from a broadside angle usually zips completely through the animal without stopping, leaving telltale blood on the shaft that indicates the liver has been hit instead of the paunch.

Animal reaction to liver hits varies considerably. There is seldom the mad dash associated with a chest-cavity hit. A more characteristic reaction is for the affected animal to hump up slightly in the midsection and either walk or trot away.

Blood from a liver hit is dark red in color. A hit here often produces little external bleeding because blood tends to filter downward into the abdominal cavity. Trailing a liver-hit animal is often a chore.

Hits in an animal's shoulder area should be avoided at all cost. It is painfully easy to mistakenly aim at a deer's shoulder instead of farther back in the vital rib-cage area, but a hunter should rigidly coach himself against this common blunder.

Shoulder hits on medium to large animals are bad news, because it is difficult, often impossible, for an arrow to penetrate the shoulder blade and reach the vital chest cavity. I have on occasion shot through the edge of the shoulder with a heavy bow matched with a heavy arrow, including one moose I took with a seventy-eight-pound compound bow. However, the more common result is a loud *thunk* as the arrow hits the blade, stops and quivers there ineffectively.

Game department checks of deer shot during gun seasons have proven that a fair number of healthy deer are running around with broadheads buried in their shoulder blades. Such heads usually are encased in gristle and cause the deer no discomfort at all. These wasted heads are mute evidence of bowhunting shots that would have killed quickly had they hit only three or four inches farther back.

A deer or similar animal hit in the shoulder normally runs away, the arrow waving wildly in the air. Blood is usually dark red and skimpy, if found at all. Inexperienced bowhunters often score shoulder hits and wonder why these "lung shots" didn't do the job as advertised. They assume they have let an animal get away and die, when in fact the arrow has probably pulled out or broken off within a few hundred yards to result in a quickly healed-over wound.

A hit in the paunch (stomach) area is something a bowhunter should avoid. Virtually every other solid body hit with an adequately large and sharp broadhead will result in an animal on the meat pole — provided the archer is a good hunter with decent trailing skills — but the paunch hit presents an especially ticklish problem that isn't always possible to solve.

Paunch hits normally result from poor shooting, but an animal occasionally steps forward as a shot is made and takes an arrow several inches farther back than where it was aimed. Unless an arrow slices the large pyloric artery running through the lower center of the paunch, death often comes slowly with the animal being difficult to find and finish off.

A gut-shot animal's reaction is generally sluggish. Deer and similar animals normally hump up slightly when hit and hobble away at a steady, ground-gobbling pace. If left alone — which they should be — such animals usually go a short distance, then lie down with a wary eye on their backtrail.

A paunch-hit animal usually leaves a little blood at first from small arteries and veins in the stomach wall. However, this blood usually falls in small drops and peters out within a hundred yards. An arrow that hits the paunch usually passes entirely through the animal, and is covered normally with sticky stomach fluids and partly digested food when recovered by the bowhunter.

I never have lost an animal hit in the paunch with an arrow, although recovery has been a pain at times. To put such an animal in the bag, follow the trailing procedures outlined in Chapter 16.

The ham area is a first-rate place to hit any animal with a shaving-sharp broadhead. Many hunters have a deep-seated negative view of hitting any big-game critter in the rear end, a view stemming from the fact that a hit here with a rifle bullet ruins lots of meat and sometimes results in a lost animal.

Not so with an arrow. A solid ham hit usually produces

*The best place to aim on an animal angling toward you is just in front of the shoulder blade and behind the neck. This shot placement is difficult, but a hit behind the shoulder is apt to hit nothing but paunch.*

*A chest-on, head-up animal should be shot squarely in the point of the chest as shown. Such a hit will catch the lungs or the heart.*

massive blood loss and a kill so quick it never ceases to amaze me even after witnessing several dozen animals hit in the butt with arrows. It must be stressed that such a hit should be in the large part of the ham, not in the lower leg area.

A broadhead hitting the big muscles in the ham produces a peculiar slicing sound similar to that of air being sucked in rapidly between the teeth. Animal reaction to such a hit varies from a frantic dash to a slow hobble away. A deer-sized animal hit solidly in one or both hams seldom travels more than two hundred yards before dropping. If the broadhead has sliced one or both of the large femoral arteries running down the insides of the legs, death usually occurs within fifty yards. A solid ham shot is a good shot to take with a bow — a shot an archer should definitely try if a hit in the chest cavity does not seem easy to pull off.

Depending upon the angle of arrow entry, a ham hit may bleed a lot or very little. A broadside hit usually leaves a lot of blood on the ground as the many arteries and veins in this area rapidly drain. An arrow that ranges forward into the paunch often creates a wound that funnels most of the blood into the abdominal cavity. In either case, the animal should be lying dead within two hundred yards of where it was hit, provided it was not chased immediately after the shot was made. (More about that in Chapter 16.)

I dislike the neck hit with a passion. Although a hit here can sever the spine or cut the carotid artery and/or jugular vein for a quick kill, there's a lot of non-vital tissue around

these body structures. A deer with a severed windpipe can go for miles without leaving very much sign and a deer hit in the fleshy part of the neck always gets away clean with no ill effects.

As a result, a bowhunter never should try a neck shot on purpose. This shot is a favorite with some riflemen because it ruins very little meat and drops an animal from bullet shock alone, but the neck shot is an extremely poor choice for the bowhunter.

The head shot is another debatable choice. A hit in the brain instantly clobbers any animal, but getting to the brain is not always easy. Anything but a square head hit on a thick-skulled animal like an elk or wild pig results in a wildly glancing arrow; a shot in the head that is not accurately placed seldom gets the hunter his game.

However, there are times when a head shot can be a godsend for the accurate hunting archer. I normally avoid this shot, but it has bagged several animals that were looking straight at me over bushes, logs or similar obstacles blocking a shot at the body. At twenty yards or less, the area between a deer's eyes represents a fairly large target that any decent archer can hit. If you think you can hit an animal's brain and don't have any other shot, by all means give the head shot a try. If the arrow hits the mark, your animal will go down like a load of bricks with the loud crack of steel arrowhead against bone.

Arrows that hit animals around the edges often produce spectacular blood trails which completely peter out within

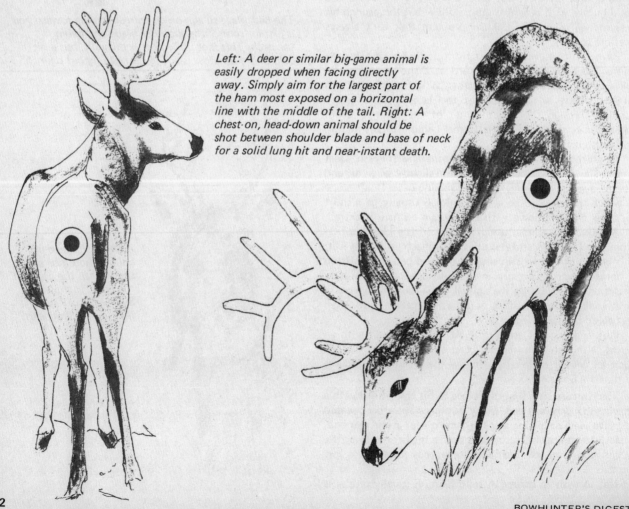

Left: A deer or similar big-game animal is easily dropped when facing directly away. Simply aim for the largest part of the ham most exposed on a horizontal line with the middle of the tail. Right: A chest-on, head-down animal should be shot between shoulder blade and base of neck for a solid lung hit and near-instant death.

two or three hundred yards. It never ceases to gripe me when I hear bowhunters describing such hits, then deciding that the animals crawled away and died. An edge hit with a bullet often pulverizes flesh and leads to infection, but a similar hit with a broadhead bleeds rapidly at first — which cleanses the wound — then seals up with no long-term damage to the animal.

Fringe hits leave a blood trail that is recognized easily by an experienced eye. Surface blood vessels are veins, not arteries, and veins are under low blood pressure, not high pressure like arteries. As a result, a fringe hit may leave a lot of blood, but this blood drips to the ground instead of spraying like the blood from a high-pressure artery. A trail with splashes of dark red blood that slowly fade into nothing is a good sign a shot has nicked an animal with no ill effect.

Although relatively rare, a bowhunter occasionally will shoot an arrow through the chest area with no immediate effect on the target animal. This baffling occurrence can be explained, although it normally blows the fellow's mind who is certain he has made a lung hit but cannot find the animal to save his life.

Normally, a shot that seems to be good but does not lead to an animal has somehow passed incredibly close to the vitals without actually touching them. I have seen this happen twice — once on an animal I shot myself and once on an animal shot by a friend.

In both cases we ended up bagging the animals, a fortunate turn of events because careful autopsies revealed exactly what had happened.

My friend's animal was a medium-sized mule deer he had shot behind the shoulder at about twenty-five yards. The buck ran away as if unhurt, the arrow buried in a log on the far side completely covered with blood. The strange part was, the deer left tiny drops of blood for about thirty yards, then the trail petered out completely.

I happened to be watching the episode from a nearby ridge, following the deer through binoculars as it barrelled down a long ridge, dove into a canyon and disappeared into a small patch of juniper. I continued to glass the patch for thirty minutes, but the deer never emerged.

Eventually my buddy and I got together. He was shaking his head in wonderment about the lost deer, but he perked up considerably when I told him I knew where his animal was. Two hours had passed, so we decided to go directly to the juniper patch and ease in from opposite sides.

It took us only ten minutes to find the deer, lying stone dead in its bed under a stunted tree. There was a neat four-edge arrow hole on each side of the body halfway between spine and brisket and well in front of the liver.

After carefully opening the animal, it was obvious what had happened. The arrow had penetrated the chest cavity, but had passed above the heart and behind the lungs. The animal had apparently exhaled just prior to being hit, shrinking the lungs away from the cavity walls and allowing the arrow to pass neatly by. The deer died as the lungs slowly collapsed from the punctured chest, but did not expire very fast. The animal lost very little blood in the process.

The critter I hit in the chest area was a small wild pig. The arrow hit slightly high of center directly behind the shoulder, and the porker squealed and raced away as if

unhit. I found the arrow in the dirt beyond, completely covered with dark red blood.

The hog left a good blood trail for about a hundred yards, but then the trail slowly petered out to nothing. The sign indicated a superficial muscle hit, but I knew I had hit the hog below the spine. After several hours of searching, I finally gave up in total bewilderment.

Three days later, I sneaked up on several pigs feeding in a thigh-deep grainfield, shot the closest one through the lungs, and trailed it down thirty minutes later. It was the same hog I had hit earlier, complete with healing broadhead holes on each side of its body exactly where I knew I had hit! A careful inspection showed that the arrow had exactly centered the thin band of muscle between the spine and the chest cavity, missing the aortic artery clean and producing

*Contrary to popular belief, a perfect hit with an arrow sometimes leaves no blood trail at all. The author shot this nice record-size blacktail buck directly through both lungs with a shaving-sharp broadhead. The arrow went all the way through, yet not one drop of blood showed along the trail the deer used to leave. Adams found the buck stone dead less than one hundred yards away, the chest cavity full of blood.*

nothing more than a harmless flesh wound. The hog was healing nicely with no sign of infection and would have been no worse for wear if I hadn't stumbled onto him a second time and slightly adjusted my aim.

Aside from an occasional fluke such as those just described, the bowhunter who knows how to shoot at game will enjoy consistent, positive results. Time your shots with care, aim at a vital zone...and your biggest worry will generally be how to lug your hard-earned trophy out to the nearest road!

# CHAPTER 16

# AFTER YOUR SHOT

## This Is When The Reality Of The Challenge May Begin!

INTELLIGENT PRE-HUNT preparation, skillful hunting on foot or on stand and a solid hit on an animal advance a nimrod three quarters of the way toward a complete and totally successful bowhunt. However, the last quarter of the way can be every bit as taxing as the first three quarters, requiring careful planning and thoughtful execution.

Finding an animal after it is hit is often easy. At times, the critter drops as dead as a stump within sight, eliminating the need to worry about trailing and tracking precautions.

An arrow seldom drops an animal in its tracks. Because an arrow does not shock down game like a bullet does, the average distance traveled by a deer-sized animal hit in a vital area with a sharp broadhead is probably between fifty and one hundred yards. In certain circumstances, a mortally hit animal can cover twice this distance before going down for good. This is not to mention the marginally hit critter that requires a longer and far more problematical follow-up to put it in the bag.

A bowhunter should cement a firm after-the-shot procedure in his mind long before he actually takes a shot at game. This procedure will give him the best chance of recovering a hit animal, leaving little to chance besides the exact placement of the shot in the vitals and the exact route the animal takes as it runs away from danger.

After a shot is taken at any kind of game, the bowhunter should do his level best to determine exactly where the arrow has hit. This determination should be based primarily on visual contact with the animal, but also can be influenced by the sound of the hit and the reaction of the critter once the hit is made. These factors are fully discussed in Chapter 15.

Knowing where the arrow has hit an animal will influence what a bowhunter does next. If the hit is a superficial one, or if the arrow has missed entirely, a bowhunter should try to nock another arrow and get off another shot if the animal lingers around.

Believe it or not, confused or lightly hunted game sometimes mills within bow range long enough to allow

*Selecting a good game area is just part of the hunting story. If you score a hit, you then must do the follow-up work that results in meat in the freezer. This chapter tells how.*

*Opposite page: This recurve bowhunter, layered with a fine powdering of snow, stands quietly waiting with sharp broadhead nocked. If he misses with first shot, he sometimes can manage a second at confused game. Above: If you shoot at game and feel you've hit the target, mark your shooting location with a handkerchief or tape.*

several shots. A friend of mine once emptied his eight-arrow quiver at a young muley buck at an average distance of under forty yards. My pal never touched a hair and he's still kicking himself over the whole episode.

If a shot-at animal thunders away, the archer should carefully watch it leave and try to track its progress even farther by sound. If a solid hit has been made but trailing clues turn out to be skimpy, being able to pinpoint the last known location of the animal can be of great value in finding it quickly and easily. Arrow-shot game often is found dead within a few yards of where it was last seen or heard, even if a blood trail is nonexistent and other signs do not allow an easy animal follow-up.

Let's say you've hit an animal, think you know where you've hit it, and watch it depart into a nearby clump of cover. The next step is simply waiting awhile to let the critter expire or at least weaken and calm down. **Do not** chase the animal or even follow it cautiously at once. Remain in the spot where you were when you took the shot for thirty minutes or more, continuing to look and listen for further sounds of the animal you have hit. If you have scored a quickly fatal hit, there is no need to follow in a hurry, and if you have not quickly dropped your prize, following at once can spook the animal into the next county. No matter what the situation, there is no percentage in following an animal at once.

Wait for at least thirty minutes after scoring a hit, then mark your shooting site and begin looking for signs of arrow impact. These include drops of blood, hair and even a blood-flecked arrow. If no blood, check for fresh tracks belonging to your animal. This is track of running deer, since dew-claw impressions are visible.

At this point, a few relatively inexperienced bowhunters may be squawking about my recommended follow-up procedures. There is a misbegotten theory among some archers that says a hunter should push an animal hit in the rear end at once to keep the wound open and blood dropping to the ground. My experience says this theory is pure bunk.

In the first place, a major wound in the rear end created by a truly sharp hunting broadhead does not quit bleeding just because an animal quits moving. In the second place, a rear-hit animal that is chased across the map will cover considerably more ground per minute than the same animal left alone, requiring the pushed animal to drop several times as much blood just to leave an identical trail to that of the animal that is left alone.

Perhaps a deer or another big-game trophy that has been

hit by a dull broadhead needs to be pushed to keep the wound bleeding, but nobody worth his salt hunts with dull broadheads anyway.

Leave your animal alone for thirty minutes or more no matter where the arrow has hit. After the prescribed time period has elapsed, carefully mark the place you shot from with a handkerchief, string of toilet paper or a length of fluorescent surveyor's tape. If you have shot from a tree stand or ground blind, this precaution obviously is not necessary. But it definitely can save time and avoid confusion if you've shot from natural terrain, cast about to find a blood trail, come up blank, and then need to return to the original shooting site to reorient yourself for another try at finding the animal.

Far too many bowhunters forget where they shot from in the excitement of the moment and end up losing an

*Author slowly and painstakingly searches for telltale signs of a hit after sending shaft toward a wild boar rooting in open meadow.*

Hunter shown on page 236 was rewarded with close-in shot on this trophy whitetail. His broadhead entered at point above shoulder and angled into the lungs for quick kill. Because of blowing snow that would soon cover up tracks and signs of blood, he followed up on his hit immediately. Nice buck!

animal entirely because they cannot pinpoint where the shooting action took place. This blunder occurs most commonly in flat, monotonous country where everything looks alike — country like a hardwood whitetail thicket or a dense stand of spruce where elk are likely to hang out.

Once your shooting position is marked prominently, the next step is to go directly to where the animal was when you took the shot. This site should be marked also with a highly visible object to further avoid confusion. From here, you should begin looking for signs of a hit that might lead you to your animal.

Unless the critter ran off with the arrow in its body, the first thing to look for is the arrow. If it can be found, the blood and/or other substances on it can help indicate where the hit has been made. If you are absolutely sure about where the arrow hit the animal, careful scrutiny of the arrow won't be necessary.

Blood types left by various kinds of hits were discussed in Chapter 15. With luck, your arrow will be covered with bright, frothy lung blood and a wide trail of this same stuff will lead away from the hit site. Actually, any easily

followed blood trail originating at the place where the animal was hit will make trailing at least initially easy and encouraging.

Unless the arrow is found covered with paunch material or similar fluid is found on the ground, the bowhunter should begin following the trail slowly and carefully. If a paunch hit has been made and blood near the hit area is skimpy or nonexistent, an archer should wait considerably longer before following to allow the animal to bed and stiffen up. I generally wait four hours before following up a gut hit, then follow with extreme caution just in case the animal is still alive and prone to leap up and run in panic.

If an arrow is covered with blood but no blood trail can be found, or if the archer knows he has scored a hit but cannot find the arrow or blood sign in the area, things quickly become more difficult. If soil is soft, tracks of a departing animal can often be followed in slow, methodical fashion. The running track of a hoofed animal like a deer or elk usually displays widely fanned toes and dew-claw depressions behind. A fresh running track normally scuffs up soil moister and darker in color than surrounding soil —

*Author doesn't put much emphasis on finding hair near hit location, since it doesn't indicate from which area of the body it has come, and there generally isn't enough present on trail leading away to help in your search.*

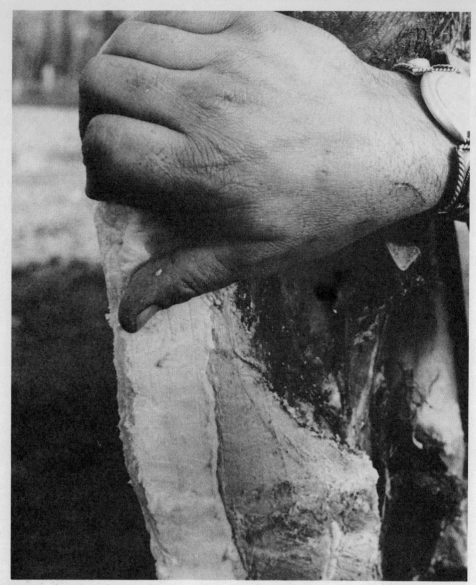

*Heat and moisture are the spoilers when it comes to meat and hides, so weather and species of animal shot dictate whether a night follow-up is required. This thick layer of fat over the rump of a whitetail would certainly lead to spoilage if the deer wasn't dressed within four hours of death, especially if warm weather conditions exist in the field*

another clue that can be important in following an animal leaving little or no blood.

If blood is present on the ground, an archer should follow the trail with care, walking to one side to prevent the possibility of destroying important sign. If a blood trail is not readily evident, the hunter should begin inspecting bushes, trees, logs and similar above-the-ground objects in the area for blood that might have been rubbed or sprayed from the body of the animal as it moved away. It is often possible to trail a hard-hit animal from blood on objects above the ground, even if none can be found on terra firma itself.

If blood and tracks are nowhere to be found, an archer can proceed sometimes by looking for other trailing clues like hair scraped loose as the target animal charged blindly through the trees, or freshly broken limbs or grass stems snapped off by the animal as it departed. A good bowhunter searches diligently for little clues that let him follow an animal.

Although some archery books make a big deal of finding hair from a wounded animal, I've discovered that animals seldom leave enough hair to follow very far and never leave enough to tell exactly where a hit has been made. A broadhead does cut hair as it enters the body, but this hair is not as important in finding an animal as some make it out to be.

If all else fails, a hunter should proceed directly to the last place he saw or heard his animal. He should mark this location as he did the shooting and hit sites, then should begin casting out in ever widening circles for drops of blood, running tracks, or the animal itself. A careful, patient search of this sort generally turns up a quickly killed animal that did not leave a blood trail and often locates a blood trail that did not begin at once because the animal's chest had not yet filled with blood to the level of the arrow holes in its body.

A paunch-hit animal is among the toughest to follow successfully. After a long wait, the hunter should attempt to trace such an animal's path, hopefully finding occasional drops of blood seeping from the muscled walls of the stomach. When following any animal, always keep an eye ahead just in case the critter isn't dead and might allow a shot before it rises and runs away. This advice is especially important when following a paunch-hit animal because the

critter very likely *isn't* dead and must be finished off after a careful, silent trailing job.

The foregoing might lead you to believe that finding arrow-shot game is a difficult and uncertain procedure. It can be at times, but most good hits with sharp arrows from adequately powered bows produce excellent blood trails and relatively easy follow-up procedures. Just remember that no matter how tough the trail happens to be to follow, your animal is very likely down within two hundred yards of where you took the shot.

Trailing game with confidence is a major key to finding this game and hoisting it on the meat pole. A typical example is a trailing episode I became involved in several years ago.

One evening I was stillhunting through a clearcut, eyes peeled for blacktail deer. Shortly before dark two nice bucks strolled out of the brush in front of me and dropped their heads to feed. I estimated the distance at forty-four

*Indian guide in British Columbia begins caping mammoth moose head in preparation for packing to camp and further preservation techniques. The snowy ground indicates that speed isn't so critical here as in other climes.*

*If weather conditions dictate a night search for arrowed game — such as warm, still temperatures or rain and snow that might obliterate tracks — you'll need a good light source. Shown here is headlamp with nine-volt dry cell, and hefty flashlight. Where possible, author favors gas lantern. Opposite page: Most deer, if not pushed, will be found dead within two hundred yards of where they were shot. Where terrain is steep, muley-dragging is difficult!*

yards, drew my old fifty-three-pound recurve bow on the bigger deer, and released the bowstring with a dull, barely audible plunk.

The shot felt right, the arrow smacked downrange with a decided thud, and both deer raced out of sight toward a brushy ravine 120 yards away. However, the light was too dim for me to see whether or not the arrow had actually hit the animal.

I knew it would be too dark to follow after a thirty-minute wait, and since the weather had been cool, I decided to return the next morning to determine what if any damage I had done. I wasn't even sure I had scored a hit because the soft dirt in the area often sounded exactly like flesh when hit with a speeding arrow. I spent a restless night, anxious to follow up the shot in hopes of a solid hit.

At dawn the next day I was examining the place where the deer had stood for the shot. The fact that I could not find an arrow nearby told me I had probably made a hit, but there was not one drop of blood visible on the ground. The deer's running tracks were readily visible in the soft soil

of the clearcut and I followed them to the lip of the brushy ravine like a beagle after a rabbit. Still no blood.

From here the going got tougher. The bucks had entered a trail in the brush, so I followed slowly and cautiously. The ground was packed too hard to see tracks. Soon I came to a triple fork in the trail, a fork presenting a difficult choice. I decided to follow each fork for fifty yards or so, snooping along with eyes close to the ground for some clue of a hit. The first two trails yielded nothing at all and I was beginning to wonder if my arrow had simply ricocheted into nearby brush or completely buried under dirt or leaves. I still believed I had made a hit from the feel of the shot and the sound of the hit, but the trailing evidence certainly wasn't encouraging. I sighed and started down the third trail at a little faster clip.

I hadn't gone ten feet when, lo and behold, there was a glimmering piece of steel lying smack in the middle of the trail. It was the razor-sharp bleeder insert from my Bear Razorhead hunting broadhead!

A few feet farther along, a big white log lay squarely

*Opposite page: Once you've found and field dressed your kill, you still have to get it back to camp. It's easier to backpack a wild boar, apparently, than to load a heavy mule deer on a pack horse that's sliding downhill (above)!*

across the trail. And directly on the other side was my buck, a fat three-by-four trophy with high, narrow antlers. He lay sprawled on his stomach where he'd fallen after a desperate leap over the log.

The arrow had lodged high through both lungs, bleeding the animal inside as it ran away completely dead on its feet. The chest cavity was full of blood and I quickly field dressed my prize, then rolled him over to drain and cool. The weather was warming up and I certainly didn't want him to spoil.

Stick-to-itiveness is a must when trying to trail an animal with very little sign to go on. So is learning how to best cope with special trailing problems that sometimes rear their ugly heads.

A bowhunter occasionally hits an animal during or just prior to a heavy rainfall. When this happens, he cannot afford to wait around, because whatever blood the animal leaves is likely to be washed away in a matter of minutes. Although not the ideal thing to do under dry conditions, an archer in the rain must take his chances and begin following a hit animal at once with a wary eye ahead in case a quick second shot is necessary.

Another problem that sometimes presents itself is what to do when a hit is made just before dark. If the animal is relatively small in body size and the weather reasonably cool, it is normally okay to leave the animal overnight and pick up the trail at first light. However, warm nighttime temperatures and/or animals with large, well-insulated bodies require a follow-up before daylight to ensure sweet, tasty meat. A small blacktail buck that expires shortly after

*Before heading into the field in pursuit of game, the bowhunter must know how he's going to care for the meat and hide. In the case of huge trophies like moose or grizzly bear, moving meat by float plane may be required.*

a hit in the evening will cool out fairly well when left for eight or ten hours at night — enough to prevent overnight meat spoilage — but a black bear, wild pig, mule deer, elk, or large whitetail deer can spoil unless found and gutted within two to four hours of the time it expires.

Trailing game at night can be surprisingly easy, provided a practical source of light is used to let you locate sign. My favorite method of night trailing is carrying a gas-powered lantern, but a strong flashlight beam also will show up blood fairly well in most terrain. A lantern provides a wider, more uniform spray of light that helps a lot when sign is sparse and difficult to follow.

One other note on trailing animals: Unless a blood trail is good enough to be followed at a fast walk, a bowhunter should always mark the last blood found with a handkerchief or a similar marker, then cast ahead for more. By leap-frogging two such markers along a trail (carrying

one ahead until more sign is found, then going back to retrieve the marker behind), a bowhunter can look ahead with nose to the ground without fear of losing track of the last sign he has found. It is far too easy on a meager blood trail to cast ahead and suddenly realize you've forgotten where the last sign was because you've become so engrossed in looking ahead for more. Such a blunder wastes valuable time and sometimes requires substantial backtracking to sort things out all over again.

Moisture and heat are the two primary enemies of wild meat. In combination, these two elements provide the ideal breeding ground for bacteria, those little devils that so quickly cause meat to spoil and the hair on trophy hides to fall out.

A competent bowhunter cares for edible game promptly and intelligently to ensure first-rate meat on the table and an attractive trophy on the wall. The first step in this

*Author realized beforehand the physical problems he'd encounter with heavyweight elk, and therefore packed along hoist to aid in lifting critter into truck. If required, game can be cut into manageable portions and packed.*

process is field dressing an animal to ensure the quick cooling of the carcass and to prevent unpleasant stomach fluids from tainting the meat. Field dressing should be completed within a few minutes after an animal is found to prevent meat from souring or becoming completely spoiled.

Field dressing is next to impossible to illustrate or describe, but the process is learned easily from any experienced hunter. This important field-care step removes the stomach and intestines from an animal's body cavity, which results in rapid chilling and drying of the meat to retard the work of bacteria.

Basically, field dressing an animal like a deer goes as follows: First, the animal is rolled over on its back to give easy access to the belly. The belly hide is carefully slit from the point of the brisket to the anus of the animal, with the incision going through a female animal's genitals and beside the sex organs of a male. Any sharp knife with a blade over

two inches long can be used to perform the field-dressing chore.

Next, the thin layer of fat and meat separating the hide from the innards must be carefully slit down the middle of the belly with a finger or two dropped between the stomach and the outer shell of meat. Exercise extreme caution during this step to avoid cutting open the paunch or the intestine. One careless slip of the blade can fill the body cavity with nasty fluids from the stomach, hurting the hunter's feelings, assailing his nostrils, dirtying his hands, and possibly tainting the meat.

Once the belly casing is slit from stem to stern, a hunter reaches forward into the head of the abdominal cavity until he finds the esophagus (the tube connecting the throat with the stomach). This tube should be carefully cut with the knife, allowing the paunch and intestine to be rolled completely out of the animal. The intestine should be cut

*No horse is capable of packing out a complete elk carcass, and this hindquarter is being covered with a tarp to prevent grime while en route.*

off where it enters the anus or the entire anus can be reamed out with the blade of the knife. In either case, the paunch and the intestine can be discarded at this point and the animal draped chest-down over a rock, log or bush so the blood can drain out of the body cavity.

In most cases, the heart, lungs and windpipe also are cut from the chest cavity in the field to further aid meat cooling. Once these basic field-dressing procedures are completed, an animal is ready to transport out of the woods to be hung in camp or taken to a cold-storage locker.

There are many ways to lug a deer, elk, pronghorn, bear, or a similar big-game animal back to a waiting vehicle. If the animal is too big to handle by yourself, there are several ways to go. Obviously one is getting help to drag or carry the critter out in one piece. Another is cutting the animal in two or more pieces to lighten individual loads.

A deer-like animal can be cut in two equal pieces with a pocket knife alone. First, a slit should be made between the fifth and sixth ribs (counting from the back rib) on either side of the animal. The knife blade should be worked between the vertebrae of the spine even with the slits between the ribs.

Once this is accomplished, a 360-degree twist on one half or the other of the animal will pop the spine in two,

leaving only a little meat whittling before the animal is in two pieces of equal weight.

When bowhunting relatively remote areas, an archer should figure out how to transport game back to civilization prior to actually packing into the back country. An elk, mule deer, bear, or similar large, fat animal can quickly spoil unless properly field dressed and promptly transported out of the hills. In many situations involving large animals, the only feasible way to avoid spoilage is using pack horses or a bush plane to quickly move meat.

I have on occasion packed elk up to fifteen miles to a waiting truck, but such an endeavor tends to be a killer because the critter must be cut into five pieces (four quarters plus the head and antlers), then each piece packed out individually. Such a process takes several days, and is only possible when weather is cold enough to chill meat thoroughly. In warm late-summer or early fall conditions, there is no way a hunter can pack out a large animal piece by piece and salvage all the meat in good condition.

No matter how you plan to get your bow-shot animal back to civilization, always remember that moisture and heat are the two things that spoil meat. A little grime on meat from dragging or carrying can always be cut away or washed off, so there's no need to be overly concerned

*Jim Easton, hunter and shaft maker, has hung this wild boar by the hind legs to permit best ventilation in warm weather. Rapid drying and cooling will ensure edible meat, if it is transported to cold storage before decay begins.*

about this. However, be sure to keep your animal as cool as possible and well ventilated to allow meat to dry out instead of collecting moisture on the surface and turning sour.

Beginning bowhunters pull some pretty dumb stunts after taking that first big-game animal. A classic boner is hauling a deer or another trophy around town for several hours on the hot hood of a car. You'd think this trick would be obviously ridiculous to anyone, but I'd wager that

several hundred deer spoil from direct sunlight and engine heat every year after being shown off in such a manner.

It is common practice to hang and skin an animal once it reaches hunting camp. This practice is generally a sound one because jerking the hide off an animal ensures rapid meat cooling and dehydration. Whether you hang your animal by the head or by the hind legs is not all that critical, although hanging game by the hind legs from a regular meat-hanging gambrel makes more sense unless the

252

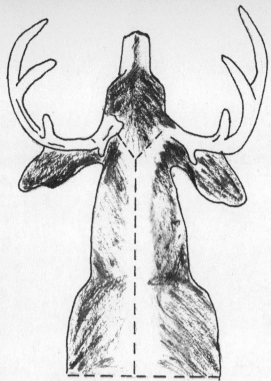

To cape antlered or horned animal: Make incision in hide completely around the animal behind shoulders, and down backs of both front legs. Make second incision up center of spine to point even with backs of ears, and two incisions should be cut from this point to each horn base in slingshot fashion. Hide should then be peeled carefully from shoulders and neck, and head cut off where neck joins skull.

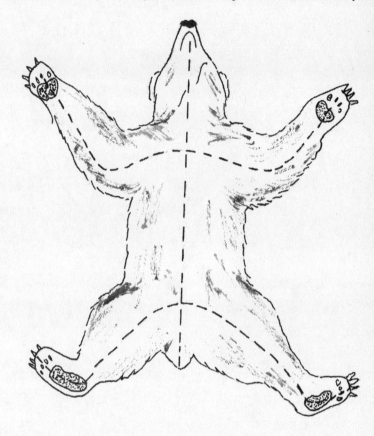

To save the whole hide on a bear or similar animal, make these incisions and carefully remove the skin with the help of a sharp knife with a blade two inches or longer in length. Avoid nicking hide for best finished job.

weather is cold, because hanging an animal by the head tends to trap warm air in the upper chest cavity and also makes removing a trophy head impossible unless the animal is taken down and hung by the hind legs later on.

Skinning an animal is a simple process similar to peeling a potato. A reasonably sharp knife makes quick work of parting an animal from its hide, allowing the hunter to slice through the membranous tissue between the hide and the meat. The only tricky part about animal skinning is making the proper incisions in a hide, if you want to save the entire hide for a rug or you want to cape out the animal for a trophy head mount.

When skinning out any bear hide, deer head or similar trophy to be tanned and/or mounted, take special care not to nick the hide as you skin it out. A few small knife holes can be repaired by a good taxidermist, but the fewer the better for a first-rate looking trophy.

As with meat, a trophy hide and head should be kept as cool as possible to prevent spoilage and irreversible slippage of the hair. Transport both meat and hide to a cold storage locker as soon as possible so the meat can be cut and packaged and the hide either sent to the taxidermist at once or frozen until convenient to have it tanned or mounted.

To adequately protect a trophy hide and/or head from freezer burning (harmful dehydration), it should be triple bagged in plastic garbage bags sealed tightly at the mouth. A trophy can be kept frozen in such a manner for up to one year before dehydration begins to damage the hide and hair.

Aside from careful attention to preventing the spoilage of meat and trophy hide, an archer also must protect meat and hide from flies, meat-eating bees and similar pests. The standard way of doing this is to cover meat and hide with loose-fitting, insect-proof bags that allow good air circulation and cooling while keeping flying critters at bay. Flies can deposit eggs (called blows) on meat and create a smelly mess, while various carnivorous bees can devour a surprising amount of meat as game hangs in camp.

If a game bag is not available, a mixture of lemon juice and pepper can be sprinkled on meat and hide to help ward off flies and other insects. If the weather is reasonably cold, some hunters prefer to leave the hide on an animal as it hangs in camp to protect most of the meat from harmful insects.

No matter what precautions you take to preserve meat and hide in the field, it is extremely important to transport a trophy to cold storage as soon as possible — preferably within twenty-four hours if daytime temperatures are averaging above 50 degrees Fahrenheit.

*Improvements in bowfishing tackle, dissatisfaction with being able to hunt only one or two months per year are two major reasons for increase in popularity of bowfishing carp and other species.*

# CHAPTER 17

# BOWFISHING & BIRD SHOOTING

## Special Equipment – Coupled With Special Considerations – Can Mean Success

ALTHOUGH BOWHUNTING is primarily devoted to the pursuit of animals, an increasingly high percentage of archers are supplementing their summer and fall big-game activities with pleasant off-season jaunts after fish and birds.

There are several reasons for the current interest in these offbeat bowhunting activities, including a gradual decline in huntable animal populations in some parts of the country, the recent introduction of quality bowfishing and bird-shooting gear, the continuing liberalization of special bird-hunting and bowfishing seasons in various parts of the country and the basic desire of many serious hunting archers to practice their sport on a year-round basis instead of only one or two months out of the year. As bowhunting continues to grow in popularity, shooting equipment

continues to improve and state hunting laws continue to become more favorable for shooting fish and birds, these fine off-season activities are likely to grow at a steady, rapid pace.

Bowfishing and bird hunting provide excellent shooting practice for the regular hunting of large and small animals, but these are also fine, fulfilling sports in their own right. Here are some important facts about how to enjoy these pastimes to the fullest.

A wide variety of so-called rough fish can be taken legally with bow-and-arrow gear. Such fish usually compete directly with game fish such as trout, bass, and catfish, making them less than popular with game officials and the general sporting public. Some of these fish — such as carp — are not even native to North America and are commonly

viewed as invaders and pests in similar fashion to the rabbits that currently infest Australia.

For whatever reason, such rough fish are fair game for the archer in most public waters. Commonly hunted species include carp, suckers, buffalo fish, alligator gar, bowfin, chub and sharks. These and similar trash species are quite abundant in most waters, providing a virtually untapped bonanza of shooting fun for the hunter who equips himself properly and spends some time in a boat or along a shore.

Necessary gear for bowfishing is not especially expensive, but it is quite specialized and sophisticated. An archer should choose this gear with care to ensure pleasant times around the water.

Opinions on what sort of bow to fish with are split right down the middle, with some archers preferring the old-style recurve bow, because it is smooth for snap-shooting and others preferring the modern compound bow because it can be held at full draw for quite a while as an archer follows the wakes of fish and waits for them to roil periodically on the surface. Both shooting tools have their points, but I personally feel the compound bow offers a decided advantage over the recurve for anyone who normally shoots a compound on other kinds of game. Such a bow allows careful aiming without undue muscle strain, and also provides the punch to penetrate fish in especially deep water.

Modern heavy-wall aluminum bowfishing arrows are replacing solid fiberglass arrows as the standard for serious bowfishing activity. The best aluminum shafts weigh as much as fiberglass for deep penetration, provide every bit as much durability and fly more accurately because they are straighter and more uniform in stiffness.

*Opposite page: In addition to the challenge of bowhunting for birds, the archer may receive another benefit — dinner! A fat Canadian goose was dispatched by this archer, who chose a recurve for this hunting trip. Below: The "rough fish" species of carp, sucker, buffalo fish, alligator gar, bowfin, chub and shark, are fair game for bowfishermen. Like many, expert bowfisherman Harvey Naslund prefers a compound bow for penetrating big carp in deep water.*

A top-of-the-line bowfishing arrow such as the Easton/Dougherty Fishgetter arrow consists of a central shaft, a screw-in plastic fish nock in the rear that trails line directly behind the shaft and some sort of bowfishing point attached to the front with epoxy and possibly a steel pin for added security on big fish. The relatively new screw-in fish nock is a major breakthrough in bowfishing tackle which greatly enhances accuracy and prevents weeds from snagging on the end of an arrow as it is reeled in after a missed shot.

Because line drag on the exact rear of a bowfishing arrow provides flight stability, rubber fletching is an optional and largely unnecessary addition to any fish arrow.

Deciding on a bowfishing head is primarily a personal matter, although certain designs definitely work better than others in particular situations. For most shooting circumstances, the best bowfishing heads are simple, durable, and very easy to remove from a fish after a shot. My personal favorite for shooting carp, buffalo and shark is the Retract-O-Blade, an incredibly rugged head with heavy steel barbs that hold a fish yet fold out of the way under a sliding steel collar when it is time to pull the arrow

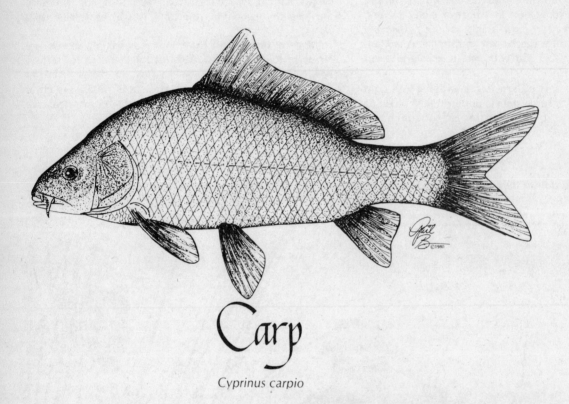

# Carp

*Cyprinus carpio*

# Bowfin

*Amia calva*

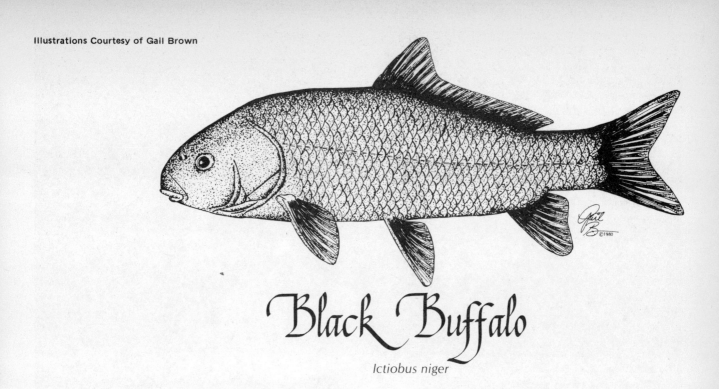

# Black Buffalo

*Ictiobus niger*

# Shortnose Gar

*Lepisosteus platostomus*

# Alligator Gar

*Lepisosteus Spatula*

This night stalker has combined a new bowfishing reel with a recurve bow and arrowed successfully large spotted gar. Special points are used.

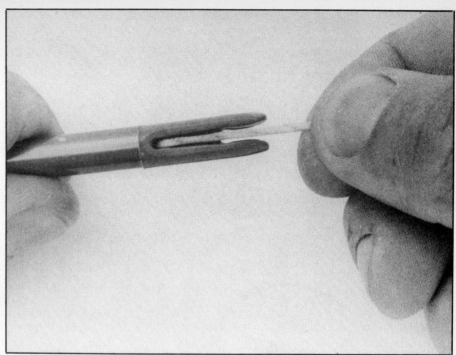

*Right: The Easton/Dougherty Fishgetter arrow features a screw-in plastic nock that trails line directly behind the shaft. Below: Although rubber fletching is used by a few bowfishermen, such fletching has little if any effect on the flight of a heavy fish arrow.*

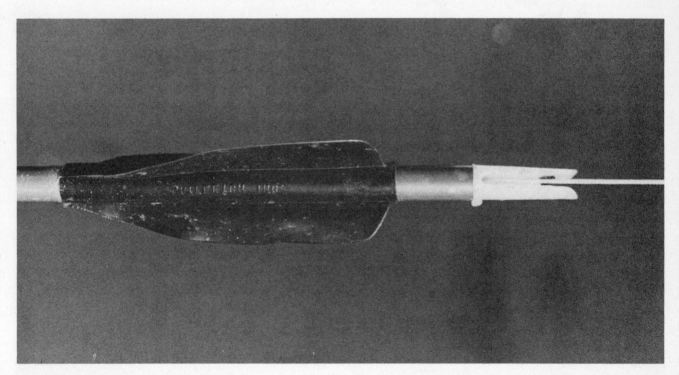

free. Other bowfishing heads also have their fans, including heads that unscrew to allow arrow removal and so-called inertia heads with barbs that fold into the arrowhead ferrule for removal and spring out on impact with a fish to hold it securely until it is landed.

Of particular importance to the gar fisherman is a head with a sharpened tip to penetrate this critter's incredibly tough hide. Special gar-fishing heads resembling oversized, barbed big-game broadheads are sold at archery shops in the Southern states where gar are normally hunted..

A bowfisherman needs some sort of reel loaded with carefully chosen bowfishing line. In times past, the

drum-type bow reel was standard equipment with archers: either a reel that screwed into the stabilizer hole below the bow grip or a larger open-center reel taped up higher to allow the archer to shoot through the middle of the reel to improve line flow from the reel as the arrow zipped away. Drum-type reels normally were loaded with about fifty feet of heavy braided nylon bowfishing line of 90 or 100-pound test.

Today, most serious bowfishermen use large, closed-face spin-casting reels instead because these provide vastly superior line flow during a shot, allow quicker arrow retrieval by cranking a handle, and virtually eliminate the

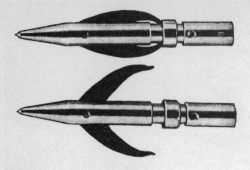

Author's favorite fish point is the Retract-O-Blade, shown here both open and closed (above). Below is an open-center, shoot-through drum-style reel that is taped to your bow's riser.

Sting-A-Ree is an alternate type of arrow point, and is shown in its three stages: closed, open, and folded back to facilitate removal of fish (above). This bowfishing reel seat screws into bow's stabilizer hole (right). It's made by Martin and available locally.

snagged or tangled line associated with old-style drum reels. A good-quality, large-capacity bowfishing reel like the Zebco Model 808 is usually attached to a commercial bowfishing reel seat which is screwed tightly into a bow's stabilizer hole.

There is absolutely no comparison between the performance of drum-type bowfishing reels and more modern push-button reels. A push-button reel is quieter and handier to operate, allows accurate shots out to twenty-five

Ken Brown, well-known bowfisherman, nailed this huge longnose gar with modern spin-casting tackle. Such a leather skinned, hard-fighting prize requires a special gar-fishing arrowhead punched deep by a heavy-draw hunting bow.

Two tournament organizers and game warden watch as bowfishermen roar into the morning light in pursuit of big fish and tournament cash. Fixed hours and prizes a la bass fishing contests make these tournaments quite a challenge!

yards when 70-pound, round-braided Dacron cod-fishing line is used, and makes fighting a fish extremely easy because of the handle-crank line retrieval. I can regularly hit a floating tennis ball at fifteen yards with my modern setup, a feat unheard of with an older-style reel because line flow was jerky and line drag extremely severe.

Although some bowfishermen after large species like gar and buffalo prefer to use a stubby bowfishing rod ahead of the push-button reel, I've been able to achieve much better arrow flight and have experienced fewer line tangles by eliminating the rod from my setup. However, a rod does take the sideways line burden off a reel when horsing in fish after fish — the major reason a rod can be a good thing when fighting big, plucky rough fish.

Rough fish generally are shot as they cruise the surface, spawn in shallow water or swim about deeper down. Shooting at carp, sucker or buffalo as they spawn can be ridiculously easy because an archer can often wade or

paddle within point-blank range of these fish and flock shoot them as several males roil with a female on top of the water. Double and even triple hits are relatively common in such a situation.

Shooting cruising fish can be a considerably tougher proposition, especially if these fish are several feet below the surface. Carp, gar and most other species can be fairly wary, requiring a slow, silent approach by boat or on foot. Paddling, poling, or using a quiet electric trolling motor is often the only way to approach spooky fish within a solid shooting range of ten or fifteen yards.

Different archers use different aiming methods on fish. Most of my acquaintances use bowsights set for five, ten, fifteen and twenty-yards — a system that works just great on top-water fish. Because a fish arrow complete with point weighs about three times as much as a regular big-game arrow and because line drag slows such an arrow down rapidly, trajectory is quite arching and requires range

estimation within a yard or two for solid hits on carp-sized fish of five to ten pounds.

Deep-water shooting can be terribly frustrating. Light refraction in water makes subsurface objects appear higher than they really are, requiring low holds for accurate shooting. When an arrow enters the water, it appears to change direction and rise toward the target fish. Knowing where to hold on deep-water fish is strictly a matter of extensive practice at such shooting and even practice does not guarantee success. Every depth and every shooting angle requires a slightly different hold.

Shooting at carp and similar rough fish at depths past three feet requires holds so low they'll blow the beginner's mind. I have hit deep fish ten yards in front of a boat by aiming nearly straight down at my toes. The difficulties involved must be experienced to be appreciated.

The past few years, organized bowfishing tournaments sponsored by various archery manufacturers, publishing houses and private archery clubs have gained widespread popularity with the country's more serious fishing

*Thirty-two-pound carp was more interested in love than survival, and was neatly arrowed while on the surface, roiling with several others (above). While carp can be taken with relative ease at this time of year, there's no such easy time in which to bag the sharp-eyed pheasant (right).*

These angler-archers have just fired two fish arrows from their different setups. The older-style drum reel is used by archer in background. Note better smoothness of spin-cast setup used by archer in foreground.

*A fat grouse may look as big as a 747 when you put your bowsight on him, but you may be surprised at how small he becomes! A razor-sharp broadhead is favored by serious bird hunters, and it penetrates heavy feathers well.*

bowhunters. Such tournaments are normally run in similar fashion to pro-bass tournaments, with set shooting hours, specific equipment rules, and a wide array of prizes plus cash rewards to the most successful bowfishermen. Tournament rules vary considerably, but the top prize generally is given for either the most pounds of fish taken within the prescribed shooting hours or the greatest number of fish shot. A special prize also is awarded normally to the individual shooter who has taken the largest single fish of the competition.

Whether you end up enjoying relaxed afternoons plunking at carp on the local slough or find that you prefer the extreme challenge and excitement of an organized bowfishing competition, shooting fish with a bow is something you really ought to try. If you're like me, both casual fish-shooting and organized competition will become a regular part of your yearly off-season archery schedule.

Bow-shooting birds is not a stunt. It is a widely practiced and highly enjoyable endeavor that regularly produces meat if an archer knows his stuff.

Many states, like my native California, have regular bowhunting seasons for such game species as pheasant, grouse and quail. In addition, varmint birds like barn pigeons and crows can also provide enjoyable shooting

A pigeon is a mighty tiny target when roosting, and is even harder to hit when winging away in fright. Some shooters prefer the smooth-drawing recurve for birds, since there's no bowstring let-off to affect fast shooting.

action. No matter what the species involved, shooting birds represents yet another worthwhile dimension to hunting archery for sportsmen willing to tackle the challenge head-on and try, try again.

There is nothing particularly easy about shooting at a bird with a bow, no matter whether the target is sitting still or winging rapidly away. Most game birds present small, difficult targets surrounded by a healthy layering of feathers. No matter how you manage to hit a bird, you deserve a solid pat on the back.

As is the case with bowfishing, serious bird-shooting archers are divided on what kind of bow is most effective.

On stationary birds such as a sitting quail, a standing turkey, or a grouse perched on a tree limb, the accurate, deliberately shot compound bow is the best choice. However, for flying birds I tend to agree with those favoring the smooth-shooting recurve bow. Such a bow allows one fluid draw and release instead of a bumpy bowstring draw. The smooth snap-shooting motion makes nailing a flushing cock pheasant or a zipping Canada goose easier for most bowhunters.

As mentioned in Chapter 6, most birds are shot with arrows tipped by sharp hunting broadheads because such heads penetrate well even as a bird flies directly away.

Two samples of oversized flu-flu fletching are shown in this photo: on left is six-fletch, on right is corkscrew. Both will slow arrow speed and prevent shaft fired skyward from sailing dangerously into the blue, and are effective at short distances. The corkscrew should not be used, author says, at distances greater than twenty yards. This avoids cripples.
Opposite page: A satisfied Chuck Adams displays dinner: two grouse bagged with his compound.

Savora broadhead enabled
quick, clean, one-shot kill
on this honker. Compound
was used successfully here.

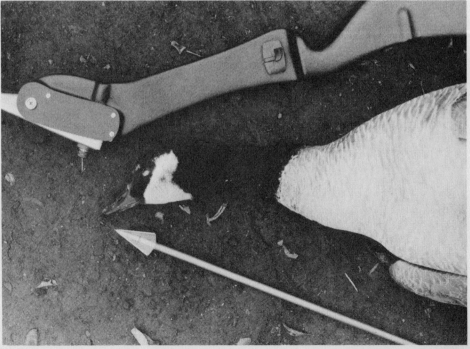

*If shooting at targets farther than twenty-five yards, such as at high-flying geese, bowhunter should use standard fletching. Ensure, however, that you have 300 yards of clear area before shooting. Opposite page: Pat yourself on the back if you're lucky and skillful enough to collect midget-sized valley quail.*

Other arrowheads like the Snaro and the Judo also are used by some, because they feature enlarged contact zones which make hits on flying birds somewhat easier than normal. However, I am prone to be skeptical of such heads for all but the smallest game birds, as they can glance off on occasion or cripple instead of kill. A Snaro head will take quail nicely at fairly close range and also will drop a pheasant if solid contact is made. However, I've seen this and similar heads glance off of ducks, geese and pheasants on many unhappy occasions.

Arrows for bird hunting normally have the same good-quality aluminum shafts as regular hunting arrows. However, most shooting at airborne birds is done with special oversized flu-flu fletching instead of conventional low-profile three-fletch. Such fletching slows an arrow fast

to allow easy arrow retrieval and prevents them from flying dangerously for several hundred yards.

Flu-flu fletching is an excellent choice when hunting flushing birds like pheasants and quail. Oversized four-fletch or six-fletch flu-flu fletching is considerably more accurate than so-called corkscrew flu-flu fletching and travels a bit farther and faster for surer kills over twenty yards. Because flu-flu fletching slows an arrow incredibly fast, shots are not recommended over twenty-five yards, because hitting birds is difficult and arrow power completely goes to pot past these distances.

When shots at birds are likely to be over twenty or twenty-five yards, an archer should use hunting arrows with standard fletching. However, he never should shoot at high-flying geese or similar overhead targets, unless he is

Snow geese and similar forms of waterfowl can be successfully jumpshot by a sneaky bowhunter. Although snows can also be shot as they fly over decoys, such shooting is trickier than snapshooting at geese jumped from land.

certain the area for three hundred yards in front of him is clear. The average hunting bow casts an arrow about 250 yards when aimed upward at a forty-five-degree angle, making shots in the air quite dangerous unless surrounding terrain is flat and easily surveyed for nearby people, animals, buildings, automobiles, et cetera.

Several hunting techniques can be used to set up shots at game birds of various kinds. Quail, grouse and other forest dwellers are often shot incidentally as a hunter slips along in search of big game. Other kinds of birds must be deliberately sought out and hunted by time-tested methods.

Waterfowl often can be shot with a bow after being called in over well-placed decoys. Such shooting is tricky, because targets usually are moving fast at fairly long range. A more productive way to bowhunt ducks and geese is to sneak up on the birds as they rest on water or land and either potting them where they are or jumping them prior to taking a shot.

Jumpshooting such birds as pheasants is the classic method of taking feathered game with a bow. A bird that flushes from under your feet often provides a fairly good target if you are fast enough to draw and release before the bird picks up speed and reaches marginal shooting range. I

especially enjoy wing-shooting pheasants over a well trained pointing dog, because birds always flush close and never catch a hunter with his guard down.

Nailing flying birds is strictly an instinctive shooting sport, a matter of feel and timing rather than deliberate concentration on step-by-step shooting form. Such shooting consists of a single fluid motion during which the hunter draws, swings on target and lets the arrow go.

Bowhunters with good hand/eye coordination can develop into surprisingly good shots on flying birds. Such skill must be acquired through lots of in-the-field hunting practice and/or considerable shooting practice on styrofoam aerial archery targets hand thrown by a friend standing to the side.

Bird shooting is an exciting and productive pastime no matter how you approach this sport. A bird-shooting flu-flu arrow stuffed in a big-game quiver can lead to lots of incidental shooting fun on grouse and other legal game birds encountered during hunts for elk, deer, and similar animals. A deliberate trip after ducks, geese, pheasants, crows, barn pigeons and other feathered prey also provides top-notch off-season sport — a brand of sport many archers look forward to when big-game seasons are closed.

A small bunch of Canadian geese, photographed through telephoto lens, are at full alert — and still far out of bow range. This eyesight and lack of good ground cover make nearly hopeless a successful stalk (above). Developing a skill at instinctive shooting in which archer simply draws and fires at moving object is purpose for this drill. Styrofoam targets are hurled skyward, and the shooter draws and fires without truly aiming. Arrowed targets on the ground indicate that this shooter has the hang of snap-shooting — and then some!

# Make Your Own Custom
# CAMOUFLAGE SHIRT

## Step-By-Step Easy Instructions For Making Your Own Special Hunting Shirt

## CHAPTER 18

**B**OWHUNTERS NEED several things working for them when they go into the hunting field. One is the ability to virtually disappear from view. This is accomplished to a great degree by using the right colors and types of camo clothing.

The following do-it-yourself project outlined by well-known bowhunter Bob Learn is typical of what can be accomplished by an ingenious hunter with a little time. The result of Learn's experiments was a practical shirt for bowhunting all kinds of game, large and small. Learn relates valuable tidbits of knowhow throughout this chapter — tidbits that will greatly help if you want to make your own bowhunting shirt. This and similar items can be made by a handy archer.

One of the first considerations in selecting camo clothing is the type of material. Brushed cotton or denim are good since such material is quiet. Hunting pants for many are

off-the-rack brushed denim in black, dark green or brown. Shirts of brushed cotton or denim are a bit harder to come by. Suede cloth shirts featuring a camo pattern are available. While quiet in the bush, they tend to be warm for early Fall hunting. Also, most have pockets that interfere with the bowstring.

Surplus military camo in different patterns and materials is readily available. However, this type was designed for military riflemen, not bowhunters. The pockets become string snaggers.

The better solution is to buy your bowhunting camo from a company that caters to the bowhunter. Kolpin marketed some great camo sweaters some years ago, but no longer offers them. Most archery shops stock a type of camo hunting outfit that is better than military surplus for the bowhunter. Martin Archery, for one, always is experimenting with new ideas.

An outfit down in Texas called the Camo Clan caters to the archer entirely and a catalog of their units verifies that they think in terms of problems of the bowhunter. They offer a catchy little Camo Clan Bow Sling for resting your bow while standing or even walking slowly if you like. They also pucker the shooting arm of the jacket for either a right- or left-hand shooter. That way, one suffers no string snags on the puffed sleeve, even without an arm guard.

Camo Clan offers full camo outfits of jackets and trousers in three camo patterns: World War II, Vietnam and tiger stripe. The firm also makes a full coverall in each of the three patterns.

The Texas firm also offers to sell just the materials in any of the three patterns, with a choice of eight-ounce duck or ten-ounce twill.

"About a dozen years ago, I had some camo made from the tiger stripe they were then using in Vietnam. It has been my favorite and is still good but is getting threadbare and a little lighter with each washing," says the venerable Mr. Learn. "I never use soap on it unless there's too much blood so it isn't the soap that is wearing it out. It is the brush and cold-water washes I use. Here was my chance to make a new set.

"I ordered Camo Clan's Tiger Stripe material in the eight-ounce duck. It runs $3.50 per yard in a forty-five-inch width. They informed me the tiger stripe is a bit harder to get so there might be a delay on this material in bolt or cut orders. The Vietnam or World War II patterns are readily available in either fabric weight."

Learn ordered three yards of material for a new bowhunting camo shirt. It was more than needed, but he could always use the excess for a camo hat, a bow sleeve or whatever.

When the material arrived, included were sample swatches of each of the other two patterns.

"All I had to do was drag out an old hunting shirt from which to make a pattern. I know of no place one can get a pattern for the type shirt I wanted to make, so it was make my own," Learn reports.

"While I worked on the pattern, I placed the new tiger stripe material in the washer, with a dab of detergent. Cold water was used, and all subsequent washings would be with cold water."

Prewashing does two things: It removes the sizing and excess dye from the material. Second, it causes shrinkage. Don't make a shirt with new material, then wash it. It might shrink to a point you can't get into it!

To make a pattern, Learn used an old brushed-cotton pullover hunting shirt that had become acutely threadbare. One can cut the shirt apart and fashion the pattern from the pieces. The second option is to lay the shirt on a piece of medium-weight hard cardboard used for signs.

Fasten the shirt to the board with pins at about every inch. Do this for the front, remove the pins and shirt. Use a pencil then to trace around the pinhole outline, adding three-quarters-inch to allow for seam width. Do the same for the back and the sleeves. Cuffs are not necessary. Bob Learn patterned the collar from another shirt since this collar was a bit low. Now we have a full front and back for the shirt and half a sleeve.

Fold the front and back and mark them, then cut them down the center. Mark the centerline with *fold*. Mark one side of the sleeve on the cardboard, flop it over and trace the other half. Both left and right are the same.

When finished, one should have a small pattern for the front and back and a huge-looking one for the sleeves. Mark the center-back for the fold the same as the front.

"If you want pockets, plan them now," Learn suggests. "I wanted sleeve or shoulder pockets, one on each side. I made a square large enough to hold a cigar for length and wide enough for my compass or a similar small object. This

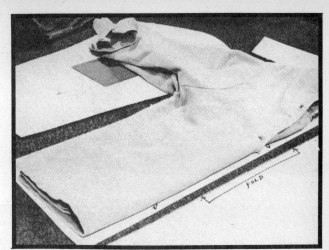

*Using an old shirt to develop your own pattern may be best and the most simple way of doing the job. This pattern was drawn on heavy show card, which later was cut out.*

**1**

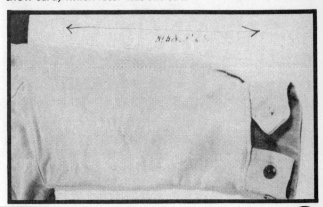

*In patterning the sleeves, it is obvious they require much more material than one would think, even if one doesn't include the cuff.*

**2**

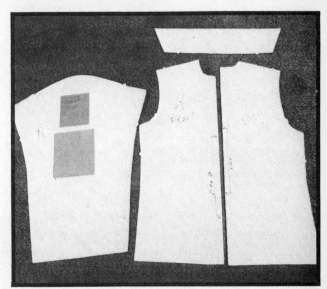

*Finished patterns, cut and marked, provide for a front, back, sleeve, collar and pocket. Note the notches to aid in installing camouflage collar.*

**3**

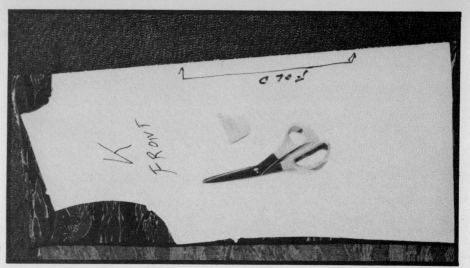

*Material should be washed to shrink, remove sizing before pattern is cut out. By placing pattern on fold one can save sewing, Learn reports.*

**4**

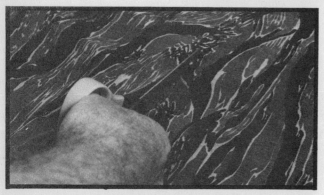

*Instead of pinning pattern to the cloth, as many do, Learn prefers to use tailor's chalk, marking out pattern, then cutting on lines.*

**5**

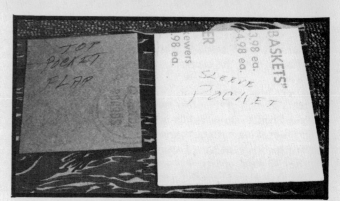

*Sleeve pockets should be large enough to hold a pack of cigarettes, compass, or small map. Flap is imperative to keep items from falling out if running or you have to bend over.*

**6**

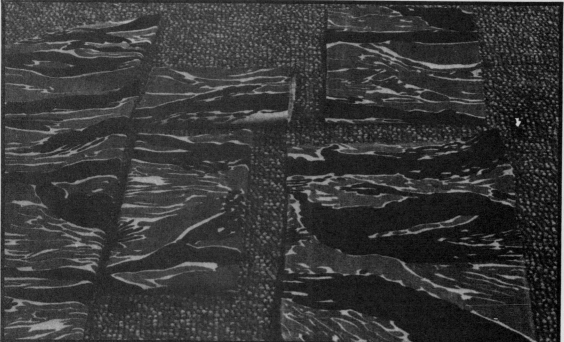

**7**

*The pockets are cut larger than actually will be needed, as part of the added material will be taken up by the seams, with additional needed for gussets. In photo, the cut material is at right, the sewn pocket at left.*

Before the sleeve is sewn, mark the position of the pocket, then sew on the main body of the sleeve pocket. If one waits until the sleeve has been closed, it will be necessary to sew pocket on shoulder by hand. **8**

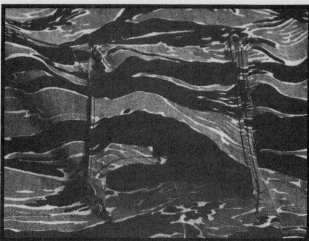

Right side of the sleeve pocket has double seam for strength. Note small section of Velcro to hold down the flap of pocket. Note matching of the camouflage stripes. **9**

is flapped, so allow for that too, with a wider pattern to cover the mouth of the pocket. So much for the outside pockets. I wanted one on the front of the shirt, but planned to put it inside."

The hidden front pocket came out 7½ inches square. Learn didn't want buttons or Velcro on it so he came up with a nylon zipper.

Learn removed the freshly washed and dried tiger-stripe material and spread it on his work table. The front was placed over the material and the pattern checked to determine in which direction the pattern should go. Learn decided to use the horizontal print pattern.

"Fold the material and place the front pattern on it matching the fold line to the fold on the material. Make certain you allow enough material on the other side for a seam. With scissors, cut the material following the pattern. When you unfold the material you will have a full front section," our craftsman instructs.

Do the same for the back using the fold technique. With front and back cut out, place them to one side.

Position the sleeve pattern with the print pattern grain direction matching that of the front and back sections. Weight the pattern down and cut the sleeves, mark them on the inside *left* and *right* with a soft pencil.

Next, use the small pieces left over to cut out the pockets, flaps and collar.

Ready to assemble, you need a sewing machine, good thread, an iron and board to keep the material flat.

"My favorite redhead, an excellent seamstress who cringed at the way I proceeded with this project, offered some interfacing, an iron-on stiffening material for collars and other uses," Learn reports.

"First cut a slot, fold back the edges and sew them for the right-side front pocket. Sew the zipper in securing the ends tightly. Sew the pocket under the zipper, make the flap, line it with interfacing and sew it on over the zipper. I allowed the flap to extend into the seam line on that side of the shirt.

"Pin the front and back sections at the shoulders and sew them together on the machine; I always use a double

The larger pocket for carrying lunches and lengths of rope, et al., is sewn on inside of the front right side of the shirt. The actual positioning is up to the maker. **10**

stitch and tack the ends. My machine in a vintage-class White Rotary on which I sew leather and nylon straps and anything I can get under the foot. It is a great old machine."

Place the sleeve pockets three inches down from the top edge and center them on the sleeve by folding the sleeve and the pocket in half, then pin it matching creases. If you want a cargo-style pocket, sew a seam all around the three edges about one inch in from the raw edge.

Place the pocket on the sleeve, pin and sew it. Using a piece of scrap material, match the pattern on the sleeve and make a flap, lining it with the interfacing. If using Velcro for a closure, this should be sewn on before reaching this point.

The sleeve pockets and flaps in place, we are ready to sew the sleeve to the body of the shirt. Pin around the edge

With zipper shown from front, edge of opening was folded over, sewn down for a clean closure, without raveling. **11**

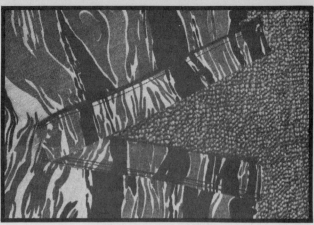

The neck opening is cut down about twelve inches, then two sections are sewn on to overlap the cut for neat, finished look. **12**

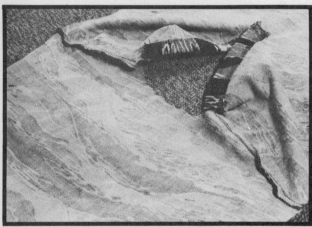

To finish the shirt after pockets have been installed, sew two top seams across shoulders. For extra strength double-stitch with nylon. **13**

For collar, place pattern on the doubled material and cut it out. For extra stiffening iron-on interfacing was applied prior to sewing, making task easier. **14**

The top flaps of the sleeve pockets and the collar were stiffened with the iron-on interfacing that can be found in nearly every yardage store. This stiffener affords the completed shirt a more professional look.

**15**

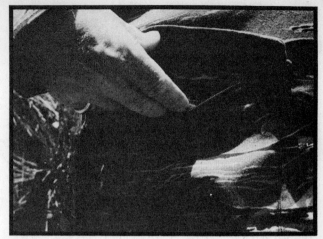

*Learn preferred to forego the difficulty of cuffs for his shirt; installed simple, non-snagging Velcro closures, as shown at left. Front pocket, right, is closed with nylon zipper and covered by flap; large but out of the way on hunts.*

of the sleeve, attaching it to the body on the inside. With the sleeve held in place in this manner, sew the sleeve to the body. Both sleeves are handled in the same manner.

"Put the shirt on like a floppy sack now to check the fit. I allowed extra material on my pattern for the seams, as my seam-sewing methods are not too exact," Bob Learn says.

"Turning the shirt inside out, I start at the underarm junction and sew out to the end of the sleeve, turn it around and sew back and down the body seam to the end, then back again. This makes the seam under the arm very strong. Do the same for the other side and your shirt is almost done."

It still is necessary to open up the front for the neck area. Fold the shirt at mid-point on the front body, mark down seven or eight inches and cut along that line. Using small scraps of material, make a stiffer front section using the interfacing. Fold this over the cut seam and sew it into place on each side for a neat, strong neck opening.

"The collar," Learn admits, "is where I get into trouble. I had cut pieces from the collar pattern, lined and sewed them. I wanted the smooth edge against my neck, so I flopped the collar over with the inside against the top of the back side of the neck opening. Pin and sew, then roll the collar back, fold the back seam under and sew that to the body and you are almost done. This collar turned out great, the interfacing keeping it stiffer, making it look better."

Fold the bottom section of the body over twice so you have no raw edge visible, then sew it completely around.

All that is left is the sleeve closure. Learn wanted Velcro closures, so he folded the sleeve under and extended the arm to check for proper sleeve length. When it felt right, he lined the fold under with interfacing and sewed it down at that point, along both the front and back edges.

Fold the cuff from inside toward the outside and you will find it gathers the sleeve and keeps it a tight, clean line from shoulder to wrist, just what you need for your

shooting arm. Fold it, pin it, then actually draw a bow before adding the Velcro. Mark the fold line with chalk and add two pieces of Velcro about two inches long to the flap section. This makes it adjustable so a shirt or sweater can be worn underneath in cold weather. Do the same for the right sleeve.

With this homemade tiger-stripe camo shirt, there are no pockets in front to snag a string. You have a cargo or large pocket well away from the bow and the zipper is hidden. You have sleeve pockets for small gear, compass, matches and other items that won't rattle.

*A shoulder pocket is favored by many bowhunters, as it is out of the way of the bowstring when shooting. This one is sufficiently large for a number of small needs.*

*Some archery clubs lease or own facilities for indoor shooting, and this is especially valuable during winter.*

## CHAPTER 19

# ORGANIZED BOWHUNTING

# FUN

### One Can Learn Through The
### Social And Competitive Aspects

*There are situations, however, where the bowhunter must shun company, as is demonstrated in this photo.*

**B**OWHUNTING IS, in many ways, a loner's sport. An archer intent on taking an animal or bird usually heads afield by himself, even if several fine hunting companions join him around the campfire each night to swap hunting stories and compare notes on the day's activities. There are simply some bowhunting goals that can't be met with someone tagging along behind.

Despite the solo nature of many bowhunting activities, there are many other bowhunting events that are extremely social in nature. These sorts of organized bowhunting fun are available to anyone who wishes to participate and many seem to be growing rapidly in popularity as more and more hunting archers discover them.

The most grass-roots bowhunting organization a hunter can belong to is the local archery club. Archery clubs are numerous around the country and vary considerably in size and structure, depending on the area and the people involved.

Most local archery clubs have regular shooting ranges where a hunter can practice his target skills with friends. Although the majority of these ranges are outdoor setups with one or more butts to shoot into, quite a few larger clubs rent indoor facilities for the purpose of shooting targets at close range (say twenty yards) throughout the winter months no matter what the weather conditions happen to be. Such indoor archery shooting is normally a highly social activity among good bowhunting friends, with abundant side bets riding for the best score shot on a given night and in many cases weekly or yearly prizes awarded for top target scores.

*Shooting at archery silhouettes is rapidly gaining popularity these days with serious archers (above). Such sport sharpens the shooting eye in a very exciting way! The large bowfishing tournaments like Clear Lake's annual contest make friends with scientists and anglers alike. Rough fish like carp (right) that compete with bass and trout are eliminated, encouraging growing populations of quality species.*

Many archery clubs in larger towns put on annual invitational field-archery shoots to test the skills of archers in the area. Such shoots usually require shooting at several dozen targets spread out over a course similar to a golf course. Standard scoring rules govern such shoots, with the top archers in various equipment divisions winning prizes. A fair number of such contests are so-called "animal shoots" with cardboard and/or three-dimensional animal targets such as deer, bear and elk. Participating in an organized animal shoot can be extremely enjoyable for any hunter, providing both excellent shooting practice and the chance to win a prize for an exceptional score.

For the archer who really dotes on outdoor target shooting as well as regular hunting for game, several large state and national archery competitions are sponsored each year by various archery manufacturers in conjunction with national archery organizations like the National Archery Association (NAA) and the National Field Archery Association (NFAA). Such major shoots definitely separate the men from the boys, and they provide the ultimate in serious shooting competition both indoors and out. For more information on major target competitions, contact your local archery store or shooting club.

One new form of organized archery competition that is

*Harvey Naslund, popular tournament director of California's annual Clear Lake bowfishing competition, awards raffle prizes here to a large, enthusiastic crowd. Bowfishing tournaments of this sort are popular these days.*

coming on strong these days is shooting at plastic archery silhouette targets. Such silhouette shooting is exciting to participate in and also exciting to watch, and promises to become an especially popular form of organized archery fun as more and more bowhunters find out about it. Silhouette shooting with rifles, handguns, and air guns has enjoyed sensational success over the past few years, and the visual thrill of seeing an upright target go down on impact is bound to turn archers on every bit as much.

As mentioned in Chapter 17, organized bowfishing tournaments with strict rules and tempting prizes are all the rage in some parts of the country. The carp is the primary target at most tournaments — a circumstance that thrills fish biologists in the area of a tournament because carp

compete directly with bass and other desirable species. One such tournament is annually sponsored by Easton Aluminum at Clear Lake, California's largest natural body of water. In a normal year, the two-hundred two-man bowfishing teams in this event take over 20,000 pounds (ten tons) of carp during fifteen hours of official shooting. The game fish in the lake benefit, local sportfishermen benefit and all the participants in the tournament also benefit.

Perhaps the most widespread form of organized bowhunting competition is held by various big-game record-keeping organizations around the country. Such groups keep records of exceptionally large animals taken with bow-and-arrow gear and periodically hold conventions

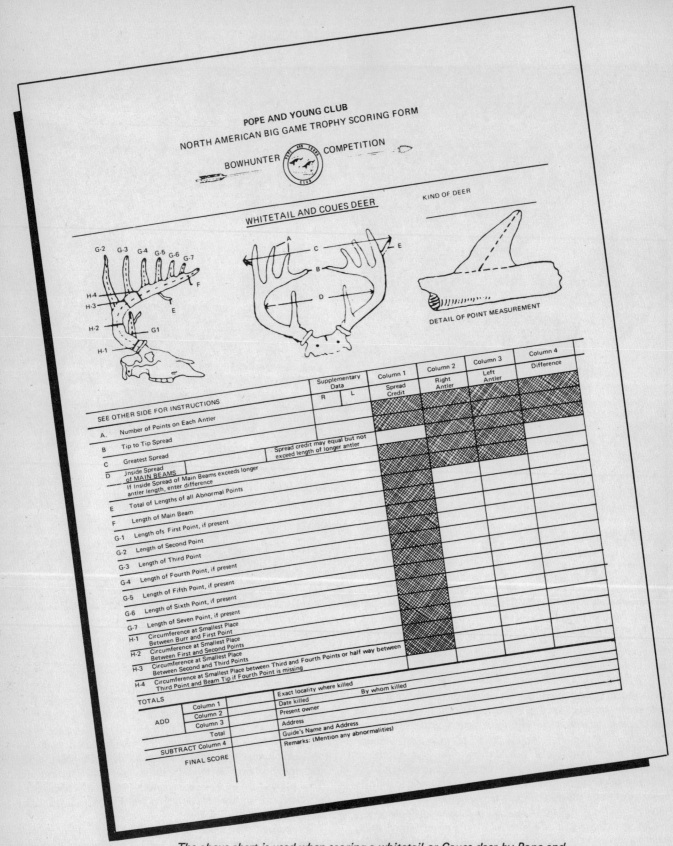

POPE AND YOUNG CLUB

NORTH AMERICAN BIG GAME TROPHY SCORING FORM

BOWHUNTER COMPETITION

WHITETAIL AND COUES DEER

KIND OF DEER

DETAIL OF POINT MEASUREMENT

| | Supplementary Data | | Column 1 | Column 2 | Column 3 | Column 4 |
|---|---|---|---|---|---|---|
| SEE OTHER SIDE FOR INSTRUCTIONS | R | L | Spread Credit | Right Antler | Left Antler | Difference |
| A. Number of Points on Each Antler | | | | | | |
| B. Tip to Tip Spread | | | | | | |
| C. Greatest Spread | Spread credit may equal but not exceed length of longer antler | | | | | |
| D. Inside Spread of MAIN BEAMS | If Inside Spread of Main Beams exceeds longer antler length, enter difference | | | | | |
| E. Total of Lengths of all Abnormal Points | | | | | | |
| F. Length of Main Beam | | | | | | |
| G-1 Length ofs First Point, if present | | | | | | |
| G-2 Length of Second Point | | | | | | |
| G-3 Length of Third Point | | | | | | |
| G-4 Length of Fourth Point, if present | | | | | | |
| G-5 Length of Fifth Point, if present | | | | | | |
| G-6 Length of Sixth Point, if present | | | | | | |
| G-7 Length of Seven Point, if present | | | | | | |
| H-1 Circumference at Smallest Place Between Burr and First Point | | | | | | |
| H-2 Circumference at Smallest Place Between First and Second Points | | | | | | |
| H-3 Circumference at Smallest Place Between Second and Third Points | | | | | | |
| H-4 Circumference at Smallest Place between Third and Fourth Points or half way between Third Point and Beam Tip if Fourth Point is missing | | | | | | |

| TOTALS | | | Exact locality where killed | By whom killed |
|---|---|---|---|---|
| ADD | Column 1 | | Date killed | |
| | Column 2 | | Present owner | |
| | Column 3 | | Address | |
| | Total | | Guide's Name and Address | |
| SUBTRACT Column 4 | | | Remarks: (Mention any abnormalities) | |
| FINAL SCORE | | | | |

*The above chart is used when scoring a whitetail or Coues deer by Pope and Young Club standards. You needn't be a club member to submit possible trophy.*

*Right: Animals like this toothy wild boar make top trophies for selective archers like well-known bowhunter Joe Johnston (on left). Below: Companionship in far-flung hunting camps is one very rewarding aspect of the bowhunting lifestyle — an aspect every serious nimrod comes to appreciate every bit as much as solo outings after game.*

to award prizes for the very best animals taken during prescribed periods of time.

Every archer who hunts big game can deliberately trophy hunt with record-book minimum scores in mind, setting an extra challenge atop the basic challenge of taking any animal with a bow. Although trophy bowhunting is not for everyone, and is not at all necessary to have a fine·time, it is a highly enjoyable endeavor for many serious and widely experienced hunters.

To find out about state and national big-game record-keeping organizations, contact your local hunting club or archery shop dealer. Each record club has different methods of judging various animals and different rules about how and where these animals can be taken — things an archer must be aware of to compete on an equal footing with other bow-benders around the country.

The primary national big-game record-keeping organization for hunting archers is the famous Pope and Young Club, named after Dr. Saxton Pope and Art Young, two forefathers of modern bowhunting. This excellent record club provides a network of official trophy measurers around the country, a biennial big-game competition and awards convention, and an excellent, periodically updated record book listing all trophies that have measured up to snuff according to minimum scoring requirements. Anyone can become an associate member of the Pope and Young Club by paying annual dues and anyone can submit acceptable bowhunting trophies whether they belong to this organization or not.

A well-rounded bowhunter takes full advantage of organized archery activities to increase his pleasure and improve his performance on game. Although bowhunting is often a sport practiced alone, it can also be a sport actively shared and enjoyed with others.

# Directory Of The BOWHUNTING TRADE

## BOW MANUFACTURERS

Allen Archery, 200 Washington St., Billings, MO 65610 (bows, accessories)

American Archery, P.O. Box 100 Indus. Park, Oconto Falls, WI 54154 (bows, accessories)

Bear Archery, RR 4, 4600 Southwest 41st Blvd., Gainesville, FL 32601

Bingham Archery, Box 3013, Ogden, UT 84403 (bows, accessories)

Boswell Longbow, P.O. Box 3061 T.A., Spokane, WA 99220 (longbows)

Browning, Rt. 1, Morgan, UT 84050 (bows, accessories)

Carroll's Archery Products, 59½ South Main, Moab, UT 84532 (bows, accessories)

Cravotta Brothers, Inc., Third St., E. McKeesport, PA 15132 (bows)

Darton, Inc., Archery Division, 3261 Flushing Rd., Flint, MI 48504 (bows)

East Side Archery Ltd., 3711 E. 106th St., Chicago, IL 60617 (longbows, accessories)

Graham's Custom Bows, P.O. Box 1312, Fontana, CA 92335 (bows, accessories)

Herter's Inc., RR1, Waseca, MN 56093 (bows, accessories)

Howard Hill Archery, Rt. 1, Box 1397, Hamilton, MT 59840 (longbows, accessories)

Damon Howatt (Martin Archery), Rt. 5, Box 127, Walla Walla, WA 99362 (bows)

Jack Howard, Washington Star Rt., Nevada City, CA 95959 (bows, accessories)

Hoyt Archery Co., 11510 Natural Bridge Rd., Bridgeton, MO 63044 (bows, accessories)

Indian Archery, 817 Maxwell Ave., Evansville, IN 47717 (bows, accessories)

Jeffery Enterprises, Inc., 821 Pepper St., Columbia, SC 29209 (bows)

Jennings Compound Bow Inc., 28756 N. Castaic Cyn. Rd., Valencia, CA 91355 (bows, accessories)

Kittredge Bow Hut, P.O. Box 598, Mammoth Lakes, CA 93546 (bows, accessories)

LongBow Mfg. Co., 1827 Stampede Ave., Cody, WY 82414 (longbows, accessories)

Martin Archery, Rt. 5, Box 127, Walla Walla, WA 99362 (bows, accessories)

Mohawk Archery, 228 Bridge St., E. Syracuse, NY 13057 (bows, accessories)

Dick Palmer Archery, 1262 College Ave., Elmira, NY 14901 (longbows, accessories)

Ben Pearson Archery, P.O. Box 7465, Pine Bluff, AR 71611

Plas/Steel Products, Inc., Walkerton, IN 46574

Precision Shooting Equipment, Main St., Mahomet, IL 61853 (bows, accessories)

Pro-Line Co., 1843 Gun Lake Rd., Box 370, Hastings, MI 49058 (bows, accessories)

Rigid Archery Products, 445 Central Ave., Montclair, NJ 07307 (bows, accessories)

Spartan Archery, Inc., 474 Wheeler N., Seattle, WA 98109 (bows)

Stemmler Archery, 984 Southford Rd., Middleburg, CT 06762 (bows, accessories)

TSS, 419 Van Dyne Rd., N. Fond du Lac, WI 54935

Woodcraft Equip. Co./York Archery, P.O. Box 110, Independence, MO 64051

Yamaha International Corp., 6600 Orangethorpe Ave., Buena Park, CA 90620 (bows)

Zebra Long Bow Mfg. Co., 231 E. Meuse St., Blue Grass, IA 52726 (longbows)

## ARROW SUPPLIES

Acme Wood Products Co., P.O. Box 101, Myrtle Point, OR 97458 (cedar)

American Archer, P.O. Box 100, Industrial Park, Oconto Falls, WI 54154 (arrows ready-made)

Anderson Archery Corp., Grand Ledge, MI 48837 (arrows ready-made, components)

Archer's View, P.O. Box 487, Linden, MI 49451 (arrows)

Archery Headquarters, 4591 N. Peck Road, El Monte, CA 91732 (made-to-order, ready-made, components)

Arrow Manufacturing, Inc., 1365 Logan Ave., Costa Mesa, CA 92626 (made-to-order, ready-made, components)

Arrow Mart, 1670 Babcock, Costa Mesa, CA 92627 (ready-made)

Bear Archery, RR 4, 4600 Southwest 41st Blvd., Gainesville, FL 32601 (ready-made, Bear Metrics, components)

Bohning Adhesive Co., Ltd., Rt. 2, Lake City, MI 49651 (components, arrow repair kits)

Bowhunters Discount Warehouse, Inc., Box 158-R, Wellsville, PA 17365 (ready-made, components)

Cabela's, P.O. Box 199, Sidney, NE 69162 (graphite)

Custom Archery Equipment, 1645 W. Sepulveda, Torrance, CA 90501 (ready-made)

Darton, Inc., Archery Division, 3261 Flushing Rd., Flint, MI 48504 (ready-made)

Easton Aluminum Inc., 7800 Haskell Ave., Van Nuys, CA 91406 (aluminum, components)

R&C Elliott Corp., Box 469, Spencer, IA 51301 (Gilmore fiberglass)

Vic Erickson, 1295 Ada Ave., Idaho Falls, ID 83401 (arrows)

F/S Arrows, Box 8094, Fountain Valley, CA 92708 (ready-made)

Gordon Plastics, Inc., 2872 S. Santa Fe Ave., Vista, CA 92083 (fiberglass, graphite)

Herters, Inc., Waseca, MN 56093 (ready-made, accessories)

Jack Howard Archery Co., Washington Star Rt., Box 220, Nevada City, CA 95959 (ready-made, components)

Hunter Arrows, 177-F Riverside Ave., Newport Beach, CA 92663 (ready-made, components)

Hunter's International, 26422 Groesbeck Hwy., Warren, MI 48089 (steel arrows, accessories)

Indian Archery, P.O. Box 889, 817 Maxwell Ave., Evansville, IN 47706 (ready-made)

Doug Kittredge Bow Hut, P.O. Box 598, Mammoth Lakes, CA 93546 (ready-made, components)

Lamiglass, Inc., Box 148, Woodland, WA 98674 (graphite arrows)

Martin Archery, Inc., Rt. 5, Box 127, Walla Walla, WA 99362 (ready-made, made-to-order, components)

McKinney Arrow Shafts, Oakland, OR 97462 (arrows)

Northeast Archery, P.O. Box 552, Brewer, ME 04412 (ready-made, components)

Norway Archery, Norway, OR 97460 (cedar)

Ben Pearson Archery, Inc., P.O. Box 7465, Pine Bluff, AR 71611 (ready-made)

Precision Shooting Equipment, Inc., Mahomet, IL 61853 (ready-made, components, PSE Pro-Fletch vanes)

Rose City Archery, Inc., Box 342, Powers, OR 97458 (cedar)

Seattle Archery, Inc., Box 120, Lynnwood, WA 98036 (ready-made)

Shaw Custom Arrows, Julie Dr., RD 4, Hopewell Jct., NY 12533 (custom-made)

Stemmler Archery Inc., Southford Rd., Middlebury, CT 06762 (ready-made)

Sweetland Products, 1010 Arrowsmith St., Eugene, OR 97402 (components)

Texas Feathers, Inc., Box 1118, Brownwood, TX 76801 (feathers)

Trueflight Mfg. Co., Inc., Manitowish Waters, WI 54545 (feathers)

Ultra Products Ltd., Box 100, Fairfield, IL 62837 (vanes)

Utah Feathers, Box 396, Orem, UT 84057 (feathers)

Wood Arrows, P.O. Box 665, Coos Bay, OR 97420 (cedar)

## BOW-SHOOTING ACCESSORIES

Accra Mfg. Co., 717 N. Sheridan, Tulsa, OK 74115 (sights, other accessories)

Accuflite, P.O. Box 101, Turtle Creek, PA 15154 (accessories)

Altier Archery Mfg., Honesdale, PA 18431 (sights)

Archer's Arm, Payne St., Elmsford, NY 10523 (armguards, accessories)

Arrow Hold Mfg., P.O. Box 2246, Rockford, IL 61111 (release/hold)

Chas. E. Babington Corp., P.O. Box 277, Vandalia, OH 45377 (release)

Barner Release, P.O. Box 382, Bozeman, MT 59715 (release)

Joe Bender, Stoddard, WI 54658 (bowstring attachment)

Bigame Products, 20551 Sunset, Detroit, MI 48234 (broadhead)

Bobkat Archery, 2312 N. 400 E, Ogden, UT 84404 (peepsight)

Bonnie Bowman, 1619 Abram Ct., San Leandro, CA 94577 (accessories)

C/J Enterprises, 410 S. Citrus Ave., Covina, CA 91722 (release)

Cajun Archery, Inc., Rt. 3, Box 88, New Iberia, LA 70560 (accessories)

Cobra Bow Sight, 6737 E. 5th Pl., Tulsa, OK 74112 (sights)

J. Dye Enterprises, 1707 Childerlee Ln., NE, Atlanta, GA 30329 (arrow guide)

Dyn-O-Mite Archery, 225 SW Western Ave., Grants Pass, OR 97526 (releases, other accessories)

Evans Archery Products, Box 40453, Cincinnati, OH 45240 (accessories)

Fine-Line, Inc., 6922 N. Meridian, Puyallup, WA 98371 (sights)

Frontier Archery Co., 3440 La Grande Blvd., Sacramento, CA 95823 (accessories)

Full Adjust Products, 915 N. Ann St., Lancaster, PA 17602 (accessories)

M.R. Gazzara Mfg. Co., 345 White Horse Pike, Hammonton, NJ 08037 (release)

Golden Key Futura Archery, 1851 S. Orange Ave., Monterey Park, CA 91754 (sights, other accessories)

Gorman's Design, Box 21102, Minneapolis, MN 55421 (sights)

Granpa Specialty, 10801 Ridgecrest Dr., St. Ann, MO 63074 (broadhead)

Hi-Precision Co., Orange City, IA 51041

J.C. Mfg. Co., 6435 W. 55th Ave., Arvada, CO 80002 (accessories)

Kolpin Mfg. Inc., P.O. Box 231, 119 S. Pearl St., Berlin, WI 54923 (gloves, tabs, other accessories)

Kwikee Kwiver Co., 7292 Peaceful Valley Rd., Acme, MI 49610 (quivers)

Lee's Archery Mfg., Rt. 2, Box 269, Sedalia, MO 65301 (slings, other accessories)

Lewis & Lewis, Rt. 1, Box 4, Nekoosa, WI 54457 (release)

Midwestern Engineering & Mfg., 2737 Expressway, P.O. Box 444, Ypsilanti, MI 48197 (broadhead)

Moto Miter Co., Prairie du Chien, WI 53821 (release)

Make-All Tool & Die Co., 1924 S. 74th St., W. Allis, WI 53219 (broadhead)

National Archery Co., Rt. 1, Princeton, MN 55371 (accessories)

National Archery Supply, 4738 Frederick Blvd., St. Joseph, MO 64506 (rest, grips)

New Archery Products Corp., 370 N. Delaplaine Rd., Riverside, IL 60546 (broadheads, other accessories)

Nirk Archery Co., Potlatch, ID 83855 (accessories)

Nock Rite Co., 3720 Crestview Circle, Brookfield, WI 53005 (bow-string attachment)

Old West Leathercraft, Inc., 2244-2 Main St., Chula Vista, CA 92011 (leather quivers, accessories)

Papoose Arrow Quiver, P.O. Box 5056, Kofa Station, Yuma, AZ 85364 (quiver)

Precision Shooter Co., P.O. Box 201, Flushing, MI 48433 (release)

RC Mfg., 3465 Woodward Ave., Santa Clara, CA 95050 (accessories)

R&D Products, P.O. Box 154, Euless, TX 76039 (accessories)

Rancho Safari, Box 691, Ramona, CA 92065 (quiver, other accessories)

Range-O-Matic Archery Co., 35572 Strathcona Dr., Mt. Clemens, MI 48043 (sight, other accessories)

Ranging, Inc., 90 Lincoln Road North, East Rochester, NY 14445 (rangefinders)

Razorback Sporting Goods Mfg., Box 367, Flippin, AR 72634

Renson Sport Supply, 6307 Long Lk. Rd., Sterling Hts., MI 48037 (broadhead)

Richmond Sports, 56 Spartan Ave., Graniteville, NY 10303 (clicker)

S&K Mfg., 11320 East Mill Plain Blvd., Vancouver, WA 98664 (release)

Safariland Archery, Box 579, McLean, VA 22101 (accessories)

Sanjo Custom Archery Products, P.O. Box 327, Marcus, PA 19061 (accessories)

Saunders Archery Co., P.O. Box 476, Columbus, NE 68601

Savora Archery, Inc., Box 465, Kirkland, WA 98033 (broadheads)

Saxon Archery, Inc., P.O. Box 1277, Bellaire, TX 77401 (broadheads)

Selector, P.O. Box 1588 VHFS, Warrenton, VA 22186 (release)

Sherwin Industries, P.O. Box 849, Port Richey, FL 33568 (broadhead)

Smith's Sports Products, 925 Hillcrest Pl., Pasadena, CA 91106 (bow sling)

Spectre Archery Ent., 17th & Northampton Sts., Easton, PA 18042 (accessories)

Sportronics, P.O. Box 09045, Detroit, MI 48209 (sight)

Sprandel's Bowsight Co., 19 Brookside Dr., Monroe, CT 06468 (sight)

Stanislawski Archery Products, 7135 SE Cora St., Portland, OR 97206 (accessories)

Stuart Mfg. Co., P.O. Box 718, Rockwall, TX 75087 (release)

Sure Shot, P.O. Box 486-B, Parowan, UT 84761 (release)

Tomar Corp., Indus. Pk. Dr., Harbor Springs, MI 49740 (accessories)

Toxonics, Inc., P.O. Box 1303, St. Charles, MO 63301 (sight)

Trueflight Mfg. Co., Inc., Manitowish Waters, WI 54545 (accessories)

WASP Archery Products, P.O. Box 760, Bristol, CT 06010 (broadheads)

L.C. Whiffen Co., Inc., 923 S. 16th St., Milwaukee, WI 53204 (accessories)

Wilson Allen Corp., Box 302, Windsor, MO 65360 (accessories)

Wilson Bros. Mfg., Kendall Branch, Miami, FL 33156 (release)

Zwickey Archery Co., 257 E. 12th Ave., No. St. Paul, MN 55109 (broadheads, points)

## MISCELLANEOUS SHOOTING EQUIPMENT

A.J.'s Targets, 267 Highland Ave., Downington, PA 19335 (targets)

Don Adams Marine, Rt. 2, Box 241, Veneta, OR 97487 (bow wood)

Aerial Archery, P.O. Box 81, Lenox Dale, MA 01242 (aerial target)

Henry A. Bitzenburger, Rt. 2, Box M1, Sherwood, OR 97140 (jigs)

Bohning Adhesives Co., Ltd., Rt. 2, Box 140, Lake City, MI 49651 (lacquers, epoxy, other materials and accessories)

Bows Unlimited, 5501 Acoma S.E., Albuquerque, NM 87108 (recurve to compound conversion)

Calmont Compound Archery Target, Box 207, Inverness, MS 38753 (targets)

Freeman's Archery, RR 3, Box 536, Plainfield, IN 46168 (targets)

Jim Dougherty Archery, 4304 E. Pine Place, Tulsa, OK 74115 (bows, arrows)

Micro Motion Inc., 2700 29th St., Boulder, CO 80301 (arrow chronograph)

Dave Miller, Rare Woods, 3180 Bandini Blvd., Vernon, CA 90023 (bow wood)

Old Master Crafters Co., 130 Lebaron St., Waukegan, IL 60085 (bow making materials)

Papi, P.O. Box 55184, Fort Washington, MD 20022 (trophy system for bowhunters)

RLC Archery Enterprises, Inc., P.O. Box 8530, Portland, OR 97207 (recurve to compound conversion kits)

San Angelo, Box 984, San Angelo, TX 76901 (bow racks, other accessories)

Tandy Leather Co., 2808 Shamrock, Fort Worth, TX 76107 (leather archery accessories, kits)

Earl Ullrich, Box 862, Roseburg, OR 97470 (bow wood)

Van's Archery Supplies, P.O. Box 929, St. George, UT 84470 (arrow puller)

Zonkers, P.O. Box 4304, Auburn Heights, MI 48057

## BOW & ARROW CASES

Alco Carrying Cases, Inc., 601 W. 26th St., New York, NY 10001

The Allen Co., Inc., 2330 W. Midway Blvd., Broomfield, CO 80020

Challanger Manufacturing Corporation, 94-28 Merrick Boulevard, Jamaica, NY 11433

Gateway Luggage Manufacturing Company, Incorporated, 820 W. Tenth Street, Claremore, OK 74017

Gun-Ho, 110 E. Tenth Street, St. Paul, MN 55101

Paul-Reed, Incorporated, P.O. Box 227, Charlevoix, MI 49720

Penguin Industries, P.O. Box 97, Parkesburg, PA 19365

Protecto Plastics, Incorporated, 201 Alpha Road, Wind Gap, PA 18091

Sloane Products, P.O. Box 56, Saugus, CA 91350

Sportscase, Incorporated, 204 Central Avenue, Osseo, MN 55368

Sylvester's Archery Supplies, 212 Hawthorne Circle, Creve Coeur, IL 61611

## VARMINT & GAME CALLS

Burnham Brothers, Box 110, Marble Falls, TX 78654

Electronic Game Calls, 210 W. Grand Avenue, Grand Rapids, MI 54494

Faulk's Game Call Company, Incorporated, 616 18th Street, Lake Charles, LA 70601

P.S. Olt Company, Pekin, IL 61554

Penn's Woods Products, Incorporated, 19 W. Pittsburgh Street, Delmont, PA 15625

Scotch Game Call Company, Incorporated, 60 Main Street, Oakfield, NY 14125

Johnny Stewart Game Calls, Incorporated, 5100 Fort Avenue, P.O. Box 1909, Waco, TX 76703

Thomas Game Calls, P.O. Box 336, Winnsboro, TX 75494

Western Call & Decoy, P.O. Box 425, Portland, OR 97207

## MISCELLANEOUS HUNTING EQUIPMENT

A&W Archer, Box 1219, Garden Grove, CA 92640 (bow quivers)

Avery Corporation, P.O. Box 99, 221 N. Main Street, Electra, TX 76360 (varmint calling lights)

Auto-Quiver, P.O. Box 771, Wayne, NJ 07470 (bow quivers)

Baker Manufacturing Company, Box 1003, Valdosta, GA 31601 (tree stands)

Belke Company, 2308 Pleasant, New Holstein, WI 53061 (saw-knife)

Joe Bender, Stoddard, WI 54658 (No-Glove finger protectors)
Vic Berger, 1019 Garfield Avenue, Springfield, OH 45504 (Berger button)
Brownell, Incorporated, Moodus, CT 06469 (bowstring material)
Buck Knives, 1717 N. Magnolia Avenue, El Cajon, CA 92022 (hunting knives)
Buck Stop Lure Company, 3015 Grow Road, Stanton, MI 48888 (insect repellent, deer lure)
C/J Enterprises, 410 S. Citrus Avenue, Covina, CA 91722 (one-piece aluminum release)
Camillus Cutlery Company, Camillus, NY 13031 (hunting knives)
Camouflage Manufacturing Company, 9075 Atlantic Blvd., Jacksonville, FL 32215 (camouflage hunting clothes and accessories)
Camp-lite Products, Incorporated, 1408 W. Colfax, Denver, CO 80204 (lightweight backpack and camping tents)
Camp Trails, P.O. Box 14500, Phoenix, AZ 95031 (backpacking and camping equipment)
Colorado Outdoor Sports Company, 1636 Champs Street, P.O. Box 5544, Denver, CO 80217 (lightweight packing equipment)
Cutter Laboratories, Incorporated, Fourth and Parker Streets, Berkeley, CA 94619 (insect repellents, snake bite kits, first aid kits)
D&D Rods, Box 206, Comstock, MI 49041 (stabilizer rods and weights)
Deer Me Products, Box 345, Anoka, MN 55303 (tree steps, tree stands, deer drags)
Dolch Enterprises, Incorporated, Box 606, Westlake, LA 70669 (telescopic bowstringer)
Federal Instrument Company, 93-36 65th Avenue, Rego Park, NY 11374 (rangefinders)
Fleetwood, 902 Ogden Avenue, Superior, WI 54880 (general line of accessories and bow racks)
Game Winner, Incorporated, 2940 First National Bank Tower, Atlanta, GA 30303 (camouflage and hunting clothes, accessories)
General Recreation Industries, Fayette, AL 35555 (sleeping bags)
Gordon Plastics, Incorporated, 5334 Banks Street, San Diego, CA 92110 (fiberglass shafts)
Gutmann Cutlery Company, Incorporated, 900 S. Columbus Ave., Mt. Vernon, NY 10550 (hunting knives)
Indian Ridge Traders, P.O. Box X-50, Ferndale, MI 48220 (hunting, skinning knives)
Jet-Aer Corporation, 100 Sixth Ave., Paterson, NJ 07524 (insect repellents, game lures, fabric and leather treatments and water-proofings)
Jim Dougherty Archery, 4304 E. Pine Place, Tulsa, OK 74115 (all bowhunting gear)
Kelty Pack, Incorporated, P.O. Box 639, 10909 Tuxford St., Sun Valley, CA 91352 (pack bags, pack frames, soft packs)
Killian Chek-It, 12350 S.E. Stevens Rd., Portland, OR 97226 (competition string release)
Kwikee Kwiver Company, 7292 Peaceful Valley Rd., Acme, MI 49610 (bow quivers)
Lawson Manufacturing Company, Rt. 3, Oregon, IL 61061 (tree stands)
Len Company, BT-101 Brooklyn, NY 11214 (survival knives)
L&M Cork Products, Mokena, IL 60448 (cork target back-stops, mats)
Magna-Flight, 212 Hawthorne Circle, Creve Coeur, IL 61611 (bowstring releases)
Mac's Archery Supplies, Incorporated, 6336 W. Fond du Lac Ave., Milwaukee, WI 53218 (bowfishing reels, arrows, points)
Marco's Enterprises, 2120 Ludington St., Escanaba, MI 49829 (deer soap)
Mini Bow, 1880 Century Park East, Suite 315, Los Angeles, CA 90067 (novel system for living room archery)
Mountain Products Corporation, 123 S. Wanatchee Ave., Wenatchee, WA 98801 (lightweight camping gear)
National Packaged Trail Foods, 632 E. 185th St., Cleveland, OH 44119 (freeze-dried camping foods)
Natural Scent Company, 1170 Elgin Ave., Salt Lake City, UT 84106 (animal scents)
New Archery Products, 107 Berrywood Dr., Marietta, GA 30060 (flipper rests)
Nock Rite Company, 3720 Crestview Circle, Brookfield, WI 53005 (bowstring attachments)
Old Master Crafters Company, 130 Lebaron St., Waukegan, IL 60085 (bow laminations)
W.C. Phillips, 2515 Magnolia, Texarkana, TX 75501 (tree stands)
R&D Products, P.O. Box 154, Euless, TX 76039 (arrow holders and bowfishing points)
Ranger Manufacturing Company, P.O. Box 3386, Augusta, GA 30904 (camouflage clothing)
Ranging, Incorporated, P.O. Box 9106, Rochester, NY 14625 (range-determining devices)
Razor Edge, Box 203, Butler, WI 54007 (hunting knives)
Ron's Porta-Pak Manufacturing Company, P.O. Box 141, Greenbrier, AR 72058 (tree stands)

Rorco, Box 1007, State College, PA 16801 (shaft spiders)
S&K Manufacturing, 1707 S.E. 136th Avenue, Vancouver, WA 98664 (hunting release)
San Angelo Die Casting Company, Box 984, San Angelo, TX 76901 (bow racks and holders)
Saunders Archery Company, P.O. Box 476, Industrial Site, Columbus, NE 68601 (complete line of archery accessories)
Schrade Walden Cutlery Corporation, New York, NY 12428 (hunting knives)
Shockalator, 12122 Monter, Bridgeton, MO 63044 (mercury bow stabilizers)
Smiths Sports Products, 925 Hillcrest Place, Pasadena, CA 91106 (bow slings)
10-X Manufacturing, 100 S.W. Third Street, Des Moines, IA 59309 (camouflage and hunting clothing)
Trail Chef Foods, P.O. Box 60041, Terminal Annex, Los Angeles, CA 90060 (lightweight foods)
Trophyland USA, Incorporated, 7001 West 20th Avenue, P.O. Box 4606, Hialeah, FL 33014 (trophies)
Trueflight Manufacturing Company, Incorporated, Manitowish Waters, WI 54545 (string silencers, nock locators and assorted accessories)
Wilson-Allen Corporation, Box 104, Windsor, MO 65360 (brush nock)
L.C. Whiffen Company, Incorporated, 923 S. 16th Street, Milwaukee, WI 53204 (bow quivers)
R.C. Young Company, Incorporated, Manitowoc, WI 54220 (feather trimmers)

## NATIONAL BOWHUNTING ORGANIZATIONS

American Archery Council (AAC), 200 Castlewood Rd., N. Palm Beach Beach, FL 33408
American Indoor Archery Association (AIAA), P.O. Box 174, Grayling, MI 49738
Archery Lane Operator's Association (ALOA), 2151 N. Hamline Ave., St. Paul, MN 55113
Archery Manufacturers Organization (AMO), 200 Castlewood Rd., N. Palm Beach, FL 33408
The Fred Bear Sports Club, RR4, 4600 S.W. 41st Blvd., Gainesville, FL 32601
Bowhunters Who Care, P.O. Box 476, Columbus, NE 68601
National Archery Association (NAA), 1951 Geraldson Dr., Lancaster, PA 17601
National Bowfishing Association, 1895 N. McCart, Stephenville, TX 76401
National Field Archery Association (NFAA), Rt. 2, Box 514, Redlands, CA 92373
Pope & Young Club, Rt. 1, Box 147, Salmon, ID 83467
PSE Outdoor Adventures, Main St., Mahomet, IL 61853
Professional Archers Association (PAA), P.O. Box 7609, Flint, MI 48507
Professional Bowhunters Society, P.O. Box 13, New Concord, OH 43762

## MAIL ORDER DEALERS
(not listed elsewhere)

Al's Sports Inc., 195 E. State St., Iola, WI 54945
Anderson Archery, Box 130, Grand Ledge, MI 48837
Archery Distributors, Box 488, Holmen, WI 54636
Archery Wholesale, 2007 High St., Alameda, CA 94501
Arrowhead Archery, 1454 Velp Ave., Green Bay, WI 54636
Barefoot Archery, Inc., 5501 Wilkinson Blvd., Charlotte, NC 28202
Bowhunters Discount Warehouse, Inc., Zeigler Rd., Wellsville, PA 17365 17365
Bowhunters Supply, Rt. 6, Box 1158, Parkerburg, WV 26101
Butler's Archery, 100 8th St. No. 1, Evanston, WY 82930
Cabela's Inc., Sidney, NE 69162
Deercliff Archery Supply, 2852 Lavista Rd., Decatur, GA 30033
Feline Archery, 220 Willow Crossing Rd., Greensburg, PA 15601
Glenn's Bow Benders' Supplies, 204 W. Main, Morganfield, KY 42437
Graham Archery Sales, 425 Faith Rd., Salisbury, SC 28144
S. Meltzer & Sons, 118-120 Outwater Lane, Garfield, NJ 07026
PGS Archery, 46 Almond St., Vineland, NJ 08360
Robert's Archery Co., P.O. Box 7, Palmer, MA 01069
Rocky Mountain Discount Archery, 3946 S. Broadway, Suite 209, Englewood, CO 80110
Sayne's Archery, Inc., P.O. Box 328, 6766 St. Rd. 128, Miamitown, OH 45041
Seattle Archery, Box 120, Lynnwood, WA 98036
Southeastern Archery, 101 Gatlin Shopping Center, Orlando, FL 32806
TJS Distributors, 110 2nd Ave., Pelham, NY 10803
West Virginia Archery Supply, 616 Chestnut St., S. Charleston, WV 25309
Western Archery Sales, 3505 E. 39th Ave., Denver, CO 80205
Western-Direct Sales, Box 1270, Moab, UT 84532